PRONUNCIATION

OF

ANCIENT GREEK

TRANSLATED FROM .THE THIRD. GERMAN
EDITION OF DR BLASS

WITH THE AUTHOR'S SANCTION

BY

W. J. PURTON, B.A.

PEMBROKE COLLEGE.

CAMBRIDGE
AT THE UNIVERSITY PRESS
1890

Printing Statement:

Due to the very old age and scarcity of this book, many of the pages may be hard to read due to the blurring of the original text, possible missing pages, missing text, dark backgrounds and other issues beyond our control.

Because this is such an important and rare work, we believe it is best to reproduce this book regardless of its original condition.

Thank you for your understanding.

PREFACE.

THE present translation of Dr Blass' work on ancient Greek pronunciation represents the third and latest German edition, and the translator has throughout its production had the advantage of the advice and help of the author, who kindly undertook to read all the proof-sheets.

A few words are necessary touching the system of transliteration adopted by the translator. As regards the consonants little difficulty presented itself. He was able here simply to adopt the transliteration used by the author, only making the necessary changes of *y* for *j*, *ch* for *tsch*, *j* for *dzh*, and so on, according to the different values of the letters in German and English. With regard to the vowel sounds however his course was not so plain. As, in spite of the labours of Mr Sweet and Mr Ellis, no artificial system of phonetic representation has obtained sufficient acceptance to be really familiar to English scholars, he has resolved to retain the vowels with what may roughly be called their continental values. The alternative plan, namely to represent them by their approximate English equivalents, presented great difficulties. To take an instance: to represent the continental long *i* sound by *ee*, not to speak of its cumbrousness, labours under the additional disadvantage that the short sound must still be represented by *i*, thus obscuring the identity of the two sounds.

Again Dr Blass has in the case of the *e* and *o* sounds adopted diacritic marks to distinguish the open and closed sounds, and it therefore seemed especially desirable here to retain simple symbols. In all cases therefore where the Greek vowels are represented by Roman letters, these must be understood to have their continental sound, that is to say roughly speaking :—

ā must be pronounced as in *father*.

ă   ,,   as in *man*.

ī   ,,   as in second syllable of *quinine*.

ĭ   ,,   as in first syllable of *quinine*.

ē   ,,   as in *fête**.

ĕ   ,,   as in *ebb*.

ō   ,,   as in *note**.

ŏ   ,,   as in *not*.

ū   ,,   as in *lute*.

ŭ   ,,   as in *put*.

The translator has already mentioned his indebtedness to the author for his kindness in reading the proof-sheets; he has also to express his gratitude to Mr R. A. Neil, Fellow of Pembroke College, for similar help.

* It ought to be remarked that these two sounds in English contain a diphthongic element which phoneticians call a *glide*—in the case of ē an *i*-glide, in the case of ō a *u*-glide—which gives them a decidedly different sound to that heard on the Continent. The nature of this difference may be suggested by saying that in the case of ō the continental sound often tends in the direction of our *aw* in *saw* etc.

June, 1890.

ADDITIONS AND CORRECTIONS.

P. 37, note 5. δινάρια for Δινάρια.

P. 47 (text) l. 12 after λῃτουργία add "κλείς for κλῄς" and substitute for end of sentence "in which cases even inscriptions shew ει and the grammarians designate ηι as old Attic."

P. 52 (text) l. 12, ἐπιτήδεος for first ἐπιτήδειος.

P. 72 (text) l. 7, υ for ο.

P. 77 (text) l. 14, a-no-si-ya for a-no-si-ja.

P. 118 (text) l. 23 after Auramazda add Μαζαῖος, Μαζάκης, Mazdai, Mazdak.

Section 1.

The theoretical and practical sides of the subject.

THE investigation of the pronunciation of Ancient Greek may be considered from the point of view of theory and again from that of practice. In the former case its object is the phonetic value, which the Greek letters and combinations of letters had in the living ancient speech; in the latter the point under discussion is, what phonetic value are we to give to those letters and combinations in reading and teaching Ancient Greek? The answer to the question of theory will influence the answer to the question of practice; not however exclusively, for in the case of the latter appropriateness and feasibility must be taken into consideration. I intend in the present work to enter but little into the practical question. For the Germans are not in need of reform either in the case of Greek or in that of Latin in the same degree as the English, and even if they were, the welfare of Greek and Latin instruction does not depend on the abolition of this misusage and this only. Our object is contact with the spirit of classical antiquity; but for the purpose of such a contact it is by no means a hindrance to me, if I say something like *Tsītsĕrō*, while the actual man called himself *Kĭkĕrō*. And there is according to my conviction nothing in our pronunciation of Greek so positively and stupidly wrong as the ordinary pronunciation of Latin *c*. If however anyone feels himself bound in the interest of what we may call a more workmanlike prosecution of classical studies to pay scrupulous regard to such things, and can in so doing guard against the reproach of straining at gnats and swallowing

P.   1

camels, for such a man I have of course nothing but praise. But the attempts, constantly repeated here as well as in other countries, to introduce in practice the modern Greek pronunciation for ancient Greek, must be withstood in view of not only practical but also theoretical and scientific interests. For even the champions of the modern Greek pronunciation appeal not to a practical superiority, which it obviously does not possess, but to a supposed scientific accuracy. A short history of the whole contest from the beginning of Greek studies in the West may conveniently be introduced here.

SECTION 2.

History of the contest about the pronunciation of Ancient Greek.

The knowledge and study of ancient Greek came to the countries of the West towards the close of the Middle Ages through the medium of Byzantine scholars, who naturally brought with them and introduced their own pronunciation, that is to say that current among the Greeks of their day.

As however these studies were prosecuted more independently and thoroughly in the countries of the West, there arose against the traditional pronunciation a reaction which started with some support in the fact, that quite a different pronunciation was customary in the case of the sprinkling of Greek words in Latin, such as *ecclesia, ethice, alphabetum.* Moreover the Byzantine pronunciation deviated so widely from the writing and confused so many sounds, that it of necessity not only appeared unpractical but also called forth doubts as to its originality. Finally, many passages in ancient authors spoke so plainly for a different ulterior pronunciation, that the fact of an alteration having taken place could not by any possibility escape classical scholars. Accordingly so early as Aldus Manutius we have his little πάρεργον[1], which has appeared in many forms in

---

[1] Aldi Manutii *de vitiata vocalium et diphthongorum prolatione* πάρεργον, first printed (1512) in the appendix to the Aldine edit. of the Ἐπιτομὴ τῶν

print, relating to the diphthongs, η and υ, and some consonants. A short treatise on the pronunciation of all the letters
was furnished by Jacobus Ceratinus[1], professor at Louvain, who
died in 1530. But the most celebrated of these early combatants was the renowned Desiderius Erasmus, in a dialogue
de recta Latini Graecique sermonis pronunciatione[2], which
appeared first at Basel in 1528. Although the author was
pleased to clothe his subject in the facetious, or more correctly
the rather insipid, dress of a dialogue between a lion and a bear,
nevertheless his treatment is so thorough and comprehensive,
that there can be no doubt whatever of his scientific seriousness.
The fact is not altered by our knowledge that Erasmus himself
continued to use the traditional pronunciation[3]: a reformer he
certainly was not. A greater stir was made by some English
scholars at Cambridge, John Cheke and Thomas Smith, moving
the condign wrath of Stephen Gardiner, bishop of Winchester,
at that time Chancellor of the University, whom we know in
Church History also as a fierce persecutor of heretics. In 1542
he issued an edict for his University, in which e.g. it was
categorically forbidden to distinguish αι from ε, ει and οι from ι
in pronunciation, under penalty of expulsion from the Senate,
exclusion from the attainment of a degree, rustication for
students, and domestic chastisement for boys. Cheke's correspondence with the Bishop on pronunciation appeared at Basel

ὀκτὼ τοῦ λόγου μερῶν by Const. Lascaris
(as R. Meister shews, *z. griech.
Dialektologie, Progr. Nikolaigymn.*
Leipzig, 1883, p. 13), then repeated in
the Cologne pirated reprint of the
Erasmian Dialogue (1529), also in the
Orthographiae ratio Aldi (published
by his grandson, 1566).

[1] His proper name was Teyng,
born at Hoorn in Holland, died
1530. The treatise was printed at
Antwerp 1527 (vid. E. Lohmeyer, *Phon.
Stud.* I. 183), reprinted in the above-
mentioned Cologne piracy of Erasmus,
also in *Sylloge scriptorum, qui de
linguae Graecae vera et recta pronunci-*
atione commentarios reliquerunt, ed.
Sigeb. Havercampus, Lugd. Bat. 1736,
p. 355—376. Title, *de sono litterarum, praesertim Graecarum*. It is
dedicated to Erasmus, but does not
make the smallest reference to his
labours on this subject, so that the
priority is evident.

[2] Reprinted 1530, pirated 1529 at
Cologne (vid. supra); see further in
Havercamp's *Sylloge altera scriptorum
qui*, etc. (Lugd. Bat. 1740), p. 1—180.

[3] S. Vossius, *Aristarch.* I. c. 28
(*Opp.* vol. II. p. 36); Ellissen, *Göttinger
Philologenversammlung* (1853), p. 108
ff.

in 1555, published by Coelius Secundus Curio[1]; the Bishop uses for the most part the weapon of authority, Cheke on the other hand that of respectable learning and intelligent critical discussion. He was seconded by his friend Thomas Smith, whose missive to the Bishop is dated in the year of the edict[2]. At this point the movement began also among the French scholars, among whom Petrus Ramus and Dionysius Lambinus[3] must be mentioned as the first combatants. Before the century had closed, the victory of the Erasmians was decided in all the chief centres of classical philology. A pretty thorough exposition was written by the well-known reformer Theodor Beza, *de germana pronunciatione Graecae linguae*[4]. He as well as Cheke was made use of in a somewhat questionable manner by the Dutchman Adolph van Metkerke (Mekerchus) in his work *de linguae graecae veteri pronuntiatione*[5], Bruges 1565, the most complete confirmation of the Erasmian system that had been written. Finally in 1578 the famous Henr. Stephanus entered the lists in the same cause, *Apologeticus pro veteri ac germana linguae Graecae pronuntiatione*[6]. Stephanus is already able to say, that in France, England, the Netherlands and elsewhere the reformed pronunciation was eagerly learnt and practised. In this there is nothing to cause surprise; for not only had the Erasmians, on the whole, the better cause, but the opposite party were very weakly represented. Joh. Reuchlin, from whom the pronunciation of the latter takes its name in Germany, gave the impulse to it only in so far as he was the founder of Greek studies in that country; for although he used and taught the modern Greek pronunciation, he could have no object in establishing and defending it, inasmuch as he never lived to see Erasmus' treatise. Bishop Gardiner cannot be reckoned a scientific combatant; and the short treatise directed

---

[1] Printed in Hav. II. p. 181—468 (the Chancellor's edict p. 205—207).

[2] Hav. p. 469—574. According to Hav.'s Praefatio this was published in 1568 by Rob. Stephanus.

[3] Both directly or indirectly victims of the massacre of St Bartholomew (1572). Their participation in the contest on pronunciation is learnt from H. Stephanus in the work to be cited below (p. 391 f.).

[4] Printed in Hav.'s *first Sylloge*, p. 305—352, appeared (acc. to Ellissen) 1554.

[5] Hav. p. 1—170.

[6] Id. p. 377—476.

against Mekerchus by the Englishman Gregory Martin[1] (died 1582) was of trifling importance. Accordingly the Erasmian pronunciation prevailed throughout the West, and the counter-efforts of Erasmus Schmidt of Wittenberg (1560—1637[2]) and of Joh. Rud. Wetstein of Basel (end of the 17th century[3]) failed to make any alteration in this result. There was now a lull in the contest, and the interest in the question waned, until the revival of grammatical studies in our century gave it new life. All our great grammarians have entered the arena either entirely or essentially on the side of the Erasmian pronunciation, e. g. G. Hermann, August Matthiae, Phil. Buttmann, R. Kühner, K. W. Krüger, G. Curtius[4]. Seyffarth and Liscovius, who published special works on the subject in 1824 and 1825 respectively[5], affect an independent attitude towards both schools, and arrive at mixed results. About the same time the Dane S. N. J. Bloch[6], who was refuted by his countryman R. T. F. Henrichsen in a justly valued book, was a zealous champion of the modern Greek pronunciation. The matter was next treated of in the Göttingen and in the Frankfort *Philologenversammlung* in the years 1852 and 1861, Ellissen supporting the modern Greek pronunciation and Bursian a mixture[7].

The hottest and most persistent combatants are the Greeks

[1] In the *Syll. altera* p. 575—622.

[2] Id. p. 631—674.

[3] *Joh. Rod. Wetstenii pro graeca et genuina linguae Graecae pronunciatione orationes apologeticae*, editio II. Basileae 1686.

[4] G. Curtius, *Erläuter.* p. 15 ff., and more thoroughly *Ztschr. f. d. österr. Gymn.* 1852, p. 1 ff.

[5] Seyffarth, *de sonis litterarum gr. tum genuinis tum adoptivis*, Leipz. 1824; Karl Fr. Sal. Liscovius *über die Aussprache des Griechischen*, Leipz. 1825.

[6] S. N. J. Bloch, *Revision der Lehre von der Ausspr. des Altgr.*, Altona and Leipz. 1826; additions in Seebode's *Archiv*, 1827 and 1829; also three Copenhagen Schul-Programme, 1829—

1831; *Zweite Beleuchtung der Matthiae'schen Kritik, die Ausspr. des Altgr. betr.*, Altona 1832. R. J. F. Henrichsen, *über die Neugriechischen oder sogen. Reuchlinische Aussprache d. Hellen. Sprache*, übersetzt von P. Friedrichsen, Parchim and Ludwigslust 1839.

[7] *Verhandl. der XIII. Vers. deutscher Philologen*, Gött. 1853, p. 106—144; id. *d. XX. Vers.* Leipzig, 1863, p. 183—195. Ellissen's treatise is valuable on account of its thorough treatment both of the history of the Greek nation and the history of the contest over the pronunciation: an index of the literature of the subject is given p. 137 f. note.

of course unconsciously adopted. Accordingly the Germans pronounce ζ as *ts*, οἴνους like εἶνους, both syllables of εἶναι with the same vowel sound, and call this the Erasmian pronunciation, although the ancient Erasmians required the pronunciations *ds* for ζ, ε + υ for ευ, ε + ι for ει.

SECTION 4.

Relation of Sound and Writing.

However, as I have said before, I shall here disregard practice and keep to scientific discovery; for as such, and indeed as a very great discovery, I regard the achievement of Erasmus and his predecessors and followers. The theoretic and scientific significance of these researches can indeed be far more easily undervalued than overvalued. The history of Greek pronunciation is the history of that phonetic change, which took place in the language so to speak covertly, but which is on that account by no means less real and important than the alteration, which became apparent in the writing. It is indeed the case with all languages, that the writing does not keep pace with the changes of sound, but remains more or less in the lurch. Writing is no conscious translation of sound into symbols, but, after this has been done once and originally, habit has stepped in, and one race hands on this habit to the other. Hence arises the well-known variation between pronunciation and writing in modern languages, which is nowhere greater than in English. Not that the present English orthography is the same as that under Henry the Eighth: but we should be entirely misled, if we were to estimate the deviation of the language of that period from that of the present day by the deviation in the writing. The matter is well known to and treated of by specialists[1]; that however need not prevent us citing here the results of the above-mentioned treatises of Cheke, Smith and others. They transcribe Engl. *mane* μᾶν, *gate* γᾶτ; Erasmus ascribes the pro-

---

[1] H. Sweet, History of English Sounds, *Transactions of the Philol. Society*, 1873—1874, p. 461 (517).   A. Ellis *on E. English Pr.*, ib. extra vol. v. 1869—1870, 1869—1878, 1871, 1875.

nunciation of *a* as *ae* to the Scotch. Further, *mean* μην, *meat* μητ, *heat* ἤτ, *wheat* οὐητ ; the η signifies the open sound, the closed sound in *me, bee* being called *e italicum*. The Scotch according to Erasmus pronounced this *e* as *i*. Βῖτ *bite*, φῖλ *file*, βὶ ἰτ *buy it*. Γῶν *gone*, γὸ ὸν *go on*. Δυκ λυτ ρεβυκ *duke lute rebuke*, the long French *u*, which was also attested for *rude, rue ;* the corresponding short sound, says Smith, is heard more frequently in central than in southern England, but would be general in *ruddy, bloody* (written at that time *bludy*), *muddy*. Latin *u* is heard according to them in *bow* the verb βου, *gown* γοῦν, *foul* φουλ ; in *bow* the substantive, *bowl* etc., the sound of the Greek ωυ (the modern *ou*). For the diphthong *ai*, i.e. *a + i*, *way, pay* are cited (in these cases however in more cultivated pronunciation more of an *ei*, in Scotch and north English almost a monophthongal *ae* was heard), for *ei neigh*, for *au claw*, for *eu few, dew*. To sum up, we find, that an extraordinary alteration has taken place in the actual language, quite as great as that established for Greek by the Erasmians. French also of that period was pronounced quite differently to what it is at the present day : mute *e* had its value, the mute final consonants were perceptibly dwelt upon at all events before a pause, in *beau* Smith heard the Greek diphthong ηυ, Erasmus and Stephanus a triphthong, all three vowels being heard. So shifting is pronunciation, and so stable writing, juggling away as it does the most important changes. But the enquirer must not allow himself to be juggled with, not even to the extent of regarding what is apparent as more important owing to its transparency than that which comes to pass covertly.

But if these sound-changes are not apparent, how can we know anything at all about them and about the earlier sound-stage of Greek? I might answer at once : in the same way that we do with regard to the earlier sound-stage of English ; for Greek too there is a whole series of similar evidences in ancient authors. But Erasmus was perfectly right in inferring a variety of sound from the application of various symbols, and a diphthongal pronunciation from diphthongal writing. The simple and natural rule, write as you speak, has never from the beginning been infringed without special reason. Such a reason existed in many instances for the Romance languages in the deference paid to the Latin mother language; French modes of writing such as *corps, doigt*, at an earlier period also *faict* for *fait* and so on, where the penultimate consonant was always mute, could never have existed but for the Latin *corpus, digitus, factum*[1]. For the *ai* in *aimer, faire* etc. Erasmus and Beza attest the living dialectal use of the diphthongal pronunciation in their time; *eu* is according to them universally a diphthong, $= e +$ (Fr.) *u*, in like manner *au* ($= a + o$ according to Beza); *eau* and *oi* have been already mentioned, and for the latter the original pronunciation as $o + i$ is guaranteed by the living English *voice* from *voix* and *choice* from *choix*[2]. Similarly English orthography, disregarding the mixture of different systems of sound-notation, has arrived at its present incongruity with the sound through deference to Latin and the permanence given by writing to sounds formerly—but now no longer—really heard. Since then the ancient Greeks were not in a position to pay deference to a previous language in a higher stage of cultivation, they must consequently have originally striven to bring their writing as near as possible to the sound. As the language underwent further development, it may well have happened both in Attic and in the other dialects that the orthography did not progress evenly; but this must have consisted much more in what was old not being entirely crowded out by what was new, than in the retention of the old to the absolute exclusion of the new. For a crystallization of orthography can only occur where the word forms have stamped themselves firmly

---

[1] Diez, *Gramm. d. roman. Spr.* 1[3], p. 442.

[2] Stephanus, p. 414, ed. Haverc., makes the universal statement as regards the French: " non solum diphthongos et triphthongos, hisque longiores recte pronuntiamus; verum etiam nullam ex vocalibus devorantes, indissoluta voce plane distinguimus *beau, lieu, ioyaux, ioyeux*....Quotum enim quemque Gallorum hodie reperias, qui aequo animo ferat μονοφωνίαν suarum diphthongorum et triphthongorum ? Id est,

si una sola enuncietur, velut quaelibet ex tribus vocalibus?" Modern Provençal still retains diphthongal *ai* (faire, paire, maire = père, mère), *au, eu* (Diéu, castèu = château) etc. Cp. Diez, p. 429 ff., who adduces for *au* from Beza's treatise *de francicae linguae recta pronuntiatione* (1584) a somewhat discrepant testimony to the effect that the pronunciation like *ao* was Norman, the ordinary pronunciation much like *o*.

by much reading and writing; where there is but little reading
and writing, as in Greece in the classical period and in western
Europe in the Middle Ages, unless the sound is very stable and
well defined, the orthography is extremely shifting.   Now it is
actually the case that in Attica towards the close of the fifth
century the entire system was absolutely changed.   Here was
the opportunity in those cases, where the living sound had here
and there deviated from the writing, to bring them again into
harmony.   Moreover, since the Athenians and also the other
races did not yet possess any grammarians or etymologists to
attach importance to a historical mode of writing, the only
principle which could have weight was the phonetic.   Accordingly it is actually the case that on Attic inscriptions
of the fourth century the orthography is by no means established in all points: τεῖ τιμεῖ and τῆι τιμῆι are written promis-
cuously.   When in the course of time the Attic dialect extended itself beyond the boundaries of Attica, and became
essentially the standard for the κοινή of Hellenized countries,
and at the same time habits of composition and literary culture
increased to an extraordinary degree, fluctuation in orthography
must most certainly have become far less easy.   To the Macedonians, the Egyptians, the Carians and Lydians, and also the
Dorians of the Peloponnese, Attic Greek was an acquired
tongue, and that in part by means of its literature, so that
sound and writing impressed themselves simultaneously.   We
soon have to add to this the influence of the learned grammarians.   However even at that period the orthography did
not yet crystallize: the ι of the diphthongs ᾳ, ῃ, ῳ, which had
gradually disappeared in the spoken language, was in the time
of Augustus consciously omitted by many in writing also, as
Strabo says[1], πολλοὶ ἐκβάλλουσι τὸ ἔθος φυσικὴν αἰτίαν οὐκ
ἔχον.   In like manner, after ει had become attenuated to a
long ι, although it was not given up in writing, it was applied
to a new purpose, namely the regular notation of long ι[2].

---

[1] Strabo xiv. p. 648, speaking of
the ι of the Dative.

[2] Cp. Quint. 1. 7. 15 (of the Romans): Diutius duravit, ut ei jungendis
eadem ratione qua Graeci ει uterentur
(for a long ι).

From the time of Augustus however Atticism made great strides, with avowed principle of restoring everywhere the genuine Attic as opposed to the barbarous corruption of the language, and it attained a supremacy in literature which it maintained throughout the whole Byzantine period. Moreover the grammarians, and especially Herodian, now took great pains to obtain fixed orthographic rules based on etymology and original writing, and subsequently, in literature at least, no considerable change was possible either in the form or the writing of words, but the standard was given once for all. Accordingly even the mute ι was reinstated, ει for long ι was supplanted, and all ancient modes of writing together with the diacritic marks of the old grammarians were preserved with the same conscientiousness which we see at the present day among the modern Greeks. For the latter, were they to write phonetically, would be under no necessity either of making a distinction between ο and ω (we owe their distinction in pronunciation to the Erasmians) or of retaining more than one mark of accentuation, or again of writing any breathing: all this is in the living language mere dead weight, indeed it only serves to mislead with regard to the actual sound conditions. How can anyone possibly think that such an orthography was originally shaped to fit such a language? No, this mode of writing is alone sufficient evidence to teach us, that the ancient Greek sounds were absolutely different; just as the French and English orthography alone sufficiently prove the alteration which has taken place from the original languages. Grimm also says in his German Grammar: "for the pronunciation of broken and diphthongal sounds I lay down a general principle, that each one of the vowels contained in such sounds was originally perceptible singly, and the condensation of both into one tone in all cases occurred at a later period," and Diez remarks with regard to this, "the history of French pronunciation will hardly invalidate his axiom[1]." Let us then allow, that what holds in general, holds also for Greek, and leave off making oral tradition our basis instead of this literary

---

[1] Grimm, 1³, 38; Diez, 1³, 417, note.

tradition. For when, to take an example, Bursian appeals to the fundamental axiom of philological criticism, that tradition is to be regarded as correct, until its incorrectness can be demonstrated, he forgets that we have here two traditions, and that it is a not less recognized principle to prefer the older and the literary to the later and oral[1]. The present sound in any language proves nothing for the earlier, although the mode of writing it may have remained the same; this testimony requires in each single case further confirmation, before it can be admitted with any certainty. And if there is an absolute incongruity of sound and writing, this forms the strongest presumption against the so-called testimony. Modern Spanish has or had a short time ago three notations for the guttural *ch, g* (before *e* and *i*), *j* and *x*. This is an incongruity, in so far as the sound is everywhere similar, the writing dissimilar. The writing of *g* side by side with *j* is easily explainable by the deference paid to Latin; that of *x* is stranger: why *relox* 'horologium,' *baxo* Fr. 'bas,' *Quixote, Xerez, Mexico, Texas,* and not from the beginning *reloj, bajo, Jerez* etc., as has been written since 1846? An explanation might perhaps be found, shewing the present value of *x* to have been the original; still there would be ample ground to justify doubts as to the original similarity of *x* on the one side and *j* and *g* on the other. For as specialists know and tell us, *x* had at all events up to the 16th century the value of French *ch, g* and *j* of French *j*[2]. The writing therefore was in this case too the true witness, oral tradition the false.

There must be added however an important point, which has been emphasized by the Greek Psichari[3]. As a matter of course that only can pass for oral tradition and evidence, which really exists in the language of the people, not anything which may have been violently foisted on the language by the learned and cultivated out of regard for writing or some other supposed standard of accuracy. Now in the case of the Greek of to-day the genuine language falls foul of the traditional writing much

---

[1] *Frankfurter Philologenvers.* (1861), p. 184.

[2] Diez, p. 371 f.

[3] J. Psichari, *Rev. critique,* 1887, p. 262 ff.

more frequently than the language of the learned. The latter it is true has in those cases, where a sound has undergone a universal transition into another, adopted the new sound, so that now this new value is actually attached to the symbol, as for instance that of *f* to *φ* and that of *i* to *η*; but where the new sound has appeared only under certain conditions occurring in a minority of cases, the cultivated language, clinging to the writing, frequently does not admit it. Every *e* (*αι*, *ε*) or *i* (*ι*, *υ*, *ει*, etc.) when followed by a vowel becomes *y* in the real spoken language: *nyos* *νέος*, *palyós* *παλαιός*, *yos* *υἱός*; but neither the cultivated nor the Reuchlinians are willing to pronounce thus, although the latter, if they want to follow the testimony of the living language, would certainly be bound to shew their adherence in this point also. Moreover the language as now spoken tolerates neither two tenues in juxtaposition nor the combination of nasal with spirant; we must therefore force on ancient Greek the rules that *κ* and *π* are to be pronounced as (German) *ch* and *f* before *τ*, and that *ν*, *μ* and *γ* must be assimilated or allowed to drop out before *θ*, *φ*, *χ*. It is of no importance whatever in this respect that educated Greeks are careful to preserve the value of *κ* and *ν*; for that takes place not as an effect of oral tradition, which they wish to make their support, but of written tradition, which they despise. The Reuchlinian therefore ought to say *eftá*, *ochtó*, *niffi* (*nifi*) for *νύμφη* etc., and arrange everything under proper rules the number of which must certainly be very great; otherwise he transgresses at every step his own principle. Finally there is no lack of points, as regards which the testimony of oral tradition is entirely at variance, according to dialects and localities; for example with respect to the pronunciation of *κ* before *ε* and *ι* (*kye, tye, chye, che, tsye, tse* = *κε*), or that of *χ* after *ρ* (*k* or *ch*): where consequently as a matter of fact we have no evidence. This is all emphasized by Psichari, and the necessary inference to be drawn from it is that the Reuchlinian principle neither is nor can be carried out in practice.

Section 5.

Method of ascertaining the ancient pronunciation.

The matter then stands thus; for the original sound writing is our evidence, for the present sound (and for this only) the living representatives of the nation, and the point to be investigated is, how long the original sound has stood its ground, and when the present sound began. This investigation must be carried on separately for every single sound, for the results may be very various. The sum of these is a piece of sound-history of the Greek language, to be supplemented from the alterations which become apparent in the writing, which latter however belong more to the prehistoric than the historic period. Looking at it in this light we first see the whole of the significance of the subject, and, it must be confessed, the whole of its difficulty. It is true the general rule, by which to decide, whether a sound at a given time retained its original value or had already passed into another, may simply be taken over from allied fields of enquiry. E.g. the fact that French *en* in the golden age of old French literature was identical with *an*, is inferred among other proofs from its confusion with *an* which already took place at that period[1]; conversely if such a confusion did not appear, it would be concluded with equal certainty that *en* still had the *e* sound. If then in like manner we say with regard to the Greek αι; it was in the Attic period a real double sound, since it is exchanged neither with η nor with ε; this is a mode of reasoning, the justness of which no one would impeach in the domain of any other language. In fact it is quite clear that, if αι was identical with *è* and also η, even in the case of a much more learned people than the ancient Athenians some confusion in writing would infallibly have occurred, especially during the course of so many centuries. We have only to notice in comparison, how shifting and uncertain the Latin writing is in the period of the Republic in spite of the exertions made by the grammarians from an early date to regulate it. Even if we suppose that αι was an *e très*

---

[1] Lücking, *d. ältesten franz. Mundarten*, p. 106 ff.

ouvert, while η was an ordinary open *e*, such a trifling difference
as that would not long have been adequate to hinder confusion.
This then is the first and most general method: investigate up
to what period the writing is constant and when it begins to be
no longer so. Next we have direct information and descriptions
in the works of the grammarians, and can also draw inferences
indirectly from the grammatical nomenclature and classifications
of sounds, from directions as to orthography and so on. Further
phonetic transitions within the word and especially in the
combination of words have weight; for if ἐπὶ ᾧ becomes ἐφ' ᾧ,
and καὶ ἔστι becomes κἄστι, this teaches us something about
the value of φ and αι, since this fact is utterly irreconcilable
with certain values of these symbols. Of great importance too
are transcriptions from and into other languages, and here
Latin is of primary value for Greek, just as Greek is for Latin.
Κέλερες Κικέρων, *Cimon Cyrus*, are in themselves adequate
evidence for the fact, which is established by other considerations, that Latin *c* was always *k* in the classical language: for
no one can doubt that this was the value of κ[1]. In like manner
transcriptions such as *Athenae, ecclesia,* κῆνσος, Λουκρήτιος are
alone sufficient proof that η was equivalent to *ē*; for that Latin
e was not equivalent to *i* is doubted by none except those who
have given their verdict after having bowed their necks once for
all to modern Greek authority. Such people are doubtless
skilled to throw doubt on that which is most firmly established, and give a plausible appearance to that which is most
questionable, according as it falls foul of or is at harmony with
this authority[2]. Much light can be obtained for Greek from

---

[1] It is true that in the 16th century
the point was not considered to be
settled; Bishop Gardiner prescribes:
in *k* et *g* quoties cum diphthongis aut
vocalibus sonos *i* aut *e* referentibus
consonantur, quoniam a doctis etiam-
num in usu variantur, aliis densiorem
aliis tenuiorem sonum affingentibus,
utriusque pronuntiationis modum dis-
cito, ne aut horum aut illorum aures
offendas...; caeterum qui in his sonus a

pluribus receptus est, illum frequentato.
[2] Ellissen, p. 136: "we do not know
how the Romans pronounced *e*; we do
know however, that in the Romance
daughter-languages an *i* has been developed out of it in numberless words."
(Diez, 1³, 150 f. states that the transition of *e* to *i* is common to the
Romance languages but not usual
outside France).

oriental languages also, for instance from Coptic. Lastly the plays on words depending on similarity of sound (analogous to rime, which in the case of Mediæval languages is certainly a far more excellent resource), also etymologies in ancient writers, imitations of the cries of animals and so on must be laid under contribution for information. This last expedient, especially the βῆ βῆ of Kratinus, furnishes a Reuchlinian like Ellissen with a handle for cheap witticism making it appear as though the contest about η was merely a contest to decide the competence of a wether as witness for the pronunciation of a Plato and a Demosthenes; with these and similar turns of speech he can wriggle successfully out of the quite unimpeachable evidence, which is contained in this representation of the cries of animals[1]. I mention this here, as I have no inclination after this to enter the lists at all with opponents, who substitute dogma for enquiry; they will not submit to refutation, and we can only take leave of them with the words recommended by the ancient Euænus for such combatants, σοὶ μὲν ταῦτα δοκοῦντ᾽ ἔστω, ἐμοὶ δὲ τάδε. They are fortunately not too numerous among us.

Section 6.

Degree of accuracy attainable.

If then all these expedients and especially the deviations of writing in the inscriptions and papyri, which have become so numerous in our time, are made use of in a critical and unbiassed manner, satisfactory results can certainly be obtained, provided that we do not look for too much. For neither can precise limits of time be given for the transitions, nor can these themselves and the original sound be denoted with mathematical precision. We find Cheke insisting that these things must be treated rather ἐν πλάτει than πρὸς ἀκρίβειαν; in fact every science has its own degree of precision attainable. For instance it is certainly not sufficiently precise, if I give the

---

[1] Cp. on this proof as well as on other methods of proof the meritorious exposition of K. Zacher: *die Aussprache des Griech.*, Leipzig, 1888.

sound of η as e; for there are two sorts of e's, the open and the closed. If however I say η was the open e, I ought not to be asked further, which open e? although, as is well known, the French distinguish three sub-varieties in their language: an ordinary open e, a more open, and a very open one. This is by no means a matter of indifference for harmony and correctness of pronunciation: but no one can expect to know anything about such subtleties in the case of a [dead] language. Lastly there are not merely three open e's, but a numberless series, and the same holds good with regard to the other sounds and combinations of sounds; for instance a diphthong can be spoken with greater or less preponderance of one or the other vowel, without regard to the possible variety in the single elements. I am perfectly convinced, that, if an ancient Athenian were to rise from his grave and hear one of us speak Greek, on the basis of the best scientific enquiry and with the most delicate and practised organs, he would think the pronunciation horribly barbarous. But if he heard a modern Greek, he would not indeed be so loud in his censure, simply because he failed to observe that this is supposed to be his own language. For where, not to mention all the other points of difference, acute and circumflex are not differentiated, and every accented vowel is pronounced long, every unaccented vowel short (e.g. $\gamma\acute{\epsilon}\nu o\iota\tau o$ yèn'ttŏ), there the language has suffered a change affecting its very essence and something absolutely new has been developed out of the old. Nor would the ancient Athenian think the language especially agreeable to the ear, I mean ancient Greek in the mouth of the modern Greek. His taste would probably coincide with that of Dionysius of Halicarnassus and Hermogenes, who both declare ι to be of all vowels the least agreeable to the ear and the most wanting in dignity[1]. But in ancient Greek, spoken according to the fashion of the modern Greek, this vowel has an unnatural preponderance. Finally, if a German came with his Reuchlinian pronunciation, observing quantities with pedantic care, the ancient Athenian would probably stop his ears at such disfigurement of

[1] Dionys. π. συνθέσ. p. 77 R. (ἔσχατον δὲ πάντων τὸ ι); Hermog. π. ἰδ. p. 225 W. 291 Sp. (τὸ ι ἥκιστα σεμνὴν ποιεῖ τὴν λέξιν πλεονάσαν).

his language (if indeed he recognized it as such) and at such discordant sounds. For who (to take an instance from Herodotus) would put up with τῖς ἀλūθῖῖς τῆς ἀληθηίης, τῖς ἰγῖῖς τῆς ὑγιείης and all the similar monstrosities, such as never appear in any real language? The ancient Greeks, as soon as ει became simple ῑ, no longer said ὑγιεία but ὑγεία, and in like manner ταμεῖον for ταμιεῖον, πεῖν for πιεῖν, just as at an earlier date πόλιι was contracted to πόλι, Διί in many cases to Δί. However we are at liberty by all means to pronounce as we please; we are perfectly secure against the censure of the hypothetical ancient Athenian, and this fiction only illustrates the fact, that we can attain perfect accuracy neither in practical pronunciation nor in theory.

After this rather long introduction I reach my subject, and first in order the history of the vowels and diphthongs.

I. Vowels and Diphthongs.

Section 7.

System of Vowels.

The relation of the vowels to one another is excellently illustrated by modern authorities, for instance R. Lepsius[1], by the well-known triangle, having at its corners *a i* and *u*. Between *a* and *i* come the two *e*'s, the open (French *è é*, Lepsius' *e̲*) nearer to *a*, the closed (French *é*, Lepsius' *ẹ*) nearer to *i*. Both *e*'s are found both long and short; the German language however wants the short closed *o*, which must be sought in the short *i* of certain dialects. In like manner between *a* and *u* come two *o*'s, an open and a closed (*o̲* and *ọ*); these also occur in French: open in *encore*, closed in *anneau, dos*; they are however distinguished by no diacritic mark.

---

[1] R. Lepsius, *Standard Alphabet* (2nd ed. London and Berlin, 1863). I see the less reason for exchanging this triangle for the vowel line which has lately won favour, since in Greek its end - *u* - has changed back again to the beginning - *i* -.

Italian grammar on the contrary uses such marks both in the case of *o* and of *e*: *òra òpera òrgano, érba étere* have the open sound, *onóre ómbra órdine, ésca ésso* the closed. The Germans pronounce the short *o* open, the long closed; a long open *o* is shown in the Low German broad *a* (English water, Danish *aa,* Swedish *å*), a short closed *o* in those dialects which also pronounce the *i* as described above. Next comes the intermediate sound between *i* and *u,* the German *ü,* Greek *v,* French *u,* and similarly between *e* and *o* come two *ö*'s, an open (*öffnen,* French *peur*) and a closed (*Öfen,* French *peu*). For these Lepsius writes *u̯, o̤, o̤,* The whole is represented as follows:—

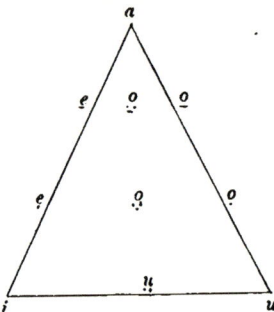

It is obvious that in this diagram there is a different vowel for every point on its lines, and consequently an endless series of vowels: but the distinction of these principal types is quite sufficient for our purpose.

The ancient grammarians distinguish seven vowels for Greek, namely two long (*η, ω*), two short (*ε, o*), and three common (*ă, ĭ, ŭ*). Sextus Empiricus[1] takes exception to this arrangement on the ground that *ε* is to *η,* and *o* to *ω,* as *ă* is to *ā, ĭ* to *ī* and so on, and that consequently only five vowels have to be distinguished, or, having regard to long and short, ten. In fact in this entire theory writing rather than sound

[1] Sext. Emp. *adv. mathem. A* p. 624 f. Bk.; see especially p. 625, 8 ff. ἀκολουθήσει καὶ τὸ ε καὶ τὸ η ἐν εἶναι στοιχεῖον κατὰ τὴν αὐτὴν δύναμιν κοινόν· ἡ γὰρ αὐτὴ δύναμις ἐπ᾽ ἀμφοτέρων ἐστί, καὶ συσταλὲν μὲν τὸ η γίνεται ε, ἐκταθὲν δὲ τὸ ε γίνεται η· κατὰ δὲ τὸν αὐτὸν τρόπον καὶ τὸ o καὶ τὸ ω μία στοιχείου γενήσεται φύσις κοινή, ἐκτάσει καὶ συστολῇ διαφέρουσα, ἐπείπερ τὸ μὲν ω μακρόν ἐστιν o, τὸ δὲ o βραχύ ἐστιν ω.

has evidently been the guide; but the point to be investigated is, how the writing has assumed this form. The names of the vowels were: ἄλφα, εἶ, ἦτα, ἰῶτα, οὖ, ὔ, ὤ. The use of ἒ ψιλόν and ὔ ψιλόν, i.e. 'simple *e*', 'simple *u*', as names ought in reason to be dropped; for when the Byzantines say e.g. τὸ παῖδες κατὰ τὴν παραλήγουσαν διὰ τῆς αι διφθόγγου (γράφεται), τὸ δὲ πέδαι διὰ τοῦ ε ψιλοῦ, they do not mean the adjective to be understood as part of the name of the symbol. 'Simple ε' is contrasted with the diphthongal writing αι, 'simple υ' with οι, as these pairs in Byzantine times coincided in sound, and we find the expressions κυ ψιλόν, φυ ψιλόν, contrasted with the writings κοι, φοι. The case is not far otherwise with the definitions ὸ μικρόν, ὼ μέγα, additions which were about as necessary to the Byzantines, with whom these two vowels had the same sound, as the definitions, "hard *T (D)*", "soft *D (T)*", to the Saxons[1]. Should the names εἶ, οὖ not be permissible as liable to be misunderstood, it is at any rate better to say with the later grammarians ἔ, ὄ (ὔ, ὄ)[2]. But the origin of these old names, which do not tally with the pronunciation, will have to be investigated. In the Greek of the present day the vowel-system has developed in the following way :—

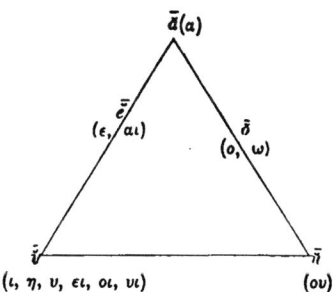

In this complete incongruity between sound and writing we see a clear indication of the transformation which has taken place in the former since classical times. The *e* is in modern Greek

---

[1] The definitions ἒ ψιλόν, ὔ ψιλόν have been disposed of by Karl Ernst Aug. Schmidt, *Ztschr. f. Gymn. Wesen* 1851 p. 433 ff.; *Beiträge zur Geschichte d. Grammatik des Griech. u. Lat.* (Halle 1859) p. 64 ff. As names of symbols they are only found in the grammarian of the *Etym. Gud.* and in Chrysoloras.

[2] For the evidence see ib. p. 62 ff.

in general open, especially in accented and long syllables[1]; *o* also tends that way, but less decidedly. The *ü* sound of *v* is heard even now according to many authorities sometimes before *r* (ἄχυρα *achüra*, τυρί i.e. τυρός *türí*)[2]; the fact of an η appearing as *e* ε before *r* in unaccented syllables (ξερός, θερί for θηρίον etc.) is not due to a retention of the ancient sound, but to a modern phonetic law, according to which every unaccented *ir* (ιρ, ηρ, υρ) becomes *er*, as *keryaki* κυριακή[3]. But, that the *i* sound has elsewhere in modern Greek different shades of tone according to its origin, is, according to competent authorities pure invention[4], in spite of the assertion of Reuchlinians.

Section 8.

System of Diphthongs.

We find in ancient Greek side by side with the vowels and having a like function of syllable-formation a large series of diphthongs, close combinations of pairs of vowels, of which the last is always either *ι* or *v*. Since these two can be combined with all the other vowels, short as well as long, and *ι* also with *v* as first element, theoretically we have in all fourteen diphthongs; these however are not all distinguished in writing, nor indeed can they all be proved even to have had an actual existence[5]:

αι (ἀγοραί)	αυ (παύω)
ᾱι (ἀγορᾱι)	ᾱυ (γραῦς ion. γρηῦς ?)
ει (λείπω)	ευ (εὖ)
ηι (τιμῆι)	ηυ (ηὔλουν)
οι (οἶνος)	ου (οὗτος)
ωι (ὀδῶι)	ωυ (ion. dor. ωὑτός = ὁ αὐτός)
υι (νέκυι)	
ῡι (θυιάς ?)	

---

[1] K. Foy, *Lautsystem d. griech. Vulgärspr.*, Leipzig, 1879, p. 84.
[2] id. p. 86.
[3] Psichari *Revue Crit.* 1887, p. 266.
[4] Foy, p. 84.
[5] The theory of the 14 vowels is developed by G. Hermann *de emend. rat. Gr. gr.* p. 49 ff.

The oldest theory preserved, that of Dionysius Thrax, numbers only six of these, αι, αυ, ει, ευ, οι, ου; later writers go as far as eleven or twelve; we nowhere find more than one υι and one αυ distinguished. According to one distribution[1] they fall into two classes κύριαι δίφθ. and καταχρηστικαί; the former are those named diphthongs by Dionysius, that is those with a short vowel for their first member with the exception of υι. The reason, why these were called proper and the others improper diphthongs, must rest in the idea, that ἡ δίφθογγος, scil. φωνή[2], is properly a more or less simple sound, which however consists of two elements; yi, ōu, ēu do not weld together into such a simple sound. For this very reason these three diphthongs are called according to another classification[3] δίφθ. κατὰ διέξοδον, i.e. those in which the voice passes successively through both vowel sounds. The second class in this classification are the diphthongs κατ᾽ ἐπικράτειαν, where the one sound prevails over the other and makes it imperceptible: ᾱι=ᾱ, ηι = ē, ωι = ō, ει = ῑ. Lastly come the diphthongs κατὰ κρᾶσιν, namely those with actual fusion, αυ ευ ου; for the later grammarians, by whom this doctrine is handed down to us, would leave αι and οι altogether out of their classification, in order thereby to explain their different value in respect of word-accentuation. Since however this distribution was certainly not originally invented with this purpose in view, αι and οι also must originally have belonged to the third class[4]. It

[1] Theodos. *Gramm.* p. 35.

[2] I do not know, what else except φωνή (or συλλαβή?) it is possible to supply; φωνή (φθόγγος) is vowel-sound as opposed to the ψόφοι, consonants (Aristoxenus in Dion. Hal. π. συνθ. p. 72 R.). The doctrine of the diphthongs will at any rate go back as far as Aristoxenus in its main features, perhaps even farther. For according to Plato (*Kratyl.* 424 c; *Hipp. Maj.* 285 c, D) in his time both οἱ ἐπιχειροῦντες τοῖς ῥυθμοῖς and the sophist Hippias busied themselves with the doctrine of letters and syllables, in which pursuit they must inevitably

have come upon the idea of a diphthong (two vowels in one syllable).

[3] Theodos. p. 34 f., Chœroboskos B. A. III. p. 1214 f., Schol. Dion. Thr. *id.* II. p. 804, Moschopulos p. 24. In Chœr. ει is entirely left out. The diphthongs κατὰ διέξ. are defined (Chœr.): χωρὶς ἀκούεται ὁ φθόγγος τοῦ ἑνὸς φωνήεντος; those κατὰ κρᾶσιν: συγκιρνῶσιν ἑαυτὰ τὰ δύο φωνήεντα καὶ ἀποτελοῦσι μίαν φωνὴν ἁρμόζουσαν τοῖς δύο φωνήεσιν.

[4] Cp. the introductory words, αὗται τοίνυν αἱ ἔνδεκα δίφθ. ἀνεμερίσαντο ἑαυτὰς καὶ ἐγένοντο κατὰ τρόπους τρεῖς. The division B. A. II. p. 803, into εὔφωνοι

must also be mentioned, that Sextus Empiricus[1] quotes from 'certain philosophers' the statement, that there are other elementary sounds, different from those usually taught, for instance αι, ου and all similar sounds. For these sounds are, according to their statement, unlike a syllable such as ρα, the same from the beginning to the end of their duration, and this is the characteristic of an element. He afterwards mentions ει also as belonging to this class, which indeed will coincide with the six diphthongs of Dionysius and with the diphthongs κατὰ κρᾶσιν according to the original numeration, to which therefore αι and ει also belonged. More discrepant, than at first appears, is the distribution of the musician Aristeides[2]: κατὰ κρᾶσιν, κατὰ συμπλοκήν, κατ' ἐπικράτειαν; of the diphthongs κατὰ συμπλοκήν he says, that coming at the end of a word they are less easily shortened before a following vowel than the others, since the tone is stronger owing to the clear pronunciation of both vowels. Now since ην ων υι scarcely ever occur at the end of words, we must understand this to refer to ευ and αυ (αὖ, εὖ, Ζεῦ etc.), and the corrupt statement about these diphthongs τῶν κατὰ συμπλ., λέγω δὲ τῶν διὰ τοῦ (a poor variant δι' αὐτῶν) συντιθεμένων, must be emended by the repetition of a letter, διὰ τοῦ < ῡ >. The class κατὰ κρᾶσιν would thus be limited to αι, ει, οι, except in so far as ει, having already become long ι, had now to be counted in the class κατ' ἐπικράτειαν. The expressions κατὰ

(the six of Dionys.), κακόφωνοι (ην ων υι) and ἄφωνοι (ᾳ ῃ ῳ) I pass over as having no importance by the side of the other.

[1] Sext. Emp. *adv. mathem.* p. 625 Bk.: καὶ ἀναστρόφως ἔσεσθαί τινά φασιν ἔνιοι τῶν φιλοσόφων πλείονα στοιχεῖα, διάφορον ἔχοντα δύναμιν τῶν συνήθως παραδιδομένων, οἷον καὶ τὸ αι καὶ τὸ ου καὶ πᾶν ὃ τῆς ὁμοίας ἐστὶ φύσεως.—ἐπεὶ οὖν ὁ τοῦ αι καὶ ει φθόγγος ἁπλοῦς ἐστι καὶ μονοειδής, ἔσται καὶ ταῦτα στοιχεῖα. Afterwards 626 after a discussion on αι:—τούτου δὲ οὕτως ἔχοντος, ἐπεὶ καὶ ὁ τοῦ ει φθόγγος καὶ ὁ τοῦ ου μονοειδὴς καὶ ἀσύνθετος καὶ ἀμετάβολος λαμβάνεται,

ἔσται καὶ οὗτος στοιχεῖον. If then in the time of Sextus (about 200 A.D.) αι was pronounced ever so decidedly as ä, we get no *new element* out of this or out of ει = ι. Accordingly the philosophers referred to in the sentence, in whose time ει was still a diphthong, must be earlier.

[2] Arist. Quintil. p. 44 Meibom. (p. 29 Jahn) (αἱ δίφθογγοι, ἃς ἤτοι κατὰ κρᾶσιν ἢ κατὰ συμπλοκὴν <ἢ> κατ' ἐπικράτειαν γίγνεσθαί φαμεν). Afterwards p. 46, εὐτονωτέρους γὰρ αὗται ποιοῦνται τοὺς ἤχους, ἀμφότερα φανερῶς ἐκβοῶσαι τὰ φωνήεντα.

κρᾶσιν and κατὰ συμπλοκήν are a marvellously happy definition
of the distinction intended; for in proper diphthongs, as Rumpelt says[1], the voice sounds during the movement from one
vowel-position to the other and only during this movement, so
that an actual 'mixture' takes place as between water and
wine; in improper diphthongs on the other hand the relation of
the sounds one to the other is an 'interweaving'. We are unfortunately not in a position, with the means at our command,
to follow up to its sources with any certainty the ancient theory
of diphthongs.

SECTION 9.

E and O sounds, their oldest development and representation.

As regards the value of these vowels and diphthongs,
since *a* admits of no doubt whatever, we will begin our investigation with a discussion of the E and O sounds.
Originally, and in most local alphabets up to the year 400,
every *e* was written with E, every *o* with O[2]. The Greeks of
the East however, and especially the Ionians of Asia Minor, at
a very early period employed the symbol H, Phoenician Cheth,
properly used to signify the rough breathing, as a vowel-symbol
for a particular kind of *e*. This was in fact very readily done in
Asiatic Ionia where the breathing was lost; the symbol in consequence of this was now called ἦτα instead of Cheth ῾Ητα, and
began with this vowel, exactly as ἄλφα with *a*. At a somewhat
later time, about the sixth century, various attempts appear in
various localities, to distinguish the corresponding O sounds by
the introduction of a new symbol. The symbol O was differentiated by leaving the circle open (C), or by a point in it (Θ),
or by leaving it open below and annexing two feet (Ω); this last
form ultimately prevailed, and was applied in the manner adopted
by the Ionians of Asia, according to which the new symbol corre-

---

[1] Rumpelt *d. natürliche System des
Sprachlaute* p. 47.

[2] For facts of epigraphy I refer the
reader once for all to the classical book
of A. Kirchhoff: *Studien zur Geschichte
des griechischen Alphabets.*

sponded to H, the old symbol O to E[1]. But that, which was so carefully distinguished in the cases of *e* and *o*, was by no means, as has been assumed since the days of Greek grammarians, the quantity. For, although H almost never and the corresponding O symbol in no instance whatever represents a short sound, E and O are as late as the fourth century used for long sounds, for those namely, which in the developed orthography are written diphthongally ει and ου respectively, without however being really by origin diphthongs arising from ε + ι, o + υ respectively. In λείπω and γένει the ι is radical, as is also the υ in οὐ and οὗτος; on the other hand in ἔστειλα, στέλλειν, τιθείς, φιλεῖτε the ει is merely lengthened *e*, and in βουλή, διδούς, μισθοῦτε, λόγου the ου lengthened *o*. On the one hand, therefore, the Greeks distinguished ε and o *together with* their lengthened forms, and on the other the sounds η and ω which were always or almost always long, and furthermore it never occurred to anyone in ancient Hellas to distinguish in script ă and ā, ĭ and ī, ŭ and ū, the natural way to do which would have been to double the vowel, just as the consonants were written doubled for similar reasons. Consequently the distinction between H and E, Ω and O was originally one of quality[2], and the only qualitative distinction which can have been intended is that which the Italians make prominent both in pronunciation and in grammatical writing in the case of these two vowels and only these, namely the distinction between open and closed *e* and *o*. The quantitative distinction came to pass accidentally and secondarily, after ε and *o* had been distinguished from their lengthened equivalents by the diphthongal writing of the latter, and it became the more obvious and finally as early as Aristotle[3] the only distinction recognized. But which *e* did the ancient Ionians intend to represent by H, and which *o* by Ω, the open or the closed? On this point the old inscriptions of Keos Naxos and perhaps

[1] In Paros, Thasos, Siphnos conversely Ω was written for *o* (ου), O for ω: ΣΩΙ *σοί*, ΤΩ *τοῦ*, ΤΟΝ *τῶν*, see Kirchhoff p. 65 ff.

[2] This was first explicitly stated, though not with the necessary general application, by Dittenberger on the subject of the old Naxian and Kean inscriptions (*Zum Vocalismus des ionischen Dialekts*, Hermes xv., 225 ff.).

[3] See Arist. *Poët.* c. 21.

Amorgos also are especially instructive; in them H and E only partially coincide with ordinary H and E[1]. For there H is only written for that *e*, which corresponds to old Greek (Doric) *ā*, and also that arising from contraction of εa: ΟΙΚΙΗ, ΔΗΜΟΣ, ΕΠΗΝ, ΘΥΗ, (τὰ θύεα from τὸ θύος)[2]; the η on the other hand which is common to the Greek dialects together with ε and *ē* is denoted by E, without admixture of diphthongal writing[3]: ΜΕ μή, ΕΠΙΒΛΕΜΑ ἐπίβλημα, ΦΕΡΕΝ φέρειν, ΕΝΑΙ εἶναι. The Naxians represent the short sounds also with H, if they have arisen from long *ā*; ΔΗΜΟΔΙΚΗΟ Δημοδίκεω, ΑΛΗΟΝ ἀλλέων[4]; in Keos ε is written in these cases. If then in these dialects that sound is written with H, which elsewhere has the value of *a*, and previously had that value universally, we must give to H the value of open *e*, that is, the *e* which stands nearer to *a*, and to E that of closed *e*, that is, the *e* which stands nearer to *i*, especially as this corresponds to the writing ΕΙ cur-

---

[1] Cp. Dittenb. l. c.; *Mitth. des archæol. Instit.* I. 139 ff., (Keos U. Köhler) = Röhl, *Inscr. Gr. antiquissimae* no. 395 ff. ; *Bulletin de correspondence Hellénique*, III. 1 ff. (Bustrophedon Inscr. on the offering of a Naxian woman) = Röhl 407 ; Bechtel 23, *Bull.* VI. 187, *Mitheil.* xi. 97 (Amorgos); Bechtel, 29 ff. ; Kirchhoff[4] 32.

[2] The two last examples on line 17 of the longer Kean inscr. (derived from a correction on the stone); in the same place occur also διαρανθῆι and line 23 θάνηι; thus in the diphthong ēi (24 ἐξενιχθεῖ) a mixture of the two E sounds appears. But this occurs in Attic also and elsewhere: ΤΕΙ for τῇ side by side with ΤΗΙ. Dittenberger's endeavours on this head are in my opinion misplaced. Röhl's restoration ΤΗ[λοῦ στά]ΝΤΑ l. 16 I consider wrong on the score of meaning; for a lustration of the interior of the house (διαρραίνειν) cannot be accomplished from a distance. The Naxian Inscr. offers only one stumbling block ΗΚΗΒΟΛΟΙ ἐκη-βόλῳ, which D. is certainly right in ex-

plaining as a graver's error for ΗΕΚΗΒ.; for H here still keeps the value of the breathing as well as the other. On the Naxian bronze published by Fränkel *Arch. Z.* 1879, 84 ff. (= Röhl 408) we find ΕΚΗΒΟΛΟΙ. I may here remark, that Merzdorf (*Curtius Stud.* IX. 202 ff.) tries to prove a double value of H in ordinary Ionic: from λαός, ληός (open *e*) came λεώς; from βασιλῆος on the other hand (*e* original and closed) βασιλέος. πόλεως however occurs twice on the tolerably old inscr. of Chios; Cauer no. 133, Röhl no. 381, Bechtel 174, cp. id. p. 107.

[3] But in *C. I. Gr.* 2363 b, Bechtel 44 (Keos) ΕΙΣ occurs twice in proper names of the 3rd declens. alongside ΕΣ (according to the earlier copies, while the later shew lacunae in the places in question).

[4] Comp. πόλῆας in verse, Abdera Röhl 349, Bechtel 162. ΙΗΡΟΝ Thasos Röhl *Imag.* 52, no. 4 is explained by Bechtel (*Ion. Inscr.* 56) as a mistake for ΙΙΡ., since ἱρός is found elsewhere in Thasos.

rent elsewhere, and the latter as early as the Alexandrian period had become *i.* Consequently ω also is open *o* (*ǫ*), and *o* the closed: in fact the lengthened equivalent of the latter became at an early period a *u.* Those then pronounce correctly, who give to μή a sound similar to French *mais*—in Keos and Naxos, it is true, the pronunciation was *mé,* but the mode of writing was also different—; no German on the other hand pronounces ἐμέ correctly, inasmuch as the short closed *e,* frequent in Italian (*féndere, elmo*)[1] is strange to that language. Ω in ὥρα must be pronounced as *o* in French *encore*; but *o* in ὁρᾶν neither with this sound nor yet with German short *o,* but one tending more to *u,* although not the same as *u.* Here again the Italians might be our instructors[2]. I am not of opinion however, that we ought in practice to exercise ourselves or our pupils in this mode of pronunciation; there could not be a more mischievous waste of time. A striking proof, that the foregoing statements are true in an especial degree for Attic, is, that the Bœotians, when about the beginning of the fourth century they appropriated the symbol H, employed it to represent their dialectal sound arising from common Greek αι ('Αρίστηχμος, κή). That is to say they gave to the symbol derived from their neighbours in Attica, the value, which it had there, and from αι came *ǫ* (*ǟ*), not *ę.* Moreover in the comic poets of Attica the cry of the sheep is represented by βῆ βῆ: ὁ δ᾽ ἠλίθιος ὥσπερ πρόβατον βῆ βῆ λέγων βαδίζει[3]. The next evidence touching ε and η is the contraction of εα to η, in Attic, Doric and Ionic: τείχη Att., ἤν, ἐπήν, θύη, Ionic, Στρατῆς=Στρατέας and Χαλκῆ=Χαλκέα on Rhodian inscriptions[4]. For we cannot get from εα the mixed sound *ę,* which lies nearer *i* than either of the two elements,

[1] Diez *Gr.* 1³. p. 333 (every unaccented *e* in Italian is both short and closed).

[2] Diez 336: "every unaccented *o* is closed."

[3] Kratinus fr. 43 Kock (from the drama *Dionysalexandros,* assigned by Meineke to the younger Kr.). The line is used by Aldus Manutius and afterwards by Cheke (p. 288) in support of Etacism. Further cp. Aristoph. fr. 642 K. θύειν με μέλλει καὶ κελεύει βῆ λέγειν. Lohmeyer (*Phon. Stud.* I. 69) compares Hesych. βηβῆν πρόβατον.

[4] Inscr. of Kamiros and Ialysos published by C. T. Newton, *Transactions of the R. S. of Literat.,* Vol. IX. N. S. Liscovius, p. 19, recognizes in this phenomenon an argument for open *e.*

but ҽα readily gives ҽ, standing as it does midway between the two. The same follows for Doric from the contraction of αε to η : νικῆν, τῆμά i.e. τὰ ἐμά. In fact for dialectal η in general we must everywhere assume the same sound of open ҽ, and accordingly the following history of the E sound for Greek becomes evident[1]. The short e had at that prehistoric time, when forms such as ποιῆσαι πατήρ ἤσθιον arose, still an open sound; for the lengthening gave η ҽ. This open sound may have been retained in those dialects, which in later formations also, such as contractions, keep η as lengthened equivalent of ε, that is in Arkadian Elean Lakonian Lesbian etc. The Dorian dialects coming under this category having ἤχον for εἶχον, ἐφιλῆτο, ἦς, are united by Ahrens under the name of the stricter Dorism. These then, and the Lesbian etc., had everywhere only one sort of e, the open, at least in the long sound, for the short may indeed subsequently have had the same development in these too, which it had long before elsewhere. In the milder Dorism, in Bœotian, Thessalian, and Ionic, ε became at an early period ҽ, hence its lengthened equivalent ει. Further the old long sound as in πατήρ remained in most dialects open; but among the Ionic Keans and Naxians and also in Bœotia and Thessaly it got the closed sound: ΜΗΤΕΡ mẹ̄tẹ̄r (Keos), ΜΑΤΕΡ and from the fourth century onwards ΜΑΤΕΙΡ in Bœotia and Thessaly. In the last two dialects therefore there was also only one kind of e, that is the closed, except in so far as an open e had been newly developed out of αι. Lastly the special Ionic η was everywhere ҽ. The case is partly analogous, partly different, with respect to the o sounds. Since ω was open, o must have been so too at the time when the nominative -ων arose from -οντ and the augment ω from o; the open sound maintained its ground still longer in those dialects, which made λόγως out of λόγονς and λόγω out of λόγοο, that is, roughly speaking, the same, which shew η for ει, and also Bœotian. In the rest o became at an early period ǫ, hence the lengthening ου. Finally the original long sound as in λέων remained open everywhere except in Thessalian, where it was represented by ου.

---

[1] I follow here the excellent essay of Dietrich, *Zum Vocalismus der griech. Sprache, Kuhn's Zeitschr.* XIV. p. 48 ff.

SECTION 10.

EI *and* OT *from* E *and* O.

I have intentionally deferred to this point the important
question, what the sounds are, which are represented by EI = ē
and OT = ō. First of all there is no doubt on this point, that
the real ει as in λείπω and the real ου as in οὗτος were originally the diphthongs ei (more accurately ẹi) and ου (more
accurately ọu); with these diphthongs at a later period,
lengthened ε and ο are universally confounded in writing,
and were so, in many places, even at an early period. This
levelling took place earliest in Corinth and its colonies, in
the sixth century or even earlier. By the Corinthians the
local symbol Ɓ was employed for ε and η, the ordinary
E for ē and ει: ΔϜΕΝΙΑ (real ει) Δεινίου, ΠΟΤΕΔΑΝ
(do.) Ποτειδάν, ΚΛΕΤΟΛΑΣ Κλειτόλας, but ΞƁΝΟΚΛƁΣ
Ξενοκλῆς[1]. In Corcyra Ɓ is the only form, and both ει's are
written diphthongally[2]. In both places and also in the Sicilian
colonies of Corinth spurious ου is denoted by ΟΤ, while Ο
serves for ο and ω[3]. This ΟΤ is found also instead of Τ in the
diphthong ευ: Ἀχιλλεούς on a Corinthian vase[4]; correspondingly
Corinthian E = ει as second element of the diphthong αι:
ΑΘΑΝΑΕΑ Ἀθαναεία Ἀθαναία[5]. All these forms of writing are
not perfectly constant; for example here and there the Corinthians resolve their E into ƁΣ (ει), as ΠΟΤƁΣΔΑΝ, once we
find even Ἀμφιτρίτα written with E ει in the penultimate

---

[1] Kirchhoff, p. 88 ff.; Röhl *Inscr.
Gr. antiqu.* no. 15, 20, 16, 23. As a
rule I intentionally refrain from giving
the epigraphic forms of the symbols.
That Δεινίας has the real ει is shewn by
the fact that archaic inscriptions everywhere else write EI in names derived
from δεινός: Δεινοδίκηο and Δεινομένεος
Bustrophedon Inscr. Naxos; Δεινομένεος Hiero's helmet, Röhl 510; Δεινα-

γόρης Naxos R. 408; ΔΕΙΝΟ Melos R.
433; Δεινίας C. I. A. I. 299, 433, 447,
483.
[2] Epitaph of Menekrates (Röhl 342)
ἐποίει. Epitaph of Xenvares (R. no.
344) M εἰξιος (real ει) εἰμ'.
[3] Kirchhoff[4], no. 104 f.
[4] Collitz *Dial. Inschr.* 3122 (*An-
nali dell' Inst.* 1862, 56 ff.).
[5] Röhl no. 20, 4 comp. 5.

syllable[1]. From all this it is quite clear, that the lengthened equivalents of ε and o had become so near to i and u respectively, that a need was felt of differentiating the real and spurious e, and in like manner the real and spurious o, while on the other hand no such need was felt of separating original diphthongal ει and ου from the newly developed mixed sound. The mixed sound was thought to be heard in diphthongs such as αι and ευ also, and a corresponding mode of writing was adopted. This sound might be represented by ẹ[i] ᵉi, ǫ[u] ᵒu; the ' i pingue' of Lucilius, which he wrote ei (puerei nom. plur.), will be nothing else but the Corinthian E. For the other Doric dialects our material is not at present adequate; but the diphthongal writing of ει and ου is to be found on one of the Lokrian bronzes of the fifth century[2]. The old Ionic and Attic inscriptions nowhere or almost nowhere shew E for real EI[3], but at a very early period EI for ε̄[4], although the Athenians in particular in by far the larger number of cases do not separate ε and ε̄ in script. We must here state our opinion: the sound which is constant in writing, that is real ει, was constant also in pronunciation; that which was shifting in writing was shifting also in

[1] On the Corinth. clay tablets, published by Röhl under no. 20, Ποτειδᾶνι is written 26 times with E, 4 times with ΒΣ (once also ΠΟΤΒ...), twice with Β = ε, twice with Σ = ι, and once with ΕΣ = ευ. The last three forms are rightly considered by Kirchhoff[4], 103 (note) as errors (omission); in fact Ποτ-<Ε>δάν, 'Αθ<ά>να etc. are also found. We have a certain example of O = ου in ΑΥΤΟ Röhl no. 329 (Anaktorion according to Kirchhoff).

[2] Cauer, Del[2] no. 229; Röhl no. 321; Kirchhoff p. 146; v. Wilamowitz Ztschr. f. Gymn.-Wesen. 1877, 642.

[3] For Attic see Cauer (in Curtius Stud. VIII. 231); he produces as examples of E = real ει only ΟΛΕΖΟΝ (so C. I. A. I. 37 (9 ??); IV. 53ᵃ, with ΟΛΕΙΖΟΝ 1 B 33; IV. 27ᵇ 18. There are found besides ΠΕΣΙΔΟΣ Πείσιδος C. I. A. IV. 373ᵃ; ΕΧΣΑΛΕΨΑΤΟ? do. 53ᵃ 22; also

(Kretschmer Ztschr. f. vgl. Sprachf. N. F. IX. 154) ΗΡΑΚΛΕΔΗΣ C. I. A. IV. 491[10]; ΚΕΤΑΙ κεῖται do. 491[27]; ΜΕΝΕΚΛΕΔΕΣ 373 [117]. These are almost all private inscriptions.—But ἀποδεκνύντες Röhl no. 381 B, 13 shews the Ionic shortening of this verb.

[4] Teos C. I. Gr. 3044 = Röhl 497 KEINO B, 7; in the same place 6 instances of E in this word. Halikarnassus R. 500 at least 4 times EINAI (with E only two certain instances); EIXON; on the other hand φεύγειν and ἐπικαλεῖν with E. The Sigean Inscr. R. 492 has εἰμί in the Ionic part with E, in the Attic with EI. Miletus 6th cent. (Kirch. p. 19 ff., Röhl 488, 485): εἰμί, Κλέσιος i.e. Κλείσιος, ἐποίεν i.e. ἐποίειν. Athens C. I. Att. I. 1 thrice EINAI; Bull. de corresp. Hell. III. 179 EIMI. Comp. Cauer C. St. VIII. 230.

pronunciation. Consequently λείπω did not tend to be pronounced as *lēpo*, but φέρειν (ΦΕΡΕΝ *phẹrẹn*) did tend to the
pronunciation *phẹrẹin*, without however the *i* in this case being
very prominent. For the different treatment of the two sounds
is a proof that they were not quite similar in the fifth century :
etymological scruples about original *i* were obviously foreign to
those writers. I am consequently opposed to the opinion, which
is tolerably general at present, being held by Brugman[1] and
after him by G. Meyer, according to which the spurious ει never
had the value of a diphthong among the Athenians and Ionians,
but was only an orthographic expression for *ẹ̄* ; A. Dietrich[2]
seems to me rather in this respect also to have seen the truth.
For distinction of quantity cannot be regarded either in this
case or elsewhere in ancient times as the cause of difference in
writing: consequently the second syllable of φέρειν was distinguished from the first in *quality*. The levelling of ει and *ẹ̄*,
that is the passing of both of them into the mixed-sound
described above, takes place for Athens and Ionia in the fourth
century ; after the first decades of this century E is very seldom
found for spurious ει, although this mode of writing can be traced
beyond the middle of the century[3]. The Bœotians write their
long closed *e* (= Att. η and ει) even in the fourth century very
frequently with E[4]; the thickened pronunciation can scarcely
here be traced back beyond the beginning of this century[5].
Subsequently the *i* everywhere prevailed over the *e* in the case
of the later (spurious) ει of the various races, just as had long
before happened in Bœotia in the case of the real ει. The view
of Zacher (p. 30 of the treatise referred to on p. 16), that real

---

[1] Brugman *C. St.* IV. 82 ff.

[2] A. Dietrich *Kuhn's Ztschr.* XIV.
67 ; Rödiger *Progr. Berl.* (Luisenst.
Gymn.) 1884 p. 6.

[3] The latest Attic examples known
to me are Ἑστιαιεῖς Ὀτρυνεῖς πρυτάνες
(341/0 B.C.) *C. I. A.* II. 872; ἀποδώσεν
and ἐς do. 804 A⁰ 33, ᵇ13, B.C. 334/3.
Ἀλικαρνασσε̂ (dative) is found in the
inscr. *Bull. de corr. Hell.* 1888, 173
(B.C. 354/3).

[4] For instance the inscr. of Orcho-

menos *Bull. de corr. Hell.* III. 454, *Dialekt. Inschr.* 470, composed soon after
330, has in five instances EI only once,
E 4 times ; that from Thespiæ *id.* p. 382,
Dialekt. Inschr. 798, never has EI.

[5] Examples on the Theban inscrip.
Röhl no. 300, which shews in essentials
the Bœotian alphabet; here EI comes
four times, E thrice ; and ΚαλλικράτEIς
on the archaic inscr. of Akraiphia,
Lolling *Monatsber. d. Berl. Akad.* 1885,
1031 no. 4, 2.

and unreal ει were united in the 4th century into a pure closed e (ē), seems untenable. For if -ειν, as we are bound to assume, was in the 5th century e'n, but in the 2nd or 1st īn, it is quite certain that it cannot in the meantime in the 4th and 3rd have been ēn. With regard to the Attic-Ionic ου=ō the case stands thus: the mode of writing was for a long time almost exclusively O, nay, isolated instances occur, where it is written for ου diphthong, as in TOTON τούτων[1]. Even after the reform of the Attic orthography the simple O held its ground with great persistency, (and got more and more to be used quite indifferently for ου and ō), isolated examples occurring up to the end of the fourth century[2]. In this case then the designation of the diphthongal sound is at an ancient period no more constant than that of the lengthened sound, and accordingly the diphthong ου had as early as the fifth century coalesced with a sound, which arising from ō̦ approximated to ū, and finally became an undoubted ū[3]. When the Bœotians in the fourth century adapted their own to the ordinary orthography, they employed the combination OT in this value, that is for their old T, for which unlike most of the other Greeks they had preserved the old u-sound. In the first quarter of the fourth century however the difference in quality between o and its lengthened form cannot have been great at Athens, since to take an instance on the document of the new

---

[1] Dietrich l. c. p. 51 ff. Cauer *Curt. Stud.* VIII. 241 ff. OT is always written for ō on the inscr. of Keos R. 395. In this dialect therefore the coalition took place very early. The Asiatic-Ionic inscr. generally distinguish correctly (Chios R. 380; Halik. 500), in Chios 382 however we have τōτο; Teos 497 b, 26 βαρβάρους. Comp. Erman *Curt. Stud.* v. 284 f. On the Attic treasurer's account *C. I. A.* I. 128 (Ol. 91, 2), TOTON and TOTO stand almost without exception, though it is true the older documents of a similar nature and also most of the later ones shew TOTTON and TOTTO quite without exception (s. no. 117—

176). Other examples of O for real ου from the 5th and 4th centuries are given by Meisterhans *Gr. d. att. Inscr.* ed. 2, p. 49. For ου=ō the oldest example on stone is *C. I. A.* I. 36 ΛO (end of the 6th century?) Ἡρακλέους, Meist. p. 21, n. 121; ηxx. on vases Kretschmor, p. 154 (cp. p. 30, n. 3).

[2] The latest Attic exx. *C. I. A.* II. 836 c—k Μαλθακίο(υ) and other genitives in -ου, Meisterh.[2] p. 6, n. 21. The inscription dates from the time of the Chremonidean War (circ. 262). See also *Bull. de corr. Hell.* III. 513 κοινō and μυλωθρō (B.C. 302, 301).

[3] Acc. to Dietrich p. 60.

maritime alliance (378/7)[1] simple O stands or stood forty
times for this ου, while ου is only written three times for it.
And nevertheless in the same document every ει is constantly
expressed by EI. In agreement with this Plato in the *Kratylus*[2]
indicates the difference between καλόν and καλοῦν simply as one
of accent and quantity. On the other hand on a stone of the year
363/2[3] ō is written only nineteen times with O and twenty-five
times with OΥ; accordingly the transition to ū made rapid
advances, so that about the middle of the century there was no
longer any very great difference between the Bœotian υ in Πύθιος
Pūthios and the Attic ου in βουλή.

SECTION 11.

Later development of the sounds EH, OΩ.

At this point I leave the diphthongs, especially ει, to turn to
the further development of the E and O sounds which remain.
It cannot be allowed that Attic η in isolated instances became
later ει, especially in late Attic βασιλεῖς as opposed to old
Attic βασιλῆς: it is rather the case that the latter goes back
to βασιλῆες βασιλέης, the former to βασιλέες, and the resolved
forms occur both in the fifth and the fourth century[4]. But in
the Dorian and Ionian islands of the Archipelago we meet here
and there in post-classical times with forms of writing such as

[1] *C. I. A.* II. 17. I consider the ου of
'Ιουλιῆται as spurious, cp. G. Meyer[2] p.
92, on Ἰουλος, and *C. I. A.* II. 546, where
in a decree of Iulis ου in every other
word is written diphthongally, but
ΙΟΛΙΗΤΩΝ (occurring three times) is
regularly written so, being evidently
the survival of an old form of writing.

[2] Plat. *Kratyl.* 416 B: λέγουσί γε
αὐτὸ (τὸ καλὸν, "in pronunciation")
ἀρμονίᾳ ("accent") μόνον καὶ μήκει τοῦ ου
παρῆκται. Cp. 396 c οὐρανία derived from
ὁρῶσα τὰ ἄνω, 402 B Κρόνος from κρουνός,
406 c ΟΙΝΟΣ from οἴεσθαι and νοῦς, all
without any notice of a difference of
sound.

[3] *C. I. A.* II. 54. The statistics
for Dittenb. *Syll.* no. 79 (likewise belonging to the year 363/2) give OΥ for
real ου 14 times, for spurious (includ-
ing 'Ιουλιῆται) 16; O for real ου 4, for
unreal 85.

[4] Old Attic ΧΑΛΚΙΔΕΕΣ *C. I. A.*
IV. 27[a]; ἱππέης Kumanud. 13 (beginning of 4th century), to be compared
with ἱππέως ἱππέᾱς. Late Attic, e.g.
Εἰκαδέες II. 609; also written εἰες as
ib. 872 Κολλυτεῖες, see Dittenberger,
Herm. XVII. 38: his view is opposed by
Wackernagel *K. Z.* XXVII. 267 f. un-
successfully in my opinion as regards
the chief point at issue.

P. 3

εἴ for ἤ, δεείσῃ for δεήσει, προνοειθήτω, ἐνεῖσαν, ἐνειρύσια¹; also in the Dorian Peloponnese τειρεῖν, εἰ μάν, συντελεῖται (conjunctive)²; which all point to at least a closed E-sound, such as arose at an early period in Keos and Naxos for common Greek η. For this η ει as yet by no means coalesces with ι, although the phenomenon signifies the progress of the sound in this direction. In Bœotia and indeed also in Thessaly the original η as in πατήρ may at the close of the second century B.C. have reached the ι-extremity³; hence it would not be wrong to call the itacistic pronunciation of this letter the Bœotian. Short ε has especially in two cases a tendency to pass into ει, firstly before σ with following consonants, as in Bœotian Θεισπιεῖες Θεσπιεῖς, Θιόφειστος Θεόφεστος, vulgar εἴσχηκα εἴσχημαι⁴; secondly and far more frequently where followed immediately by vowels: MANTEION ἱδρύσειως Κιτιείων βασιλεία (accus. of βασιλεύς) Λειωγόρου εἰαυτόν, in Attic as early as the fifth and fourth century⁵. It has been remarked that an i can very easily be

¹ Epikteta's Will Thera *C. I. Gr.* 2448 (Cauer² no. 148) not infrequent; ἐνεῖσαν and ἐνειρόσια often in the Delian inscr. *Bull. de corr. h.* II. 570 (only in these two words and not without exception in them).

² Mystery-inscr. of Andania Cauer no. 13 (2nd ed. 47), Dittenb. *Syll.* 388; Mantineia Le Bas 352ʰ (τειρεῖν by ἐτήρησεν); do. 352¹ 43, εἰ for ἤ. Εἰ μάν however appears to be rather a jussum speciale of the language than to rest on a universal principle; for it is found also (as εἰ μήν) in the Septuagint and quoted in the *Etymol. M.* s. v. (Lachmann, *N. Test.* 1, p. XLI). Also συντελεῖται προσδεῖται conjunct. Athens Dittenb. *Syll.* 337, 11 (Psephism of Demades).

³ Kumanudis 'Αττικῆς ἐπιγρ. ἐπιτ. 1826 'Ισμυνίχα—Θηβαία. 'Αθήναιον IX. 362 (Lebadeia) Νιομνίω by Νιομεινίω; ἀδικῖ conjunct. for Bœot. ἀδικεῖ, *Dial. Inschr.* 425 (Lebadeia) λειτωργίμεν; 1329 II. aˡ⁰ (Thessaly shortly after 196

B.C.) Χρισίμου for Χρεισ. an accidental omission of the E.

⁴ In Thespiae itself Θεισπ. is the regular orthography, in the writing of the dialect; likewise Orchom. *Bull. de corr. h.* III. 463 in the Bœotian part of the document always Θεισπ. and actually (line 91) Θεισπιειεις τὸ, in the same place Θιόφειστος i.e. Att. Θεόθεστος; on the other hand in the part composed in the κοινή both names are written with ε.—As to εἴσχηκα see G. Meyer *Gramm.²* § 112; εἴσχον Telos *Bull. de corr. h.* III. 42; εἰστήληι, *C. I. A.* II. 563 (elsewhere ἐστήληι i.e. ἐν στήληι).

⁵ *C. I. Att.* IV. 373⁹⁹, II. 168, 263, 352, 553,115ᵇ. Meisterhans 2nd ed. p.35. In like manner we find on the Ionic inscr. of Zeleia *Mitth. d. arch. Inst.* VI. 229 (Ditt. 113) εἰάν and ἐννεία, and I have no doubt, that Æolic πρέσβεια = πρεσβέα πρεσβευτήν and in general -ειος as gen. to ευς assigned by grammarians to the later Ionians and Æolians, are so to be explained (Meyer² § 149).

developed after a preceding vowel from the sound of the s, and in like manner a weak i (or y) is a natural result when the voice passes directly from ǫ to another vowel. For the quality of ε as ῐ in the Hellenistic and Roman period we can cite, besides the confusions with ει, of which there are isolated occurrences before other consonants also[1], the fact that Latin ῐ in many positions was expressed by the Greeks in the earlier period with ε; Τεβέριος and Τέβερις, Δομέτιος, Καπετώλιον, Καικέλιος, λεγεών, λέντιον =linteum[2]. The Latin sound hovered between i and ǫ; if therefore the Greek ε had been ǫ, the ι would certainly have been nearer the Latin sound. In like manner Latin ŭ too, which hovered between u and ǫ, was in Greek prevailingly represented by o, until in the time of the Empire ου appeared, having been before avoided[3]. This also agrees well with the pronunciation of o as ǫ, although indeed it might also be explained as having arisen from necessity. Here and there ου is substituted for o in Greek popular dialects; Νικοκράτεους by -εος in Thessalian, Δάμωνους Νίκωνους in the Peloponnese, Τιμουρρόδου on Rhodian vase-inscriptions[4]. But the Hellenistic popular speech, as spoken in Egypt for instance, confuses o and ου far less than o and ω: the latter as early as the time of the Ptolemies are correctly distinguished throughout on the papyri by very few scribes, and cannot have had any considerable difference in sound in the ruder speech[5]. In this case therefore

---

[1] So (in Dor. inscr. Ahrens II. 190) C. I. Gr. 2140 φανειρός, ἐπιφανείστατος, εἰν τῶι; 1840 πειδίωι by πεδίωι; 1699 εἰνδογενῆ.

[2] Dittenb. Herm. VI. 130 ff.

[3] Id. p. 281 ff.

[4] Heuzey Mission archéol. en Macédoine Inscr. no. 214 = Dial. Inschr. 1461 (Halos). Le Bas 159 e (Hermione?) C. I. Gr. III. p. XIII. no. 447—452, 5673 b, 5751 (also isolated Τιμουρρόδου Τιμορρόδου). υ for o also once in these vase-inscriptions: Ἀθήναιον III. p. 231 Ἀγαθυμβρότου, cp. Ἀγαθυρρόδη Rhod. inscr. Bull. de corr. h. v. 333. Περιούντος Delos ib. VII. 8.

[5] I note in Papyrus 1 of the Louvre collection (Notices et extraits de manuscrits XVIII. 2, cp. Eudoxi ars astron. Kiel, 1887): col. 3 μεῖξων. 8 ἔχων for ἔχον. 14 ὠκταετηρίδα. ὦ for ὅ. τὸ αὐτὸ τρόπωι. 15 ὡρᾶται. κύκλων for -ον. 20 μεῖξων. 2 and 22 f. μεθοπορινός often. This ms. containing a sketch of astronomy was written before 165 B.C.; for a fragment of a public document on the reverse side is dated in this year, on which also mistakes such as ἐνοπίοις and ὥπως occur. But the writer of no. 40 (B.C. 156) is guilty not only of Μακεδώνος, ὥντος etc. but even of πολόντος (πωλοῦντος), βολομένου, and in no. 41 (the same date) we find παρ' Ἀπολλωνίωι (i.e. Ἀπολλωνίου) τοῦ Γλαυ-

the subsequent development consisted entirely in the cessation of the qualitative and finally also of the quantitative distinction between o and ω.

The case is not quite the same with η and ε: these sounds also are, it is true, frequently confounded by the Papyri[1], and on the latter as well as on inscriptions ε no less than η is used for the e arising from αι[2], but in other localities η followed the tendency to become i, while ε remained stationary or actually moved in the reverse direction. In this period however we must make a very sharp distinction between the cultivated language and that of the people: the transformations in the latter passed by no means at once into the former. For instance, it is certain that η preserved the e sound among cultivated speakers up to the fourth century A.D.; for this fact we have the clearest evidence in Greek and Latin authors. Dionysius of Halikarnassus[3] puts forward in respect of agreeableness of sound the following descending scale of long vowels; a, η, ω, υ, ι, i.e. he denotes ι as the least agreeable, η the most agreeable after a. The description, which he gives of the production of η and of ε, is unfortunately not of such a kind, that we can with any certainty infer the distinction of an open or closed sound[4]. At a later period the qualitative distinction between the two letters is absolutely denied; this of course must be taken as a general statement and not extended to the distinction between e̱ and e̤.

κίου. Of course ω and o of inscriptions also occasionally interchange, but in the early period not by any means frequently.

[1] Pap. Louvre 1 shews the following: col. 5 πυροειδές twice for -ῆς. 11 οἰκέσεως. 12 δισκοειδές and σκαφοειδές. no. 40 ἀπελλάγην; 46 ἤζημίοται. Inscr.: Μηλησίππου and Ἐμπήδου Delos Bull. de corr. h. II. 341.

[2] See below under αι.

[3] Dionys. Halik. π. συνθ. p. 75 ff. R.

[4] P. 76. δεύτερον δὲ τὸ ῆ, διότι κάτω τε περὶ τὴν βάσιν τῆς γλώττης ἐρείδει τὸν ἦχον ἀλλ᾽ οὐκ ἄνω (as has been before said of a, τοῦ πνεύματος ἄνω φερομένου πρὸς τὸν οὐρανόν), καὶ μετρίως ἀνοιγομένου τοῦ στόματος (farthest in the case of a).—p. 77. τῶν δὲ βραχέων οὐδέτερον μὲν εὔμορφον (on account of their shortness) ἧττον δὲ δυσειδὲς τοῦ ε τὸ ο (thus Usener Ind. schol. Bonn 1878; the mss. give some τὸ ε some τὸ ο). διίστησι γὰρ τὸ στόμα κρεῖττον θατέρου καὶ τὴν πληγὴν λαμβάνει περὶ τὴν ἀρτηρίαν μᾶλλον. I think, that it is rather ε which is preferred; for of ω it is said before, that the πληγὴ takes place περὶ τὸ ἀκροστόμιον: would it then in the case of o be περὶ τὴν ἀρτηρίαν μᾶλλον?

Sextus Empiricus (about 200 A.D.) declares, that there are naturally only five vowels, not seven; for if ă and ā are to be reckoned as one letter, this will be not less the case with ε and η, o and ω, since ε and o lengthened give η and ω, the latter shortened ε and o[1]. In like manner Terentianus Maurus (end of the third century) says: litteram namque ε videmus esse ad ῆτα proximam, sicut o et ω videntur esse vicinae sibi: temporum momenta distant, non soni nativitas[2]. Marius Victorinus, Ausonius and Martianus Capella[3] also in the fourth century bear witness to the universal quality of η as e; the same may be said of Ulfilas, in whose translation of the Bible η is prevailingly represented by Gothic e, seldom and then only owing to the fault of the East-Gothic scribes in Italy by i[4]. Isolated examples of confusion of η and ι, which have been cited from inscriptions of the period of the Empire or even earlier, have the less weight as opposed to these evidences, inasmuch as such examples in many instances do not bear a critical examination[5]. And even those instances, which do bear such an examination,

[1] Sextus Empir. *adv. mathem.* p. 625 Bk.:—ἀκολουθήσει καὶ τὸ ε καὶ τὸ η ἐν εἶναι στοιχεῖον κατὰ τὴν αὐτὴν δύναμιν κοινόν. ἡ γὰρ αὐτὴ δύναμις ἐπ' ἀμφοτέρων ἐστί, καὶ συσταλὲν μὲν τὸ η γίνεται ε, ἐκταθὲν δὲ τὸ ε γίνεται η (there follows a corresponding statement with regard to o and ω).

[2] Terent. Maur. v. 450 ff.

[3] Mar. Victorin. *Ars gramm.* p. 39 Keil: quam (the syllable *Ther* in *Thersandrus*) si produxeris—, ut pro e η Graeca littera audiatur, quae semper natura longa est. Auson. p. 202 ed. Bip.: ῆτα quod Aeolidum (i.e. Graecorum, see Henrichsen p. 145) quodque e valet, hoc Latiare E. Mart. Cap. III. § 235: E autem vocalis duarum Graecarum litterarum vim possidet. Nam cum corripitur, ε Graecum est, ut *ab hoc hoste*; cum producitur, ῆτα est, ut *ab hac die.*

[4] *Aunisimus* 'Ονήσιμος, *Filippisians* Φιλιππησίους. In Koptic also the letter ﻪ signifies in the earlier period e and is confused with ε; only in a later period

with I; vide Stern's *Koptic Gramm.* p. 32.

[5] Thus IPΩΩN is said to stand on the inscr. of Karpathus in Ross 3, no. 264, as the editor himself makes prominent. If however we look more closely we find that this word stands by itself in a line and is preceded by an empty space, and moreover that there is a serious gap in the sense. I therefore have no doubt that the first half of H has disappeared in this gap. Dittenberger *Herm.* VI. 147 cites *C. I. Gr.* 2588 (Gortyn) Κυντήλιος *Quintilius*, Κυρίνης, 2790 (Aphrodisias) ἐψηφησμένα, 6672 (Rome) Καλλήστρατος ἀνέθικεν. He says in general, that such instances become more frequent according to the various localities towards the end of the second, or as in the case of Athens, not till the third century. Meisterhans p. 15 places the transition at Athens 150—250 A.D. Δινάρια appears twice on the inscr. of Gytheion Le Bas 243[a] (161—169 A.D.), without any other

are with regard to the general statement convincing only for the popular dialect, not for the general pronunciation.

Incomparably more valuable than a few dozen of such isolated scriptural errors is the fact, that in the Alexandrine mss. of the Bible belonging to the fourth century, the Sinaitic and the Vatican, ε and αι (ę), ι and ει (ι) and indeed υ and οι are not infrequently confused; but not η (ę) and ι; the pronunciation of these symbols is consequently established beyond a doubt for this period and locality. Moreover in the *Psalterium Veronense* of the fifth to sixth century, which gives the Greek text in Latin letters, e stands for ε η αι, i for ι ει and y for υ and οι[1], from which we may infer, that in the West the old pronunciation of the η maintained itself for a very long time. In like manner Egyptian documents of the Byzantine period in the signatures written in Latin letters regularly transcribe η with e[2]. On other points there ought to be no disagreement as to the pronunciation of the real Byzantines; the followers of Erasmus are wrong in attempting at all to rebut the proofs which their opponents have drawn from Eustathius. However the pronunciation as e seems to have maintained itself to this day in the popular dialect of Trapezus[3]. Very few confusions between ι

interchange of η and ι. Bursian, who with regard to η is entirely on the side of the Erasmians, gives on p. 185 as the oldest evidence for η = ι Steph. Byz. s. v. Νάξος : τὸ δὲ κριτικὴ ἀκόνη, ἐὰν διὰ τοῦ ι γράφηται, ἡ διακρίνουσα καὶ φανεροῦσα σημαίνει. It will be found to be an addition of the epitomator Hermolaos, consequently of the date of Justinian. On the numerous Syrian inscr., ranging from the second to the sixth century A.D., communicated by Wetstein *Abhandl. d. Berl. Akad.* 1863 255 ff., ει—ι, αι—ε are very often interchanged, η—ι hardly ever. But the fact, that καὶ here is commonly written κέ, seldom (no. 118) κή, must be explained from the open sound of the ε and the closed sound of η already current then. A similar result is given by the inscriptions of Asia Minor

collected by Sterret (*Archaeol. Instit. of Amer.* vol. III., κή for καὶ no. 395, an inscr. of Christian period with very corrupt orthography). I remark against G. Meyer *Gr.* p. 89, that ποισάμενοι Pap. L. 41, is not itacistic for ποιησάμ., but a plebeian contraction from ποιησ.; comp. πεποίκει and ποῖσαι on the leaden tablets of Knidos, Wachsmuth *Rh. Mus.* XVIII. p. 569 f. The word being much used underwent an especial shortening.

[1] Lachmann *Nov. Test.* vol. 1, p. XLI. In a transcript of the *Symb. Apostol.* belonging to the 9th century η is represented sometimes by e sometimes by *i*.

[2] Wessely *Wiener Stud.* VIII. 112 (*strategiu, esemioth. = ἐσημειώθη* etc.).

[3] Foy *Lautsyst. d. gr. Vulgärspr.* p. 85; Deffner *C. Stud.* IV. 286. Cp.

and η have perpetuated themselves in our mode of writing, but according to the testimony of inscriptions (καθ)ημερίσιος, νυκτερίσιος appear to be correct, a fact which explains away the anomalous use of the η after ρ[1].

Section 12.

Pronunciation of Υ.

Of the two remaining vowels, ι and υ, only the latter demands any description. At the present day it is pronounced like ι, except dialectically, where the sound ü, or ιου, is still heard[2]; the classical pronunciation is ü, but the original sound u, and it was with this latter value that the symbol V (Υ) was taken over by the Italians from the Chalcidians of Kyme. The Chalcidian HVΠV (ὑπό) will accordingly have been pronounced hupu, and the use of Koppa before the nearly allied υ u as well as before o on Chalcidian vases appears quite natural: ϙύϙνος, λήϙυθος[3]. This use of Koppa occurs, it is true, in Corinthian inscriptions also, although in Corinth to all appearance the pronunciation was at a very early period the ordinary modified one. At least I do not know, how the forms on the latter vases Ὑσμήνα = Ἰσμήνη, Κιανίς apparently = Κυανίς[4] admit of any other explanation.

It is quite possible however, that the writing ϙυ was continued into the period when the modification was beginning or even after it had become general. In Euboea the native land of the Chalcidians the place-names Kumi = Κύμη and Stura = Στύρα

Appendix. On νερό, ξερός etc. cp. above p. 21, n. 3, G. Meyer, § 73.

[1] Καθημερίσια C. I. A. IV. p. 76 (col. III. 25); for νυκτερήσιος νυκτερείσιος also has mss. authority (as in Aristoph. Thesm. 204). Cp. νυκτερινός ἡμερινός. In Plin. xxxv. 11, § 124 mss. Bamberg. and Voss. have hemerisios.

[2] Foy p. 86; Meyer[2] § 93. Cp. Appendix.

[3] HVΠV Bechtel Inschr. d. ion. Dial. 3 (Kirchh. 121); ϙύϙνος λήϙυθος C. I. Gr. 7611, 8337; likewise ϙλυτώ 7381

(but Κλυτώ 7459), ϙλυτίος 7382; that is, the interposition of a consonant does not remove the influence on the K-sound (or on its representative). Cp. Ἀρϙύλης (?) Röhl no. 520 (Chalc.) and from Doric Magna Græcia do. 513 ϙυνίσϙος. Corinth Röhl 7, 47 ϙυλοίδας, Dial. Inschr. 3123 (3129) ϙύλλαρος, 3135 ϙλύτος Περιϙλύμενος etc. Cyrene Röhl 506[a] ϙυρα(ναίων). But in Attica Κυνόρτης side by side with ϙόραξ, Meisterh.[2] p. 22.

[4] Dial. Inschr. 3130, 3135.

remain to this day. That the *u*-sound was preserved in the neighbouring country of Bœotia, we know from the transliteration with *ov*, which became usual there after the adoption of the common Greek modification of the Ionic alphabet; this *ov* was in the course of the fourth century already employed for the short sound also: Πουρρῖνος, Φάουλλος[1]. This is another proof, how little the ancient Greeks troubled themselves about the differentiation of short and long vowels in script. The popular Lakonian also still possessed the *U*-sound, as is shewn by glosses[2], such as κάρουα, τούνη i.e. σύ, οὐμαί ὑμέτεραι. It must be stated however that on inscriptions and in the literary monuments of this dialect no such form is found[3]; accordingly the cultivated language of the Spartans may have had the ordinary *ü*, in support of which the interchange of *v* and *ι* on inscriptions such as Τινδαρίδαι, Ἐλευΰνια (Ἐλευσίνια)[4] may be cited.

In Cyprian and Pamphylian also the sound appears to have been the original one[5]. But in general the *u* was modified at a very early period in the same way as Latin *u* in France and northern Italy[6]: this pronunciation is established for the Attic of the fourth century in particular by the Bœotian manner of writing; for the *ov* would not have been introduced, if the Athenians had given the same value to Υ as the ancient Bœotians. Moreover if that had been the case, as *ō* became nearer and nearer in sound to *u*, a confusion between the symbols O (OY) and Υ would have been inevitable. But on Attic and other inscriptions of the fifth and fourth centuries it is rather I and Υ which interchange: βιβλίον and βυβλίον,

---

[1] Orchom. *Bull. de corr. hell.* III. 454 = *Dial. Inschr.* 470 (about 330 B.C.); *v* is written here as well. The Theban inscription on the contributions to the Sacred War ('Αθήναιον III. 479, *Dial. Inschr.* 705) has *ov* only for *ū*. Cp. R. Meister *Gr. Dial.* I. 231 f.

[2] Ahrens *D. D.* p. 124 ff.; G. Meyer[2] p. 103 f.

[3] But Κονοουρεῖς = Κυνοσουρεῖς on the very late Lakon. inscr. *C. I. Gr.* 1347 and 1388 comes under this head (Ahrens l. c.). Among literary monu-

ments Alcman's poems come particularly under consideration, since the *ov* has been introduced into the Bœotian poems of Corinna; the Lakonian in the *Lysistrata* indeed shews throughout *v*, but the same may be said of the Bœotian in the *Acharnians*.

[4] Τινδ. Röhl 62[a]; also *Bull. de corr. hell.* III. 365 (Cythera). Ἐλευΰνια R. 79, 11, cp. Ἐλευσυνίω Crete *Bull. de corr. hell.* III. 292 l. 8 (name of month).

[5] G. Meyer[2] p. 105 f.

[6] Diez *Gr.* p. 85 f.

τρίβλιον and τρύβλιον, Μουνιχιών and Μουνυχιών, ἥμυσυ very frequently for ἥμισυ¹, Ἀμφικτύονες and Ἀμφικτίονες. Added to this the treatment of the diphthong υι, which at Athens in the fourth century was simplified to υ almost without exception, would be perfectly incomprehensible, if the latter had been not ü but u: the Bœotians write ουιός. But in Athens even the archaic inscriptions shew ὑύς without ι, the old nominative form corresponding to the genitive υἱέος, and a confusion of sense is created by the coalition of the two υ's, which the composer of an inscription reading from right to left has not even avoided in script (ΗΤΣ), but which was generally got rid of by the transference of the nominative and accusative to another declension². It would seem to me just as unlikely that *huiús* should have become *hus*, as that *οἶος* should ever become *οὖς* in spite of the occasional shortening of the οι. In the next place, if a Greek transliteration like Κυρήνιος from *Quirinius* is only possible on the assumption of the modification of the υ, the same may be said of the υ of the Asiatic Ionians of the fifth century, considering the treatment of Persian names such as *Vištaspa* Ὑστάσπης, *Vidarna* Ὑδάρνης. That the Thessalian pronunciation was *ü*, is shewn by their writing ου instead of the ordinary ω. In the case of the κοινή there is no room for doubt; indeed the modified

¹ *Att. Inschr.* Meisterh.² p. 22; even in the tribute lists of the fifth century Κυδνῆς and Κυνδῆς are interchanged. Βιβλίον *C. I. A.* II. 1ᵇ; βίβλος *Mitt. d. arch. Inst.* VII. p. 368, of the year 346. The writing with υ has no evidence from inscriptions earlier than the first century B.C. but nevertheless appears to be the original (Birt *Buchwesen* p. 12). Quite analogous to βιβλίον is τρίβλιον for τρύβλιον Delos 364 B.C. (*Bull. de corr. hell.* X. 461, l. 16, 23). Μουνυχ. first *C. I. A.* II. 247 (306 B.C.); ἥμυσυ II. 17 A, 45 (378/7 B.C.) and in all later Attic examples; further, *Bull. de corr. hell.* II. 580 (Delos), Pap. Louvre 1, col. 4 and in general here without exception; but in the more correct documents no. 22 and Pap.

Taur. 1, 5 ἥμισυ. In Ἀμφ. the υ appears first 410 B.C. (*Bull. de corr. hell.* VIII. 283). On the inscr. of Halicarnassus *Bull. de corr. hell.* IV. 295 (circ. 400) Σιδύλημις and Συδύλημις; the stone of Sigeion Röhl 492 (6th cent.) Συκεεῦσι Σιγενεῦσι Σιγειές. Examples from Delian inscr. (circ. 180 B.C.) Homolle *Bull. de corr. hell.* VI. 114 (κυλύχνιον cp. κυλίχνη, Κυνθυκῶι -ικῶι, Χοιρύλος assimilation like ἥμυσυ). Δυνδυμέν[ηι Artake *Bull. de corr. hell.* XII. 108. Megarian αἰσιμνάτας, Bechtel n. on *Dial. Inschr.* 3016.

² ΗΤΣ *C. I. A.* IV. 373⁹⁴; ΗΤΤΣ scanned as one syllable do. I. 398, as two syllables IV. 373¹⁰⁰ (-υ). Cp. § 14 below.

pronunciation is proved even in the case of the later Bœotian, only there it takes a different form which coincides with the present English representation of French *u*. That is to say an *i* is prefixed, and there arises an improper diphthong, which so far as the writing is concerned was in Greek actually a triphthong, capable of being scanned either short or long: Πολιούστρατος, τιούχα, Διωνιούσιος. This mode of writing is however never constant, and is generally only found after δ τ θ ν λ[1]. A similar development of sound has taken place also in popular dialects of modern Greek, for instance in that of Trapezus, and in the descendant of the ancient Lakonian, the Tsakonian, from the latter of which are cited λιούκο λύκος, κιουρέ τυρός, νιούτα νύξ and others[2]. In this case the modification, which is strange to the ancient dialect and even in the modern has by no means become general, seems to have established itself in a manner analogous to that in Bœotia; but in Trapezuntine and in the other localities, where a similar phenomenon is found[3], the transition may have been similar to that in English, that is *yu* may have appeared in the place of a *ü* which was disappearing. In ordinary Greek however the *ü* has maintained itself for a very long time, not only through the Roman period, where the Latin representation with *u* and then with *y* is in evidence against its identity with *i*, but also on into the Byzantine era.

For long after the extinction of the diphthongs and the transition of η to ι, υ and οι (which by that time coincided with υ in sound) kept themselves distinct from ι η ει, even the most uneducated masons never confusing them. Accordingly in Suidas' Lexicon, where ει η ι stand together after Z and before I, οι and υ are put by themselves in the alphabetical position of the latter; at that time every one knew by the light of nature, that οἶκος and ὑγρός were not to be looked for under ι or η[4].

---

[1] R. Meister *Gr. Dial.* i. 233. But also ιουιῶ (Tetraphthong!) Chaeronea *Dial. Inschr.* 382.

[2] Foy p. 86; Deffner *C. Stud.* iv. 298 ff.; G. Meyer[2] p. 108.

[3] Meyer produces from the modern Greek of southern Italy χyuno = χύνω χέω, áχyuro áχυρον, from Church Sla-

vonic the borrowed words, kyuminü κύμινον, myuro μύρον, zmyurna σμύρνα.

[4] This is not contradicted by the fact, that confusion between η- οι- υ- ι etc. appears occasionally in a Papyrus of a much older date, see Psichari *Rev. crit.* 1888, 381. For the Byzantine period, where we have such abund-

Lastly we must not omit to mention, that Quintilian sees an especial euphonic superiority of the Greek over the Latin language in the possession of the v-sound[1].

SECTION 13.

Diphthongs having the first vowel long (HY, ΩY, ĀI, ΩI, HI).

So much for the simple vowels; we have now to speak of the diphthongs formed from them. These have in the lapse of time altogether lost their distinctive character, by no means however simultaneously, but rather one sooner another later. I begin with those improper diphthongs, the first element of which is a long vowel, that is *āι ηι ωι (āυ) ηυ ωυ*; these indeed were the first to lose their distinctive character. We must in accordance with what has been said. before lay down as their original value: *āi, ēi, ōi, ēu, ōu*; the *u* when occurring as the second member of a diphthong having in general, as will be shewn later, the value of *u* proper. Now these semi-diphthongs are one and all inconvenient to pronounce, because the component parts do not coalesce to a proper unity, and hence the tendency of the language, either to fuse them more closely together by shortening the first element, or to simplify them by rejecting the second. In the former way we may suppose that *āu*, if this sound was indeed heard in such a word as Attic γραῦς = Ionic γρηῦς, at an early period was identified with *ău*; in the Attic ναῦς in spite of the Ionic νηῦς a short vowel must be assumed, since an *ā* would in these cases in Attic also have become *η*[2]. ΩY hardly occurs in Attic (πρωυδᾶν = προαυδᾶν,

---

ance of evidence, it is not only allowed but incumbent on us, to sift this evidence more than elsewhere; it is impossible that an obscure Egyptian scribe should be taken as an authority for the general cultivated pronunciation in the Byzantine realm. The great mass of evidence certainly shews the long continuance of a separation between *ü* and *i*. See also Krumbacher *Ber. d. bayer. Ak.* 1886, 444,

who draws the conclusion that the 9th and 10th centuries were the period, in which the transition from οι and υ to the I- sound was completed. Hatzidakis Ἀθήναιον x. 42 ff.

[1] Quint. xii. 10, 27: jucundissimas ex Graecis litteras non habemus, vocalem alteram, alteram consonantem (υ and φ), quibus nullae apud eos dulcius spirant.

[2] G. Meyer[2], p. 134.

ωὑριπίδη = ὦ Εὐριπίδη), is more frequent in Ionic and Doric, but even here is almost confined to crasis: ἑωυτοῦ, ὡυτός. Now we find on an Ionic inscription ἐουτῶν[1], with shortening and at the same time also approximation of the first sound to the second (ǫυ instead of ǭυ); κοὐ = καὶ οὐ also may be ascribed to this shortening, since κωὐ would have been the regular crasis and is actually recorded in Sappho and Epicharmus[2]. In the middle of the fourth century the Athenians retained ηυ in the augments of verbs with initial ευ, and it is therefore rightly replaced in texts; at a later period these verbs were augmentless, that is ηυ ǭυ had passed into ἔυ[3]. This also may be regarded as an accommodation of the first element to the second, in so far as ę lies farther than ę from the original sound *a*, although not in the direction of *u* but of *i*. ηυ maintained itself as augment of *au*, chiefly perhaps owing to the Grammarians, if an inference may be drawn from the augmenting of αι to ει, to be mentioned immediately, and from εὐχούμην (from αὐχέω) εὔξησα (from αὐξάνω) of later inscriptions[4].

Far more important in the language are the corresponding diphthongs with ι, in which the other method also, that of simplification, is employed more vigorously. We have an instance of this at a very early period in the nominative of feminines in -ώ, originally -ώι, as is shewn by the testimony of the Grammarians from old manuscripts and by a few inscriptional examples; as a general rule on quite old vases and stones we find only -ο (ω)[5]. The next instance to be produced under this

[1] *C. I. Gr.* 2909 (Mykale) = Bechtel *Inschr. d. ion. Dial.* 144. The reading of this inscription is however by no means certain.

[2] Sappho I. 24 κωὐκ ἐθέλοισα, Epich. 19 Ahrens κωὐδὲν δεῖ. On the other hand κουκ on a Papyrus of the Ionic dialect edited by Petrettini, *Pap. Greco-Egizj* (Vienna, 1826) line 15 (cp. p. 55, n. 2), and more accurately by Wessely, *d. gr. Papyri d. kais. Sammlungen Wiens* (Vienna, 1885).

[3] O. Riemann *Bull. de corr. h.* III. 500 f. (after Wecklein *Cur. epigraph.* 33 ff.). We find, it is true, εὔχθαι in

Köhler *C. I. A.* II. 57[b] (B.C. 362/1), but only owing to an error, since the stone, as Riemann assures us, has HT. On the other hand we have εὐεργέτηκε and εὐεργετήκασι, id. 271 and 283 (end of the fourth century).

[4] Kaibel *Epigr.* no. 192 (Thera, in Roman period, in epic dialect); also v. 3 ΕΥΧΩ is certainly to be emended to εὐχο(υν) not ἔσχον or ἴσχω. Εὔξησα ἐπεύξησα in Greek text of Monum. Ancyranum col. 4, 8; 14, 4.

[5] Meyer[2] p. 315. In Röhl's *Inscr. Gr. ant.* I find only three instances of ι: no. 415, 433 (Melos), 558 (Akrai

head is the -ησι -ασι of early Attic inscriptions by the side of
-ηισι -αισι (i.e. ᾱισι) in the dative of the first declension: this -ᾱισι
-ασι occurs only after ι or ρ, while the form -αις which appears
subsequently following all sounds alike has the a short[1]. The
Dorians, Bœotians, etc. had -αις already in the earliest period ;
the ancient Bœotians having also ᾰι in the dative singular, as
we may gather from the analogy of their οι in the dative of
the second declension ; the same is true of the Arcadians and
Eleans. In the case of these races indeed the diphthongs ᾱι ωι
had in general become αι οι ; for πατροῖος is recorded by the
Grammarians as a Bœotian form[2]. Or again, they kept the
vowels separate, Bœot. Πτωΐων Ὁμολώϊχος Εἰρωΐδας, like
Καραΐων Ἑρμάϊος Νικολάϊος. Among the Thessalians we find in
like manner Εἰρουίδας and πατρουέαν[3], where no one will assume
diphthongs ουι and ουε ; in the other cases this dialect rejects
the ι tolerably early ; τᾶ for τᾶι, τοῦ for τῶι[4]. The Lesbians also
as early as the fourth century begin to dispense with the ι of
the dative[5]. Conversely the Eubœan and Oropian Ionic of the
fourth century weakened final ωι and ηι to οι and ει, reducing
internal ηι before a vowel to the simple sound : ἱερῆον[6]. In the

---

a colony of Syracuse). But the Corinthian vases (*Dial. Inschr.* 3130, 3137,
3143, 3146, 3148, 3152, 3156) furnish
12 examples of OI and none of O.
Conversely the vases in the Chalcidian
alphabet (Kirch.[2] 124) in eight examples
of such names have only one with ι
(Ξανθώι), the Attic vases not one
(Meisterh.[2] p. 109).

[1] Cauer *Curt. Stud.* VIII. 403 ff. ;
Meisterhans p. 94–5. I may remark that
δραχμαῖσι *C. I. A.* I. 48 is by no means
certain, since the remainder of the
line after ΣΙ is wanting. But μυριησι
C. I. A. IV. 53ᵃ, 20 (418 B.C.) is an
error ; χιλιασι stands do. 10, ταμιαισι
17. Also Ionic δεσπόνησιν Röhl 501 ;
but elsewhere -ησι.

[2] Ahrens *D. A.* 193 f. Meister
Gr. Dial. I. 249.

[3] *Dial. Inschr.* 326, 4 ; III. 50 ; IV.
9 ; Εἰρουΐδαιος 345, 86 f. With Bœot.
πατροῖος compare Thessal. Κερδοΐου,
Ahrens, p. 221.

[4] With the article still earlier than
elsewhere : Röhl, no. 327 τάφροδῑται
τᾶ Πειθοῖ (*Dial. Inschr.* 325).

[5] Ahrens *D. A.* p. 99 ; Meister 87 ff.
Still earlier in the case of the article :
Röhl, no. 503 ΤΟ for τῶι twice. Like-
wise in the dat. plur. of the article
τοῖς ταῖς, in other cases -οισι, -αισι.
Ἡρωΐδας *Dial. Inschr.* 281 A, 37 ; 262 ;
Ἡροΐδα Assos *Arch. Inst. of America*
I. p. 75.

[6] Bechtel *Inschr. d. ion. Dial.* p.
9, 13 (Inscr. of Eretria no. 15, Olyn-
thus no. 8, Oropus 18). Ἱερῆον Orop.
18, 33, 36. Bechtel would assume
quantitative metathesis, as in the case

case of the Athenians on the other hand ωι and αι hold their ground almost entirely in the classical and also in the period immediately following; with λῶον and σῶῶ, i.e. no doubt σωιῶ from σωίζω as νομιῶ from νομίζω[1], we must compare the numerous instances where αι and οι lose their ι before a vowel; οι for ωι is hardly more frequent than the converse ωι for οι[2]. The Asiatic Ionians distinguish correctly the conjunctives λάβωισιν (Aorist II. with long thematic vowel) and πρήξοισιν (Aorist I. with short)[3]; exception might be taken to κοινοπίδης on the same Chian inscription, since καὶ οι- must by rights give κὼι; on the other hand τοικόπεδον on the same is correct, as ο + οι cannot give ōι[4]. The case stands otherwise however with HI both for Attic and the other dialects. Dorian inscriptions shew very early for ηι, in the conjunctive for example, sometimes η (E) sometimes ει[5]; in Bœotia ει is indistinguishably confounded with η and ηι; on Ionic inscriptions the dropping of the ι in the dative, and the use of ει in the

---

of εω from ηο: ηῖ to εῖ, and then to ει. In any case in this dialect it is impossible to consider the οι to have been an original locative, as many do in the case of Bœotian etc. (Eretria Ἐφημ. 1888, 83 ff. l. 180c ΣΟΙΝΑΡ-ΓΟ[Τ], i.e. Σοιναύτου=Σωιν.?).

[1] C. I. A. II. 162; 12ᵇ, 7. (Others, as Cauer, p. 416 ff. and G. Meyer[2], p. 470, take σῶω as present form with future sense; cp. σῶον, θωά, Meisterhans p. 52.)

[2] τοῖ δήμοι, C. I. A. II. 277 (ΤΩΙ-ΔΗΜΩΙ Pittakis); τοῖ δήμοι τοῖ Διονύσοι τραγοιδοῖς by side of six instances of ωι Ἐφ. ἀρχ. 1884, 69 ff. (in the same are two instances of ο for ου; ει always for ηι); κωμοιδίαι, Kaibel no. 38 (ivth Century); conversely οἰκοσίτωις, C. I. A. II. 834ᵇ; II. 24 (B.C. 329/8), ἑκάστωις (for ἑκάστωι sing.? Meisterh. p. 52) 258 (B.C. 304), ωἰνοχόη 403 (iiird Century); στεφανῶι 3rd sing. ind., Bull. de corr. hell. III. 120 (ivth Century). Epidaurus Ἐφημ. ἀρχαιολογ.

1886, p. 147, line 56 Ἀξιόχοι. 69 τοῖ. 238 Τιμασιθέοι. 254 Ἀριστόνοι. There are however in this inscription other instances of confusion between Ο and Ω, as Λυσίοι alongside Λυσίωνι.

[3] Röhl, no. 381 (Bechtel, no. 174); the correct explanation for the alteration of ωι, ηι and οι, ει in the conj. on inscrip. of Asiatic Ionia (and Crete) was given by Schulze, Herm. xx. 491.

[4] The modes of writing such as ῷνοχόος and ῷνος, Eur. Cycl. 560, I cannot consider correct. Comp. μισ-θόοι, μισθόει=μισθοῖ, διπλόοι=διπλοῖ.

[5] Ahrens D. D. 293 ff.; G. Meyer[2] p. 86. On the Xuthias inscription (Sparta?) Röhl, no. 68; ΖΩΕ, ζώη occurs twice by ΑΠΟΘΑΝΕΙ. On the pillar of Damonon (Sparta) R. 78, ΠΕΠΟΚΑ. The inscription of Gortyn however, which always has ι in the subjunct., has ΟΠΕ, so that these adverbs must be placed in a separate category.

conjunctive. is strikingly frequent[1]; at Athens from about 376 B.C., although the usage of Ionic H was in other respects correct, EI (in isolated instances even E) was often written, and this orthography at the close of the fourth century actually prevails for every HI, e.g. τεῖ βουλεῖ, Αἰγείς for Αἰγῆς, ἐπεινέκασι, εἱρέθησαν[2]. It occurs also on inscriptions and Papyri[3] in the Hellenistic period, and that it existed in manuscripts, is shewn by isolated remnants on the Herculanean rolls, such as ἐκίνει for ἐκείνηι[4]. But with some exceptions, such as the 2nd pers. of the pres. mid. where an endeavour was made to distinguish indicative and conjunctive by -ει and -ηι, and words such as λειτουργία for ληιτουργία[5], it was done away with by the Grammarians. In fact this is a domain, where the current rules of orthographic distinction may here and there be challenged. For instance we write the feminine derivatives of words in -ευς in Attic with -ής or (which is certainly wrong) with -ηΐς, but the corresponding masculine forms (patronymics) with -είδης; are we then, in an inscriptional instance like Ἀριστηίδης[6], to assume that ηι is wrongly sub-

---

[1] Chios R. 382 αὐτῆ; other examples of ι omitted in Röhl ib., Bechtel, *Inschr. d. ion. Dial.* p. 72.

[2] Since EI for HI is commoner the later the period, we cannot consider it a remnant of the pre-Euclidian orthography. It is rightly explained by Ahrens, l. c.; there is an accurate enumeration in Meisterhans, p. 30; complete statistics, Hecht, *Orthog.-dial. Forsch.* II. Simple E, *C. I. A.* II. 61 (after 357) χαλκοθήκε and αὐτê (also ἔχε for ἔχει?), in other instances in the same ει and ηι. If we suppose ηι = ει, the writing E is analogous to o for real ου, which also occurs at that period. (E, i.e. ŷ *where*, ancient Attic, *C. I. A.* IV. 53ᵃ, 35; the inscr. is in other respects also not very accurate.)

[3] Inscr. of Delos, *Bull. de corr. h.* II. 331 always ει, ib. 570 ff. ει and ηι without any rule; Samos ib. v. 482, Ἑρμεῖ ib. 307, Delphi εἱρέθησαν.

Papyr. Louvre 22 (2nd cent. B.C.) Μεννίδει τῶι ἐπιμελητεῖ, 15 ἐπιμελητεί καθειρημένος Ἡρακλείδει; similarly in Pap. Taur. 1. II. All these documents are in other respects very correct.

[4] Gomperz, *Wiener Akad.* vol. 83 p. 91, also in Philod. π. θανάτου (Scott *Fragm. Herc.* p. xxxvii s., ed. Mekler, col. 36, 1; 37, 13); cf. 3.

[5] On λητουργία (written everywhere in Attica as late as the 4th century) Foucart, *Rev. de Philol.* N. s. I. 37; Meisterhans², p. 30. This ει remained in the language also in Αἰγείς etc., where inscriptions of the Roman period give Αἰγίς, Meisterhans² p. 30. In these cases the η had not the support of any cognate form as it had in τιμῇ (cp. τιμή, τιμῆς, τιμήν). The grammarians introduced the poetical form Αἰγηΐς.

[6] Example given Meisterh. ed. 2

stituted for ει, or shall we consider Ἀριστηίδης and Αἰγηίς alike the correct writings? We have also Ἀρχενήιδης, Ἀρρενήιδης, Χαιρελήιδης from Ἀρχένεως, Ἀρρένεως (for -νηος)[1], Χαιρέλεως; in the datives γραμματῆι, πόληι[2], cp. γραμματέως, πόλεως for -ηος. Since the -ηι in the third decl. appears considerably earlier than the -ει in the first we cannot regard the former as due to this confusion of ηι with ει. Still inscriptions of the fourth century do occur, which correctly distinguish in these cases, just as we do, Ἀριστείδης, ἀκροπόλει, but τῆι βουλῆι and so on[3]; consequently if πόληι is original, the transition to πόλει under the influence of the other cases (?) (πόλεως, πόλεις, πόλεσι) may yet have taken place at an earlier time and have been more general than that of τῆι to τεῖ. According to what has been said there has taken place in this transition an approximation of the first element to the second, e͟i for e͟i, simultaneously with a shortening; in the case of the Dorians, with whom -ηι was in general far more rare of occurrence, it was the more readily done away with, and indeed with the result that for e͟i sometimes e͟ sometimes e͟i was heard. Arcadian, which also does not know ᾳ ῳ, always shews η in the conjunctive. With the close however of the third century B.C. came the period, in which the ι of the diphthongs ᾱι ηι ωι began to disappear altogether from the language. Private documents of the second century, such as the emancipation inscriptions at Delphi and the ordinary sort of Papyri, shew more or less numerous errors in this respect, τὸν ἱερῆι, ἐχέτωι, ταυτάι (neut. pl.) with improper ι, Ἐρυμάνδρα as dat., ἐφ᾽ ὧτε, ἐν κατοχῆ

---

p. 29, n. 179; cp. Bull. de corr. hell. 1888, 136.

[1] Meisterh. p. 29, n. 180—182.

[2] γραμματῆι, C. I. A. II. 90 (about 356); πόληι ἀκροπόληι IV. 51 f. (410 B.C.); II. 25, 35, 42 (all before 376), 50 (372); last example according to Meist. p. 108, n. 991, 162 a, 12, B.C. 335. Add Bull. de corr. hell. XII. 139 (378/7), 142, 153 ff., l. 30 (393), 161 f. (399). πόληι, Iasos Bull. IV. 497 = Bechtel, n. 104, 3 (4th century);—κ]ράτηι, C. I. A. II. 644 (B.C. 400/399); also ἔτηι for

ἔτει C. I. A. II. 1059 (321 B.C.), Ἀπολλοφάνηι 834, 6, II. 54 (329 B.C.), Meisterh.[2] p. 31. Meisterh. considers γραμματῆι also erroneous, because there is only one instance of it, while there are many of γραμματεῖ and much earlier.

[3] Bull. de corr. h. III. 474. Attic documents of 369 and 363 deposited at Delos (HI in dat. 1st decl. and in conj. in 11 instances; ἀκροπόλει twice; Ἀριστείδης once).

without the proper ι[1]. Among these irregularities we still find the earlier ει and οι also, for instance at Delphi once in the same line τῶ and οῖ i.e. ῶι[2]. Similar uncertainty prevails e.g. on the Cretan inscriptions in Teos, which likewise date from the beginning of the second century[3]. Still it is possible that the cultivated pronunciation of this period still maintained the ι, although for the common people it was a mute letter: at least on carefully composed inscriptions and Papyri there is as yet no uncertainty in its use, except that it is added (and indeed consistently) to the optative, as for instance εἴηι, θείηι[4]. It is certainly allowable, although some caution is necessary, to take good documents of the second century as evidence in doubtful cases; on the other hand hardly those of the first, and certainly not those of the Empire. For it actually came to pass, that even the educated no longer knew, except perhaps in the case of the dative, where the mute letter ought to stand and where not, and that the Grammarians disputed among themselves and tried to ascertain scientifically, as for instance

---

[1] See the Delphian documents published by Wescher-Foucart and similar examples in *Bull. de corr. h.* v. 397 ff., from the latter of which I have taken my examples. Pap. Louvre 63 (B.C. 165), col. 7 ταὐτάι; col. 3 λόγω τινί, 4 ᾽υτηιρᾶι, 6 βραβευθῆ and τύχη conj., no. 22 (tolerably correct) ἐν κατοχῆ and ἐπαναγκάσῃ, 23 (a sort of rough draught of the foregoing) the ι commonly omitted.

[2] *Bull.* l. c. p. 430; Wescher-Foucart no. 304, τρόποι οἵ κα θέλη.

[3] Cauer[2] no. 122 ff. The Delian inscr. *Bull. de corr. h.* vi. 6 ff. has ᾱι and ωι correct, but never ηι, instead either η or ει. Cp. the letters of the kings of Pergamos (middle of 2nd cent.), Domaszewski *Arch. Epigr. Mitth. a. Oest.* 1884, 95; Wilamowitz *Lect. Epigr.* [1885], p. 16: ᾱι, ωι regular, ηι with errors. As further examples I cite: *Bull.* iii. 290 (Cret. document at Delos; end of 2nd cent.) entire confusion. iv. 50 (Abdera) Θρακῶν, ἠτεῖτο; in other respects correct. Ib. 164 (Teos, middle of the 2nd cent.) Σαμοθρακιασται. v. 42 (Phokis, after 181 B.C.) = *Dial. Inschr.* 1539, Dittenberger *Syllabus* 294, τᾶ, τῶ etc.

[4] Papyr. 24 (Dialectics) is correct in this respect, also 1 (Astronomy), where in other matters there are very bad orthographical blunders; it must be admitted however that it has, col. 14, τὸ αὐτὸ ὕδωρ τὸ αὐτὸ τρόπωι. Further, 15 (legal verdict); Pap. Taur. 1 (do.), but ἠρεῖτο col. 3; 7 and 8 θείηι; 9 εἴηι. This mode of writing occurs also on the Tean inscr. *Bull. de corr. h.* iv. 113, where εἴηι appears line 50 and 65. The inscription shews Ionic forms but the style of the writing belongs to the 2nd cent. On another Tean inscr. Le Bas v. 86 (Rescript of King Antigonus, between 306 and 301), the constant writing ληττουργεῖν is noteworthy.

by comparison of dialects, the rights of ι ἀνεκφώνητον. In consequence of this there is at the present time much doubt on the subject, though the investigations of Usener especially have done us great service[1]. In ancient times indeed many omitted the ι on principle as useless, as Strabo says, "many throw overboard the entire custom, as having no reason grounded on Nature[2]." The Latin transliterations also are instructive for the distinction of the pronunciation of the late period from the earlier. In words which were taken over at an early age ωι is treated just as οι, ᾱι with ι ἀνεκφώνητον just as αι δίφθογγος ἡ ἐκφωνοῦσα τὸ ι: *citharoedus, comoedia, tragoedia*; *Thraex*[3]. At a later period on the contrary the ι was not regarded: *ode, melodia, Thracia*. The Musicians how- ever maintained against the Grammarians, that the letter was really pronounced, and only drowned by the preceding long vowel[4], and to this perhaps may be ascribed the fact, that Dionysius of Halikarnassus on the subject of the Pindaric ἀγλαΐᾳ ἴδετε speaks of the ι, which in pronunciation precedes the ι of ἴδετε[5]. For the rest the mute ι was written, so far as it was written, after as well as before in the same line with the rest of the letters, and it is not until manuscripts of about the seventh century that we meet with ι written a little higher or a little lower (*a·aι*), not until those of the twelfth century with ι *subscriptum*[6].

---

[1] Usener *Fleckeisen's Jahrb.* 1865, p. 236 ff. But ὦδε without ι is shewn to be correct by the metrical inscr. *Bull. de corr. hell.* VII. 61 (Thessaly, poetical dialect; σώιζων in the same); ἄνω κάτω εἴσω προτέρω by the docu- ments relating to the building of the Arsenal, *C. I. A.* II. 1054, 78 f. 24, and the inscr. Röhl 552ᵃ (Olympia).

[2] Strabo XIV. p. 648: πολλοὶ γὰρ χωρὶς τοῦ ι γράφουσι τὰς δοτικάς, καὶ ἐκβάλλουσι δὲ τὸ ἔθος φυσικὴν αἰτίαν οὐκ ἔχον.

[3] *Thraex, Thraecius, Thraecidicus* in Cicero (only *Sest.* 94 and *Rep.* II. 9 with *a*; the writing with *e* is a cor-

ruption of that with *ae*).

[4] *Bekk. Anecd.* III. 1186: οἱ μουσικοὶ τῆς ἀκριβείας φροντίζοντες λέγουσιν ὅτι ἐκφωνεῖται μέν, οὐκ ἐξακούεται δὲ διὰ τὸ μέγεθος τῶν μακρῶν φωνηέντων.

[5] Dionys. π. συνθ. p. 162 R. παρά- κειται δὲ καὶ—τῷ ἀγλαΐᾳ, εἰς τὸ ι λήγοντι, τὸ ἴδετε, ἀρχόμενον ἀπὸ τοῦ ι, comp. what is said 156 f. on Ὀλύμπιοι ἐπί; οὐ συναλείφεται ταῦτα ἀλλήλοις (the ι with the ε). σιωπὴ δή τις ἡ μεταξὺ ἀμφοῖν γίνεται κτέ.

[6] Gardthausen *Gr. Palaeogr.* S. 193, 203. I found the *a·aι w·wι* in a Papyrus ms. of about the 7th cent., see *Ztschr. f. Aegypt. Spr.* 1880, p. 35.

SECTION 14.

Value and treatment of ΥΙ, ΕΙ, ΑΙ, ΟΙ.

The remaining diphthongs with ι, that is υι αι ει οι, have all of them this in common, that from a very ancient time they tend to simplification before following vowels: the ι then in many cases disappears in script, and in pronunciation had at most only the value of a weak *y*[1]. Of the spurious diphthong υι, which from the earliest period and during the whole history of the language appears only before a vowel, there is in Attica so early as the fourth century no trace whatever: there ὑός is written for υἱός, Ὠρείθυα, κατεαγῦα[2]. In all cases however, in ὑός from υἱός just as in ἰχθύδιον from ἰχθυΐδιον, the υ is long, so that it is open to doubt, whether the process is to be regarded as a rejection of ι, or as a coalescing of the two vowels[3]. The Bœotian pronunciation was in any case *ui* (one syllable)[4], but the writing was subsequently triph-thongal, ουι οὐιός; even a tetraphthongal form ιουι (ἰουιός) = *iui* occurs[5]; in Doric there certainly appears a shifting between οι and υι, for instance in the adverbs meaning " whither ? " οἶ οἶς and υῖ υῖς (also without ι πῦς), while we find ει in the participle as ἐρρηγεῖα[6]. In Hellenistic υι is

---

[1] G. Meyer *Gr.*[2] p. 164 ff.

[2] On Attic ὑός P. Foucart *Revue de philol.* N. S. 1, 35; Baunack *Curt. Stud.* x. 89; with υι on the altar of Peisistratus, *C. I. A.* iv. 373ᵉ; also in the 5th cent. ib. i. 374; iv. 373⁹⁰, ¹³¹. In this period also ἐσεληλυθυίας occurs repeatedly (apparently side by side with -ύας) no. 273; but in the 4th cent. Ὠρείθυα, ἐκπεπλευκυῶν, πεπλευκύας, κατεαγῦα, παρειληφῦα, Meisterh.[2] p. 46. Comp. Lobeck *Pathol.* ii. 25; υἱόν in the *Epigr.* Kaibel 86.

[3] Thus Cauer *C. St.* viii. 275. In Attic poetry only ὑ(ι)ός etc.; also in

metr. inscr. as *C. I. A.* iv. 373²¹⁸. In Homer we certainly find ὑ(ι)ός, but Meisterhans (p. 46, n. 407) ought not to make use of this for Attic, in order to write there κατεαγύα etc.

[4] Δέρμυι (dative of Δέρμυς) dissyl-labic in a hexameter in Röhl, no. 265 (Tanagra).

[5] Cp. p. 42, note 1.

[6] Ahrens *D. D.* 364, 367. Υῖς I have restored in the inscr. of Abu-Simbel (R. no. 482), *Herm.* xiii. 381; υῖ Crete Cauer, ed. 2, no. 117, 22; 118, 16.

again written before a vowel, although not always[1], and has consequently been again introduced into the Attic authors. As the Grammarians reckon it among the diphthongs κατὰ διέξοδον, they in any case pronounced it as *üi*. And this pronunciation must be assumed for ancient times in all places where υ had become *ü* uniformly[2]. For the simplification of ει αι οι before a vowel it is sufficient to mention a few facts. Thomas Magister quotes τὰς ἡμισέας from Thucydides, θρασέα γυνή was found in Philemon[3]; we ourselves write πλέον τέλεος; Attic inscriptions shew ἐπιμελέας πρυτανέας ἱερέας (from ἐπιμελεία πρυτανεία ἱερεία) Διομεεύς and other instances[4]. βραχέα is Ionic for βραχεῖα, ἐπιτήδεϊος for ἐπιτήδειος; Lesbian ἀλάθεα = ἀλήθεια[5]; Doric ἀσάλεα = ἀσάλεια, ἡμίσεα[6]. The same holds good with αι: Lesbian has Ἄλκαος Ἀλκαῖος, Thessalian Γεννάος, in the Ionic Styra in Euboea we find Αἰσχράος Σπονδάος[7]; old Attic Ἀθηναία passed through Ἀθηνάα to Ἀθηνᾶ[8], φιλαθήναιος ἔμπαιος δείλαιος Πειραιεύς shew the αι shortened in Attic poets[9], which comes to the same thing as the inscriptional writings Πειραεύς Κυδαθηναεύς etc.[10] The case is different with ἐλάα, κάω, κλάω etc. Here perhaps ᾳ was original, which was simplified to ᾱ, as ῳ in λῷον to ῳ, or again the ᾱ may have been a mistake of the grammarians for αι, just as the supposed Attic ἀετός, which has no support from inscriptions, all of them shewing

---

[1] Pap. L. 61, col. 4 προελπλυθυιῶν; 63, 2 γεγονυιῶν. On Attic inscriptions also υι appears again during and even more after the 2nd century B.C., and in the period of the Empire this is much more frequent than the simple υ, Meisterhans, p. 47. Cp. also ὑειόν (Asia Minor) Sterret *Arch. Inst. of America* III. p. 331, ὑγειοῦ (υἱοῦ) Assos do. I. p. 85 (Christian).

[2] Cp. § 12 above.

[3] Thuc. VIII. 8 (Thom. Mag. p. 172 R.); ἡμίσεας is given also by our mss. except B (which has ἡμισείας). Philemon *Bekk. An.* 99, 24 (IV. p. 8 Mein., fr. 20 Kock).

[4] Meisterhans, p. 31 ff. Examples for α ε ο from old Attic inscriptions given by Cauer *C. Stud.* VIII. 268 ff.

[5] Ahrens *D. A.* 100; Meister *Gr. Dial.* I. 90 f.

[6] Ahrens *D. D.* 187 f.

[7] Röhl *I. Gr. ant.* 372⁴ ᵃᵃᵃ. Bechtel *Insch. d. ion. Dial.* 19¹ᵘ˒¹ᵃᵃ.

[8] Meisterhans, p. 24, n. 138.

[9] Ar. *Vesp.* 282 etc.; δικαίαν Kaibel *Epigr.* 95. Schol. Hephæst. p. 107 W. cites Ἀθηναίων from Eupolis (fr. 85 K.); αἲ and οἲ are especially frequent in Hipponax.

[10] *C. I. A.* II. 50 Κυδ. twice; 573 Πειρ. four times with α, once with αι. Meisterhans, p. 25.

αἰετός[1]. Lastly for οι the best known and most frequent example is ποεῖν ποητής, from which comes Latin *poeta* ; στοιά also became στοά[2], and in the Attic poets scansions such as τοιοῦτος, οἶος οἴει with the first syllable short are frequent.

If then in their final development the diphthongs αι οι ει coalesced into the simple sounds ē (that is ancient Greek η), ü (i), ī, yet it follows from this fact of the alternation between αι and a, οι and o, ει and ε, that so long as this took place so freely, the first elements a o e were still clearly present. A shifting also occurs in the converse direction: on inscriptions of the third century and on Papyrus we find written βοιηδρομιών βοιηθόν ὀγδοίης[3], in Ionic are found Δαναίη Παμφαίης Φαιεννός, and ει stands for ε in ἐννεία and the examples, Attic and others, mentioned above[4]. Less frequently before consonants (στ, σδ = ζ); παλαστή in Attic, not παλαιστή[5]; Γεραστός and Γεραιστός in manuscripts[6]. Τροζήνιοι has inscriptional warrant[7]. Should any one on the other hand be inclined to

---

[1] Ἐλαῖαι, *C. I. A.* iv. 299ᵃ, 7 (before 403); elsewhere with simple a, also iv. 53ᵃ, 33 (B.C. 418). According to Cauer *C. Stud.* viii. 270 the origin is ἐλαι-ία, cp. also on αιι=αι q̄ Wackernagel *K. Z.* xxvii. 278. For κάω, κλάω (Voemel *Dem. contiones* p. 36) we have no examples on inscript. (the mss. waver); on αἰετός Meist. p. 24, n. 142. The proper name Ἀετίων occurs as early as 4th cent. at Iasos (Bechtel *d. Insch. d. ion. Dial.* 104, 16); but nothing obliges us to take the a in this case as long.

[2] στοιά Ar. *Eccl.* 684, 688; στωιά Mitylen, *Dial. Inschr.* 273; Curt. *Etym.*⁵ 216. Attic inscr. have only στοά, Meisterhans, p. 44, n. 384; στοιά Chalkid. Ditt. *Syll.* 369, 25.

[3] Meisterhans, p. 45 f.; βοιηθόν Pap. L. 27 (2nd cent. rather incorrect); καταβοιῆς by δόη on the Papyr. in Ionic dial. (p. 44, note 2), which I place in 4th cent. Also Πραξινοίη *Bull. de*

corr. hell. x. 340 (epitaph of a woman of Halikarnassus in Rhodes), βοίηθος Calymna, *Gr. Inscr. Br. Mus.* ii. 298, 9.

[4] Bechtel *d. Inschr. d. ion. Dial.* no. 99 (Miletus); do. *Thas. inscr. in the Louvre,* p. 26, 28. ει for ε ceases according to Meisterh. p. 46 as early as B.C. 250, accordingly much earlier than οι for o; M. refers this to the degeneration of the ει to a simple sound.

[5] *C. I. A.* ii. 167, 1. 321 f. etc.; also 834ᵇ, 11; in 16, 33 αι in Köhler's transcription is only a mistake.

[6] O. Riemann *Bull. de corr. h.* iii. 497.

[7] Besides appearing on the snake-pillar at Delphi (cp. Thuc. i. 132) it is also constant, *C. I. A.* ii. 614; Wescher-Foucart, *Delph.* 4, 50; *C. I. Gr.* i. 106 (whence?); *Dial. Inschr.* 3014 (Megara). Coins shew Τροιζ. not before Empire, earlier ΤΡΟ, which points to Τροζ., Foucart on Le Bas, ii. 38ᵃ.

infer from the Attic Ποτειδεᾶται from Ποτείδαια[1], that αι had the same sound as ε, the answer would be obvious, that Ποτειδαᾶται is wanting in euphony and out of all analogy, and that in Ionic also ἐπιστέαται ἐδυνέατο were used instead of ἐπιστάαται ἐδυνάατο[2]. In like manner we are not by any means to conclude from the censure which occurs in Aristophanes of an inelegantly broad pronunciation of κρέμαιο, that the elegant pronunciation was already at that time κρέμηο[3], but rather that a drawling of the diphthong is the object of the reproof, or perhaps, since the latter is in this case followed by a vowel, a strictly diphthongal pronunciation as opposed to the more careless, which allowed the ι to become more evanescent. It is certainly possible to pronounce ai as well as ä in very different ways. For that αι was so early pronounced e and had become identical with η, appears to me in the face of the constant separation in script a pure impossibility, as also an identity of ει and ι, of οι and υ; a historical mode of writing running counter to the pronunciation is only possible, where there is a strict grammatical code, which at that period did not exist, and isolated blunders and shiftings make their appearance in spite of such a code, especially in the course of so many centuries. The only examples however which are brought are Ποτειδεᾶται, a mode of writing which is as invariable as Ποτείδαια on the other side, and next in the third century a supposed inscriptional γένητε, which does not exist, as the right reading is ὅπως γένητ᾽ ἐφρόντισ[ε[4]. This leads then to the

---

[1] C. I. A. i. 240, 241, 242, 244; but no less also in 238, where the no. of letters shews that Kirchhoff is wrong in supplying Ποτειδαι]ᾶται. There is absolutely no example for the latter reading; for Ποτειδαι-, 236, can just as well be completed as Ποτείδαια (as in the preceding list, 235).

[2] Merzdorf C. St. viii. 188; Cauer do. 268.

[3] Bücheler Rh. Mus. xx. 302; Aristoph. Nubes 870 ff.: ΦΕΙΔ.—εἰ κρέμαιό γε. ΣΩΚΡ.—ἰδοὺ κρέμαι᾽, ὡς

ἠλίθιον ἐφθέγξατο καὶ τοῖσι χείλεσιν διερρυηκόσιν. Curtius argues against Büch. in Stud. i. 2. 275.

[4] C. I. A. ii. 379, 18, where Köhler reads γένητε φροντίς; cp. Rh. Mus. xxxvi. 617. In like manner v. Wilamowitz in the letter of Attalus to the priest of Pessinus (Domaszewski Arch. Epigr. Mitt. a. Oest. 1884, 95) c. 16 has corrected the ἐπιστραφήσεσθε κείνους of the editor into -σεσθ᾽ ἐκ. (Lect. epigr. p. 16).

arguments to be drawn from elision crasis etc. The αι of most verb-endings is, as is well known, not only in Homer but also in the Attic comic poets and indeed in prose subject to elision[1]. This fact is explainable without difficulty from the pronunciation *ai*: in the first place *légeta'en* was pronounced as *ka'en* and as *Peiraeus*; but afterwards the *a* of this *legeta'* was treated like that of ταῦτα, λέγετ' ἐν like ταῦτ' ἐν, though *ka* was as will readily be understood not in general allowed to shrink up into *k'*, but here crasis was employed. If on the other hand it had been *legetē* (λέγετη, as in Bœotian), I see no possibility of the long vowel being elided. Further, crasis furnishes, as G. Curtius shews[3], especially strong arguments for diphthongal pronunciation. Καὶ ἐν = κὰν, *ka' en* becoming *kān*; how could *kē en* become *kān*? The same applies to κἀκεῖνος, κᾆτα, κἄστιν etc. Now no doubt, where there is a frequent occurrence of a certain word-combination, a definite form of crasis might be handed down to a period, in which its elements, having in the intervening time suffered change, ought properly to give a different result: for instance θάτερον is good Attic, though the form in use there is no longer ἅτερος but ἕτερος. But this is clearly not applicable to the crasis of καὶ with any chance word beginning with ε or ει. For οι we have to consider, μούστίν from μοι ἐστίν, μούδόκει, μούγκώμιον, σούδωκεν, καίτούστιν, then ὤζυρέ, ἐγῷδα, also θοἰμάτιον like θαἰμάτια, all phenomena as easily comprehensible on the assumption that οι = ọι ọ, as they are absolutely incomprehensible supposing οι to be *ū̃*. With regard to the other dialects, giving a passing notice to the Lesbian diæreses such as ὄϊδα ὄϊκην (οἰκεῖν)[4] I call especial attention to the Cyprian writing. This peculiar script, which is entirely independent of that of the ordinary Greek, being not an alphabet but a syllabarium, nevertheless expresses all the diphthongs in a manner entirely analogous to the ordinary script, a clear indication, that this was conformable to the pronunciation, and a

---

[1] E.g. Deinarch. 1, 40 παρακρούονθ' ὑμᾶς (according to cod. N and A pr.); 2, 3 γενήσεσθ' αὐτὸν (according to N pr., A pr.).

[2] κὰ ἐν found in *C. I. A.* II. 50; on the Ion. Papyr. (see p. 44, note 2) KEN i.e. κ' ἐν twice (l. 6).

[3] G. Curtius *Stud.* I. 2, 277 ff.

[4] Ahrens *D. A.* p. 106. Meister *Gr. Dial.* I. 96.

certain proof, that the pronunciation was diphthongal in Cyprus. For instance *a-i-ve-i* αἰϝεί (ἀεί), *ta-i* τᾷ, *pe-i-se-i* πείσει (i.e. τείσει from τίνω) (η is wanting), *ma-to-i* Μᾶδοι, *to-i* τῷ, *o-na-sa-ko-ra-u* 'Ονασαγόραυ, *a-ne-u* ἄνευ, *a-ro-u-ra* ἄρουρα.

SECTION 15.

Transformation of EI, AI, OI, *in Bœotian.*

The above however does not hold good for *all* dialects, and it is the Bœotian, in which we have already recognized the beginning of itacism in the case of H, that in the case of these diphthongs also has anticipated by centuries the development as it took place elsewhere. The Bœotian sound-system, as referred to the Æolic, shews the following changes:

Æol.	η	αι	ᾱι	ει	ηι	οι	ωι
Bœot.	ει	η	η	ι	ει	υ	υ.

These alterations however did not all arise simultaneously, and it is not till the inscriptions of the third century that we find them all complete. ει, wherever it is really ε + ι and not ē̄, is in many cases in the earliest monuments and at a later period without exception simplified to ι; in those cases, where it maintains itself, as in δανεῖον Δορκείδας, ηι appears to be original, and accordingly we find also ειι (= ηῖ) in such words, μαντειία 'Αντιγενείιος[1]. AI is retained in the earlier period, for instance the older coins of Thebes shew ΘΕΒΑΙΟΝ; only in Tanagra and Hysiæ AE is written for αι and ᾱι quite in the Latin manner: 'Αβαεόδορος i.e. -δωρος; ἐπὶ 'Αμεινοκλεῖαε[2]. The old Corinthian writing also had this diphthong, there however the E was equivalent to ει; ΑΘΑΝΑΕΑ, ΠΒΡΑΕΟΘΝ

---

[1] Ahrens *D. A.* 185. Meister *Gr. Dial.* I. 223 f. Δορκείδας Orchomenos about 330, *Dial. Inschr.* 470 (ib. 502; as regards the formation cp. Meister in *Bezzenberger's Beitr.* VI. 61).

[2] Foucart *Bull.* III. 136; Meister *Gr. Dial.* I. 238; Plataiai Lolling *Berlin. Monatsber.* 1885, 1031 no. 22 ἐπὶ Δαμαενέτοε. Terent. Scaur. VII. 16 K.: antiqui quoque Graecorum hanc syllabam per *ae* scripsisse traduntur.

'Αθαναϵία Πϵραϵίοθϵν¹; ΑΕΘΡΑ² also is found on a vase
which is probably Attic; on the other hand the Thessalian
Λαρισαέων on coins of Larisa comes not from Λαρισαῖος, but
from Λαρισα(ι)εύς³. At Tanagra we find also corresponding to
AE the writing OE for οι and ωι: ·Μοέριχος, Πολυαράτοϵ;
even Priscian compares this Bœotism with Latin oe⁴. I consider
AE OE as real diphthongs; for not only in Latin but also in
Cymric (Welsh) there is a diphthongal ae oe, distinct from ai oi,
though nearly approximating to them⁵; the Corinthian writing
however corresponds exactly to the Oscan ⊣A, ⊣V, ⊣ being
the sound midway between i and e, just as Ⅴ expresses that
between o and u.—Afterwards however the Thebans adopted
the Ionic H for αι, even before the introduction of the common
alphabet, Τϵλϵστῆος, 'Αρίστηχμος⁶, and this is subsequently
the regular mode of writing everywhere in Bœotia⁷. At this
time therefore tẽ tīmẽ was pronounced with the simple sound ẽ
both in the dative singular and in the nominative plural; for ἄι
and ᾱι also at this time were not distinguished. οι on the
other hand remains, if we except Tanagra, not only in the fifth
but even in the fourth century, and even subsequently was
not ousted by the simple writing υ⁸. On very late Bœotian
inscriptions we find ϵι, which in other instances appears on
these with the evident value of ῑ, alternating with υ as in τϵῖ,
Δὶ τϵῖ βασιλϵῖ (for βασιλϵῦι pron. basīlī), κὴ τῦ Τρϵφωνί[υ] (or
Τρϵφωνῖ⁹?).

¹ Röhl I. Gr. ant. no. 20, 4, 5; cp.
above, p. 29.
² C. I. Gr. 7746; on the other hand
Ϙόραϵ (Ahrens 1. 199, 3) is a wrong
reading for Ϙόραξ, C. I. Gr. 7374,
Dial. Inschr. 3127.
³ Fick Dial. Inschr. 360; Beermann, Curt. Stud. IX. 34, compares the
two forms Πϵλιυναιϵων and Πϵλιυναιων
from Πϵλιυνα.
⁴ Prisc. Instit. 1 § 53. Κροϵσοϛ on
a vase, probably Attic, C. I. Gr. 7756,
Welcker Alte Denkm. III. 481 ff.
⁵ R. Lepsius Standard Alphabet
p. 172.

⁶ Foucart Bull. III. 136, 140 (Röhl
no. 300, Dial. Inschr. 700).
⁷ Accordingly it must be regarded
as due to intermixture of the κοινή,
that in the Theban Proxeny decree
in favour of a Carthaginian (Dial.
Inschr. 719) αι is written throughout.
⁸ Ahrens D. A. 194 ff., shewing
the local differences; Foucart l. c.
133 and IV. 88; Meister Gr. Dial. I.
235.
⁹ Dial. Inschr. 382 ff. (Chaironeia),
429 f. (Lebadeia); these are all dedi-
catory documents relating to slaves.
The example cited 429, Τρϵφωνῖ Meist.

EI for OI occurs also sporadically in late Attic; οἴκει for οἴκοι occurs in Menander, δυεῖν is frequent, τοῖς λοιπεῖς is found on an inscrip. dating 100 B.C.[1] The Bœotians did not readily admit υ instead of οι before a vowel, e.g. in Βοιωτοί[2]; according to the Grammarians also οι not υ was substituted in Bœotian for ωι[3]. All this is very mysterious and perplexing. If the Bœotians finally pronounced ti Di, one cannot understand, why in the first word they always added the E, against the pronunciation and against custom. The EI must it would seem have been an attempt to imitate the sound, which appeared to their ear something like ei, just as in the Attic δυεῖν. If this is the case, we shall have for the foundation of this ei in a preceding stage a diphthongal oi, not a monophthongal ü, and we must suppose, that the early fluctuation between OI and Υ represents a fluctuation of pronunciation. For οι and υ are closely related to one another both in ancient Greek pronunciation and that of the κοινή, as we shall shew hereafter. But EI is confined to the endings: ποιομένει or πο-ιομένει = ποιούμενοι; in these endings (as indeed also in the stems) in Latin also oi has become ei (i); Nom. plur. oi -ei -i, Dat. ois -eis -is.—The view held by Curtius and Dietrich[4], that in Bœotian oi first became ui and then ü, is contradicted both by the ancient OE, as also by the fact that ΤΙ was never written[5], although, in accordance with the value of the Υ prevailing there, this would have been the adequate expression for ui.

(383 οἰῶν stands for υἰῶν, with omission of υ, which we meet with frequently elsewhere, Μικόλος Εὐφροσόναν 386).

[1] οἴκει Herodian I. 504, 16; II. 463, 31. Δυεῖν on Attic inscr. Meisterhans, p. 124. Τοῖς λοιπεῖς C. I. A. II. 467, 12 f. = Dittenb. Syll. 347. Cp. Φαληρε̄, p. 32, n. 2.

[2] Βυωτῶν, title of Athena Itonia, Bull. de corr. hell. IX. 430. The case form τοιι can become τυι as well as τοι.

[3] Ahrens D. A. 193 f.; Meister Gr. Dial. I. 249 f. The case will be found to stand thus; πατροῖος etc. (οι before a vowel) was always found in Corinna; that in the same τοι for τῳ could have stood by the side of ἐμύ τύ (=τοι, οι) is not credible.

[4] Curtius Gött. Nachrichten 1862, p. 495; Grdz.[5] 706; Dietrich Fleckeisen's Jahrb. 1872 p. 24. On the other hand Beermann (Stud. IX. 41 f.) decides for the transition oi, ö.

[5] Μέτυικος is said to be found on one of the tablets of Styra (Röhl, no. 372 [280]); see however Bechtel Inschr. d. ion. Dial. p. 18 (no. 19 [70]).

SECTION 16.

Later Simplification of EI *to* i (e).

We must now with reference to the remaining dialects and the Greek language as a whole separate the diphthongs which have hitherto been treated in common and first of all give our especial attention to EI. Outside of Bœotian the examples for an early simplification of this diphthong to ι are not numerous nor are they sufficiently trustworthy. We must of course place in a separate category abbreviations in particular words, as for instance in the month-name Ποσιδεών, which in Attic also is always so written; the same is true of recurring forms such as Χίρων for the Centaur, which may lay claim to pass as correct[1]. The ending -κλίδης for -κλείδης may be derived from -κλος not κλῆς, accordingly even on the lead tablets of Styra[2] in Eubœa, which seemed to furnish the most numerous examples of ι for ει, nothing more is left which can be considered trustworthy. But without doubt from the end of the third century onwards, EI, and that both genuine and spurious without exception, was simplified in this way in the most diverse regions of Hellas. Our evidence for this is drawn from the same documents, from which we gained our information on the fate

---

[1] *C. I. Gr.* 7400, 7687, 8185, 8287, 8359, (7870). For Χείρων there is only one untrustworthy example. Cp. Meisterhans, p. 43.

[2] Kretschmer *Ztschr. f. vgl. Sprachf.* IX. 159, on Χ]αρικλίδας of a Corinthian vase (*Dial. Inschr.* 3121); Bechtel *Inschr. d. ion. Dial.* p. 36 (Lead tablets). On Φιλαιγίρης on a tablet (Röhl 372[382]; B. 19[145]) it must be noted, that Αἴγειρα in Achaia, whence the name comes, appears when correctly written to have an ι just as Στάγιρος, ΑΙΓΙ, Αἰγιρατᾶν on coins (Friedländer *Z. f. Numismatik* p. 6; *Catalogue of Greek coins Peloponn.* p. 17), Αἴγιρα Inscr. of Lagina *Bull. de corr. h.* IX. 444 frg. M, 2 col. 3 (81 B.C.);

Αἰγίρων proper name Inscr. Epidaur. 'Εφημ. ἀρχ. 1887, p. 9 ff. l. 38; Αἰγιράτα Wescher-Foucart 109. On the other hand Αἰγειράτης Oropus 'Εφ. 1885, p. 97 ff. l. 2 and 31 (soon after 115 B.C.). The Bœotian Φιλαιγίρα[ο] Röhl no. 382 (*Dial. Inschr.* 566) is not evidence for either side of the question. On the lead tablets there still remains Πιριθος (Πειρίθους) R. 312, but guarantee for this reading is wanting, cp. Bechtel on no. 297 (p. 29). I may also cite: δαρικός Sparta R. no. 69 (only in a bad copy of Fourmont); 'Αριστίδας Sparta ib. 84; 'Ηρακλίδης Halic. *Bull. de corr. h.* IV. 297 B, 8 (elsewhere the same occurs with ει; cp. 'Αρχαγόρω for -ρεω ib. l. 3).

of the diphthongs ᾱι ωι ηι, namely the Delphian manumission documents and the Egyptian Papyri. These writers of the second century were in perfect ignorance, where they ought to put ι and where ει, and wrote Εἶρις, τειμάς and conversely παραμινάτω and ἱερῖς[1], and if the Delphian masons at least left the short ι to itself, the Egyptians allowed this to be mixed up in the universal confusion, ἰμί and ἐστείν, συμφωνοῦσειν, ἥλειος, ὅτει, μείζονει[2]. There are however two exceptions. First a ρ following exercises a certain protective power over the E-sound, which is seen also in Latin and in modern Greek (ξερός); accordingly Σωτῆρᾳ and χέρα are written, just as ἐκεχηρία is found on an early Delphian record with what appears to be strict Doric η, for which however the Delphian dialect has ει[3]. Secondly the ordinary equivalent before vowels is η or ε, μηνιήα πληάς παιδήα οἰκηότης, πορέαν εὐθέας διδασκαλέα[4], and this holds its ground for a long time, so that e.g. in a decree from Byzantium of the time of Tiberius[5], χρήας, πλήονας, ἐπιτάδηον,

---

[1] Wescher-Fouc. no. 108, 435, 82, 365. Cp. Bull. de corr. h. v. 42, = Dial. Inschr. 1539, Dittenb. 294, Phokian official record from beginning of 2nd cent. (after 181 B.C., Dittenb.), in which Στίρι occurs (by Στειρίων) and κλαρωσῖ, and further what was said above on the final confusion of Boeotian ει with ι.—For Athens cp. Meisterh. p. 38 f.

[2] Papyr. 1 of the Louvre, which is by no means the most incorrect, furnishes these and other examples. In the Papyrus published by H. Weil 1879, which contains fragments of Euripides and other poets, we find ἐπεί = ἐπί, περεί, χάρειν (χάριν), βασειλείσσης, Κύπρειδος and others without number.

[3] Σωτήραι (-ραν) C. I. A. II. 469, 22; III. 368; χέρα Papyr. L. no. 50 τῆ χερεί, χέρας, χερός (and χῖραν); 61 col. 5 χέρα; do. Pap. Lond. (Wessely Wiener St. 1886, 203) XLIV. 11. Cp. ἄπηρον

Scott Fragm. Herculan. p. 219 f. (col. 15, 29); but the same gives also δηρα for δεῖνα twice Append. XXXVIII. l. 9 (Philod. π. θανάτου Δ col. XXXVII.). This calls to mind the Lat. i pingue, written ei e i.—Lat. cyperus (-um) κύπε(ι)ρος; but Epirus pirata etc.—Ἐκεχηρία Amphictyonic decree C. I. A. II. 545 l. 48, 49 (the H which was suspected by Ahrens has been confirmed for both places by U. Köhler and by myself); Εὐχήρου Delph. Dittenb. Syll. 198, 73.

[4] The examples are from Pap. 1. both sides (on reverse side = Pap. 63, col. 2 χρίας). Μηνιήαν Pap. 1, col. 15, wrongly read μηνικαν by editor and wrongly emended to μηνιαίαν; cp. μηνιείοις Pap. 61, col. 8.—At Delphi ἀνδρέον, γυναικέον, Καλλικράτηα etc.

[5] C. I. Gr. 2060, Dial. Inschr. 3059. (Ἐπαινῆσθαι ib. not = ἐπαινεῖσθαι but a perfect, cp. Dial. Inschr. 3078, Dittenb. 246, 92 etc.) οἰκῆον πολιτήαν (Amorg.) Bull. de corr. h. VIII. 445.

ἀσαμήωτον are written consistently. In like manner an inscription of Cos shews Καισάρηα, Ἀγρίππηα, Ἡράκληα, on the other hand Ἀπολλώνεια, Ἀσκλαπεῖα, Διονύσεια, Δώρεια¹, where the pronunciation was -ia, being in some cases original, in some cases owing to contraction, Ἀσκλαπίεια *Asklapīa*. For in those cases where this ει is preceded by an ι, either ιη can arise, as in μηνιήαν and Σαραπιῆον on the Papyri, or again ῑ, as in vulgar ὑγεία (*hygīa*) instead of ὑγίεια, ταμεῖον instead of ταμειον². There is no especial degree of consistency to be found in the Latin representation of ει before vowels; *Aeneas, Medea, Alexandrea* and *Alexandria, Dareus* and *Darius, Clio, Iphigenia*; in words taken over at an early period shortening occurs: *platea, balineum* βαλανεῖον, in general even at a later period *e* predominates³. The uncertainty of the Greek pronunciation is sufficiently established by ἐπιτήδιος and ἑρμηνία on a Papyrus of Herculaneum⁴; in the times of Terentianus Maurus an *i* was heard in Greek in Μήδεια, Αἰνείας⁵, and this agrees with the fact that η is no longer written in such words on Attic inscriptions of the second century A.D.⁶ But that previously the E-sound predominated, may fit in with the fact, that ει from the earliest times had a tendency to lose the ε before a vowel. For the rest the simplification to *i* was already complete over the whole Greek speech-area before the beginning of the Christian era⁷, and

---

¹ Dittenberger *Syll.* 399, cp. 400 (where Ἀπολλωπεια occurs, as Ἐλευθερμεῖ for -ρεῖ -ρῑ Athens, Meisterh. p. 39).

² So also in late Bœotian Θεισπείων i.e. Thispion for Θεισπιείων, *Bull. de corr. h.* III. 385 = *Dial. Inschr.* 816.— Τγῖα Athens, Meisterh. l. c.

³ Cp. Priscian I. § 54 f.; K. L. Schneider *Ausf. Gr.* I. 69 ff.

⁴ Gomperz *Wiener Akad.* Bd. 83, p. 91 f.

⁵ Terentian. Maur. v. 441, 458.

⁶ Meisterh. p. 37, n. 306 (we must however notice here νειόν = νηόν, ναόν on the Roman inscript. of Herodes Attikos, *C. I. Gr.* 6280, v. 96; also ἀτρεῖες v. 77).

⁷ To avoid useless prolixity, I will only refer to the inscr. of Halæsa *C. I. Gr.* 5594, where ῥεινός ῥεῖνα occurs by the side of ῥινός ῥῖνα. On this point it must be remarked, that according to *Etym. Gud.* 30, 48 Aristarchus affirmed that ῥεῖς was the spelling, on account of the derivation from ῥέω; also θεῖς instead of θίς on account of θείνεσθαι. As regards the supposed confusion of ει and η there is need of greater discrimination; for instance I cannot admit, that on the Pap. in Wessely *W. Stud.* 1882, 175 ὑπολήψεων ἕνεκα (sic) is = ὑπολείψεων (cp. ib. p. 196). Of von Herwerden's examples some may be

even if in the second century B.C. care and culture were still able to give not only ωι and ᾱι, but also ει its due and no more than its due[1], nevertheless this soon ceased to be a possibility, and the distinction of ει and ι had become a *crux orthographica*[2]. In many cases the resource adopted was to write ει in all cases for long *i*, as on the inscription of Byzantium, which has been cited, τειμᾶς and πολείτας[3] regularly; this however never became a universal and fixed mode of writing, and the Grammarians, especially Herodian, took pains in the opposite direction everywhere to ascertain and carry out the historical method. Even at the present day an orthographic correction is nowhere more frequently necessary than in the case of ι and ει. For instance we write ι wrongly instead of the diphthong in the following words, ἔτεισα τείσω and in all the derivatives of τίνω[4]; μείγνυμι, μείξω, Μειξίας, etc.[5], Φλειοῦς, Φλειάσιοι,

---

explained grammatically, very many contain η for ει before a vowel (ρ); ῆτα for εῖτα *C. I. A.* III. 39 is found in an inscription which is very imperfectly handed down; finally Χολλῄδης II. 82 shews η for ηι.—In Latin there are certainly some examples, where the E sound has remained even when followed by consonants (hypotenusa, Polycletus).

[1] Of the Papyri of the 2nd century the following are correct and trustworthy in disputed questions: Louvre 2 (dialectica), 15 (judicial verdict), 22 (petition); Taur. I. (verdict). Also on inscriptions: Olbia *C. I. Gr.* 2058; Delphi *Bull. de corr. h.* v. 157 (State-record). The inscription of the Mysteries of Andania (93 B.C.) has only one blunder ἀποτισάτω l. 78; for the writing εἱμάτιον εἱματισμός is conformable with the dialect. With regard to Attica in 2nd cent. see Dittenberger *Herm.* I. 414; Meisterh. p. 38, according to whom the confusion properly begins there about 100 B.C.

[2] Mar. Victor. p. 17 K. says, orthographia Graecorum ex parte maxima in ista littera consistit. nam...et in quibusdam mediis interponitur verbis, ut "Aιδης, et in extremis, ut εὐχηι et τορεύηι, et dativis casibus adjungitur, quamvis non enuntietur; et eadem subjecta ε litterae facit longam syllabam ει.

[3] In like manner e.g. *C. I. Gr.* 1798 (Epirus), 2059 (Olbia), 2335 (Tenos). Cp. Quintil. I. 7. 15 (cp. p. 10, n. 2 above); Priscian I. 50: quam (*ei* diphthongum) pro omni *i* longa scribebant more antiquo Graecorum. (Fairly regular in the Greek text of the *Monum. Ancyr.*)

[4] Sauppe *de duobus titulis Tegeat.* (Gött. 1876); Blass *Praef. Isocr.* vol. II.

[5] Examples in proper names are frequent; *C. I. A.* II. 575 Μειξίας; Kuman. Ἐπιγρ. ἐπιτ. 97 Μειξιάδου, 105 do., 102 Μειξιππος, 1284 Μειξιδημος; *Bull. de corr. h.* III. 575 Μειξιγένην, VI. 482 Μειξιγένην. Herwerden *Lap. Testim.* 29; Meisterh. p. 40. Many examples also for σύμμεικτος, Meisterh. p. 142, n. 1253; Riemann *Rev. de phil.* IX. 91; ἀμείκτοις Pap. L. 22 (ἐπιμείξει 63, 8 and συμμείξαι 49 of small value as evidence on account of the incorrectness of this

Ποτείδαια, Εὐτεαῖοι and consequently also in εἰτέα (willow)[1], in the names of the letters πεῖ, χεῖ, ξεῖ, etc. Conversely we keep ει wrongly instead of ῑ in οἰκτίρω ᾤκτιρα[2]; σιρός[3]; Σιληνός[4]; Κάμιρος Στάγιρος[5]; from the name of the deme Ἐρίκεια may be inferred ἐρίκη (heath). Besides ὑγεία and ταμεῖον, ἐπείκεια and πεῖν for πιεῖν, Hyginus ὑγιεινός[6] may be cited as vulgar modes of writing to be explained by the contraction of ι and ει. It appears then from so many indirect testimonies added to those which are direct (such as Quintilian's remark, that the Greek ει had the same value as the ei of the early Romans, that is to say long i[7]), and further from Latin equivalents, such as Pisistratus Dinarchus, that already in the Roman period, before our era, there was no distinction in pronunciation between ι and ει[8]. Let us now see, whether the state of affairs is even approximately the same in the case of the other diphthongs of a similar kind and first of all in the case of αι.

piece); letters of the Pergamenes (p. 49, note 3) D, 10 συμμεῖξαι. See also Curtius Vb.[2] 165.

[1] Meisterh. 39 ff.; G. Meyer[2] p. 128. Φλεοῦς inscrip. of Lagina, p. 59, note 1.

[2] Four examples for οἰκτίρειν; C. I. A. I. 463 (by means of which the fact was first established by Kirchhoff), Suppl. 477[c], 477[h], Röhl I. Gr. antiq. 325 (Thessaly). (On the other hand ἐποίκτειρον Epidaur. Inscrip. of Isyllus Ἐφημ. ἀρχ. 1885, 69 ff. l. 67, which with σώζοντι l. 70 serves as a proof, that the Philippos of the inscr. is the son of Demetrius, and accordingly the inscrip. dates from the beginning of the 2nd cent., Fleckeisen's Jahrb. 1885, 822.)

[3] Inscr. of Eleusis Bull. de corr. h. IV. 226; see also Voemel on Dem. VIII. 45.

[4] Numerous exx., for instance Bull.

de corr. h. II. 570 ff. (Delos); Halik. ib. IV. 303; Messene (Σιλανός) ib. V. 151; Korkyra Dial. Inschr. 3220; see Meisterh. 43[2], 3 ff.

[5] See the Attic tribute lists (Herwerden 25, 35, Meisterh. n. 357, 373). As regards μάγειρος the testimony is contradictory: ΗΟΜΑΓΙΡΟΣ Epidaur. Ἐφ. ἀρχ. 1885, 197; μάγιρος Corcyra Dial. Inschr. 3212; but μαγειρικόν C. I. A. II. 163, 28 (time of Lycurgus).

[6] ἐπείκεια e.g. C. I. Gr. 2264 (Tenos); on πεῖν see Jacobs A. Pal. III. p. 684; Fleckeisen in his Jahrb. 1870, p. 71.

[7] Quint. I. 7. 15 (see p. 10, n. 2 above). The passage of Nigidius in Gellius XIX. 14. 8 is unfortunately corrupt.

[8] This was recognized by Ceratinus (p. 3, n. 1 above) p. 374 ed. Haverc.

Section 17.

Later history of AI.

Outside of Bœotia the oldest example, which G. Meyer produces, for the confusion of αι with ε ι η, is ἀναιρερημένου (i.e. ἀνηρημένου) by the side of [ἀναι]ραιρημένος on a Thasian inscription of about the fourth century[1]. It is thought then, that the Ionians of Thasos said αἱραίρημαι, instead of ἀραίρημαι of Herodotus; but I can think of nothing more intrinsically suspicious, than a form which not only is very clumsy, but is not even really read (on the stone). It is certainly much more likely, that in this dialect too shortening has taken place, ἀνεραίρημαι or ἀναιρέρημαι[2]; in any case the example is isolated and not such as to warrant general inferences.

In the next place for the third century the Reuchlinians have that great crowning proof, the epigram of Callimachus, where Echo returns the words ναιχὶ καλὸς with ἄλλος ἔχει, that is *nechi-echi*[3]. The lines run according to the traditional reading, Λυσανίη, σὺ δὲ ναιχὶ καλὸς καλός· ἀλλὰ πρὶν εἰπεῖν τοῦτο σαφῶς, Ἠχώ φησί τις "ἄλλος ἔχειν." I however think with Henrichsen[4], that Callimachus was far too subtle a poet, to present to us such an absurd Echo, as to repeat the words addressed in reverse order. Since moreover τις is unsuitable as applied to Ἠχώ, we shall probably be right in accepting E. Petersen's[5] emendation, Λυσανίη, σὺ δὲ ναιχὶ καλὸς καλός·

---

[1] Bergmann *Herm.* III. 233 (Bechtel *Inschr. d. ion. Dial.* no. 71). 'Αναιρερ. stands there twice,...ραιρημ. once. (To explain the Lesbian αἱμισυς = ἥμισυς from the orthographical representation of ἄ by αι, as is done by G. Meyer[2] § 37, 113, is more than questionable, since this dialect shews elsewhere not the slightest trace of such confusion, and it is evident that in αἱμισυς αἱμίονος Αἱσίοδος we have a peculiar *phonetic* development.)

[2] Bechtel supposes ἀναίραιρ. and sees in the 2nd form inner reduplication as in ἠνίπαπον.

[3] Callim. *A. P.* XII. 28.

[4] P. 134, ff.

[5] E. Petersen *Progr.* Dorpat 1875; Schneider suggests ἄλλον ἔχειν. Wilamowitz *Hom. Unter.* 350 considers Echo as the reply which necessarily follows and denies any intentional jingle.

ἀλλὰ πρὶν εἰπεῖν τοῦτο σαφῶς Ἠχώ, φησί τις ἄλλος ἔχειν. Accordingly the mention of *echo* applies to the repetition of καλός and there is no longer any question of a harmony of sound between ναιχί and ἔχει. Should any one however prefer to take it as an instance of parechesis, nothing is easier than by reading φησί τις ἄλλος "ἔχω" to restore such between Ἠχώ and ἔχω. But a positive refutation can be given in the following manner. If in the time of Callimachus there was no distinction in the most cultivated court speech between the sounds αι and ε, in the vulgar speech of the second century there can have been absolutely no difference whatever. In that case however uneducated writers must of necessity confound αι and ε (or η) in the same degree, that they intermix ει and ι ῐ, o and ω and so on. What then are the facts of the case? The somewhat incorrect astronomical papyrus in the Louvre has ὁρᾶτε[1] for ὁρᾶται once. The fragments of writing on the reverse side of the same shew no error. The same may be said of papyrus No. 23, where besides ἐστείν etc., ἀσπασάμενος τὴν μάχαιραν stands for σπασάμενος and πίνοντες for πεινῶσαι. On the other hand on No. 43 we find ἔρρωσθαι for -σθε and εἰδῆται; on 40 αγορασεδωκε = ἀγοράσαι ἔδωκε, with which may be compared χρῶνθ' ὡς, περιωκοδομηκέν' αὐτοὺς on another Papyrus[2]. On Weil's large papyrus[3] πιστεύσεται stands for -σατε, ἐκτέτατε for -ταται, βαίνεται for -τε; for του μεν ξεναικειν for τοῦ (τὸ) μὴ 'ξενεγκεῖν[4] is an unintelligible corruption and cannot be regarded as evidence. And nevertheless these bungling copies bristle with the most crying confusions of ει and ῑ and such like errors. Accordingly it is quite plain that the αι of the verb-endings -σθαι -ται sounded in the speech of the uneducated like the ε of the endings -σθε -τε; but then these are cases, where the diphthong was from of old liable to elision and had no influence on the accent; the representation by ε not by η may be to some extent connected with this weakening. But we nowhere read ἡμέρη (-ρε) for -ραι, or κή (κέ) for καί, or ἥρω for αἱρῶ; on the contrary ἔλαν is the

---

[1] Pap. L. 1, col. 17, 11.
[2] Wessely *W. Stud.* 1886, 206.
[3] Col. 5, 13; reverse side col. 4, 5, 19.
[4] Col. 4, 17.

shortened form of ἔλαιον, as Σαραπιῆν of -πιεῖον[1]; it is therefore quite impossible, that αι was at that time universally
confounded with ε η and had ceased to preserve the *A*-sound.
The contemporary inscriptions are perfectly free from examples
of interchange, even those from[2] Delphi in other respects so
incorrect; on those from Attica the confusion of αι and ε
cannot be proved before the second century A.D.[3] It may
be mentioned that where in the period of the Empire αι is
written as *e*, this is expressed not only by ε but also by η, for
instance on an inscription from the Thracian Chersonese we
find κή twice side by side with γυνεκί, Ήφηστος[4] on a papyrus.
Dionysius of Halicarnassus furnishes an unmistakeable testimony
for the correct pronunciation of the Augustan period; he says
that καὶ ᾿Αθηναίων in Thucydides is a case of harsh composition, since the sounds of the ι of καὶ and the α of ᾿Αθηναίων
could not blend into one[5]. Demetrius the rhetorician declares
the name Αἰαίη to have a particularly harmonious sound[6],
surely however not pronouncing it *eee*. In the next place the
Grammarians describe αι in contra-distinction to ᾳ as ἡ αι δίφθογγος ἡ ἐκφωνοῦσα τὸ ι[7], an expression which, to say the least
of it, is very ill suited to αι = *e*; for in that case why should
it not be ἡ ἰσοδυναμοῦσα τῷ η? This description caused even
Aldus Manutius[8] to recognize and insist on the distinction
between the modern Greek pronunciation of the diphthongs
and the genuine ancient sound.—If then in spite of all this the

---

[1] Pap. L. no. 31.

[2] That I may pass over nothing,
I notice the Rhodian verse inscription
Απαιλου (=᾿Απελλοῦ?) in ᾿Αθήν. III.
226. On the inscr. of Mylasa *C. I.
Gr.* 2693[e] (Rhodian money; no Roman
names), 2693[f] κέ, ᾿Αριστενέτου, ᾿Επένετος
do not occur at all; see more correct
copy Le Bas v. 416, 414.

[3] Meisterhans, p. 26[2].

[4] *Bull. de corr. hell.* IV. 514; Kaibel
Epigr. 372; Pap. L. no. 19. Cp. however p. 38, n. 1 above, p. 69, n. 2 below.

[5] Dionys. π. συνθ. p. 167: ἡ τῶν
φωνηέντων παράθεσις — διακέκρουκε τὸ

συνεχὲς τῆς ἁρμονίας καὶ διέστακε, πάνυ
αἰσθητὸν τὸν μεταξὺ λαβοῦσα χρόνον.
ἀκέραστοί τε γὰρ αἱ φωναὶ τοῦ τε ι καὶ τοῦ
α, καὶ ἀποκόπτουσαι τὸν ἦχον.

[6] Demetr. π. ἑρμην. § 69: πολλὰ δὲ
καὶ διὰ μόνων τῶν φωνηέντων συντίθησιν
(scil. ἡ συνήθεια) ὀνόματα, οἷον Αἰαίη
καὶ Εὔιος, οὐδέν τε δυσφωνότερα τῶν
ἄλλων ἐστὶ ταῦτα, ἀλλ᾿ ἴσως καὶ μουσι-
κώτερα.

[7] *B. A.* p. 1214; more correctly
elsewhere ἡ αι δίφθ. ἡ ἔχουσα τὸ ι ἐκ-
φωνούμενον.

[8] Cp. above, p. 2.

opinion prevails with regard to this very diphthong, that it had become simple *e* at an early period, the real reason must be sought in the fact, that it represents Latin *ae* and is represented by *ae*[1]; for even Corssen gives to this *ae* the value of German *ä*. But it is just as reasonable to draw inferences from Greek *αι* with regard to the pronunciation of Latin *ae*, as the converse, since express testimony to *ae = e* is only to be produced from the period of the late Empire[2]. In the first place it seems to me certain, that AE was originally intended to represent a diphthong, just as much as the Cymric *ae* mentioned above. In old times the spelling *ai* prevailed in Latin also; afterwards however an *e*-sound was thought to be heard in the second element, or rather the intermediate sound between *e* and *i*, often written *ei*; hence arose about 200 B.C. the spelling *ae*, about 130 B.C. *aei* as in *conquaeisivei, Caeicilius*[3]. This latter corresponds exactly to the Oskan, where the *i* tending to become *e* (Ｙ) stands as the second element. Now the difference between such an *ae* and *ai* is sufficiently slight, to cause the one to be readily substituted for the other in transcription. Moreover the Greeks are not the only people who have heard in *ae* a diphthong similar to *ai*, but also the Ancient Germans, as is unmistakeably shewn by the living pronunciation of German *Kaiser* derived from *Caesar*. If so early as Varro's time there was a fluctuation in isolated words between *e* and *ae, sceptrum scaeptrum, faenerator feneratrix*[4] (and *pretor* and *Cecilius* are given even by Lucilius as examples of countryfied language[5]), this is in no way different from the fluctuation prevailing at the same period between *au*

---

[1] Except in words borrowed at an early period such as *Aiax, Maia, crapula κραιπάλη*.

[2] So Terent. Maur. v. 490: hanc enim (the diphthong *eu*)si protrahamus, *a* sonabit, *e* et *u* (that is *ae* (ē) the lengthening of *ĕ* (ḗ) will be the first element). Sergius in Donat. i. 520, 28 κ of *e*; quando correptum est, sic sonat quasi diphthongos. But Terent. Scaur. vii. 16 κ: sed magis in illis (words with *ae*, formerly written with *ai*) *e novisssima* sonat. At that period then (that of Hadrian) it was not yet sounded as a simple *e*, but *a* followed by *e*. Seelmann *Ausspr. d. Lat.* 224.

[3] Corssen *Ausspr.*[2] i. 676; Seelmann 167.

[4] Varro *L. L.* vii. § 96 (cp. v. 97); in *fen. e* is original, Corssen[2] 327.

[5] ib.

—o (u): *plaustrum plostrum caudex codex, claudo cludo, Claudius Clodius.* Whoever then does not deny, that the Romans pronounced *au* as a diphthong, must allow to *ae* the value of a real diphthong. Moreover Varro by no means says, that the *writing* fluctuates between *sceptrum* and *scaeptrum*, but: partim *dicunt* sceptrum, partim scaeptrum, and we must interpret what precedes in accordance with this: in pluribus verbis A ante E alii ponunt· (in pronunciation) alii non[1]. Should the question be asked, why the Romans made *scaeptrum scaena* out of σκῆπτρον σκηνή, if they did not pronounce the sound as *skēna*, but rather as *skaena*, I suggest that these forms shew an intermediate form between the σκᾶπτρον σκανά of Magna Graecia, which the Romans received first, and the σκῆπτρον σκηνή of the κοινή which reached them at a later period. For although η = ē, no Roman of ancient times thought of writing *Daemaetrius* or *thaesaurus*, but *ae* for η is confined to the two words in question, in these however and especially in *scaena* the writing is almost without exception. Diphthongizing has also taken place sporadically in *austrum* = *ostrum* (ὄστρειον) and in Latin words such as *ausculum* (*faenus faenum*); just as *ai—e*, so *au—o* lie very near together in sound, and foreign words adapted to popular use are especially liable to peculiar treatment[2]. It is also worthy of mention, that Latin poets occasionally scan *Phaethon* as a dissyllable, by no means however with a pronunciation so remote from the original sound as *Phethon*; Quintilian calls this συναίρεσις[3]. At the period then, in which Latin *ae* became the simple sound, that is in the third and still more in the fourth century[4], the Greek αι also had suffered the same fate[5]; but up to that time αι and *ae* may be considered to have preserved their

---

[1] See also Gellius XVI. 12. 8: (Varro) M. Catonem et ceteros aetatis eius *feneratorem* sine *a* littera *pronuntiasse* tradit.

[2] Prisc. I. 52; Seelmann p. 163 f.

[3] Quintil. I. 5. 17: quod συναίρεσιν et συναλοιφήν Graeci vocant—, qualis est apud P. Varronem: *tum te flagranti*

deiectum fulmine Phaethon. Nam si esset prosa oratio, easdem litteras enuntiare veris syllabis licebat.

[4] Corssen I.[2] p. 692 f. Seelmann 224 f.

[5] In Coptic loan-words ε was written, Stern *Kopt. Gr.* 36.

character of double sounds, not indeed in the mouths of the people¹, nevertheless in the cultivated speech. The oldest testimony as regards $\dot{a}\iota = \bar{\epsilon}$, corresponding to that of the later Latin Grammarians on *ae* as the lengthened form of the open $\breve{e}$, is to be found in the treatise of Aristides Quintilianus περὶ μουσικῆς, which is placed by some in the second, by others in the third or even the fourth century, but which judging by the names of those to whom the author dedicates it, Eusebius and Florentius, certainly cannot belong to the second². The evidence drawn by the followers of Reuchlin from transcriptions in the Septuagint is quite worthless. For the fact of *Bethel* being written Βαιθήλ and *Elam* Αἰλάμ³ does not shew that *aι = e*, but rather, if indeed it shews anything at all, that Hebrew Tsere with Yod *quiescens* was represented by *ai*. In the first place it ought logically to have been written Βαιθαίλ, if the sound were the same in both syllables, and in the second place the combination of Cholem with Vau *quiescens* is perfectly analogously represented by *au*: Αὐνάν *Onan*, Ναβαύ *Nebo*⁴. Finally this point too does not appear to me proven, that so early as the second century A.D. Herodian had given orthographic rules on *aι* and ϵ⁵. For why not also on η and *aι*? H was at that period certainly still *e*. There are moreover at the

---

¹ The wall inscriptions of Pompeii shew the greatest confusion, both between *ae* and *e*, and between *aι* and ϵ. For example, sometimes *cinaedus* sometimes *cinedus*; no. 1684 etati maeae, haberae; 733 ἐνθάδαι κατοικεῖ, μηδὲν εἰσειαίτω (i.e. εἰσιέτω, εἰσίτω) κακόμ (here too it is evident that Lat. $\bar{e}$ Gr. $η = \bar{e}$, Latin $\breve{e}$ Gr. $\epsilon = \underset{.}{e}$, cp. p. 37, n. 5 above).

² Aristid. π. μουσ. p. 56 Jahn (93 Meibom.): τὸ δὲ $\bar{\epsilon}$ θῆλυ μέν ἐστι κατὰ τὸ πλεῖστον ὡς προείρηται ("has a feminine character in contra-distinction to the masculine *o* and the neutral *a*"), τῷ δὲ τὸν ὅμοιον ἦχον ἐπιφαίνειν, εἰ ἐκταθείη, τῇ $\bar{a}ι$ διφθόγγῳ, γραφομένῃ διὰ τοῦ $\bar{a}$, ἐπ' ἐλάχιστον ("in a very slight degree") ἠρρένωται.—As regards the period of Aristides, cp. Jahn in the intro-

duction; what the latter says p. xxx. f. against Cæsar's argument from the names, has not the least significance.

³ Frankel *Vorstudien zur Septuaginta* p. 115; O. de Lagarde *Onomastica sacra*. Βηθ- (Βεθ-) is found for Βαιθ- in other names, but -ηλ (simple Tsere) is never written -αιλ.

⁴ Frankel ib. p. 116.

⁵ I must here run counter to the authority of Lenz, who tries to prove (Herod. p. cI.), that H. has given such rules, and who accordingly collects from the Byzantine writers everything having reference to this in the fragments περὶ ὀρθογραφίας, while he sets aside their rules on η -ει -ι, οι -υ, ο -ω (cp. p. cII. f.). But the proofs are neither numerous nor sufficiently strong.

present time hardly any instances of uncertainty of writing with regard to αι and the E-sounds. It is a ridiculous thing, that the name of the well-known Athenian, who fell at Marathon, is written Κυναίγειρος instead of Κυνέγειρος, in which latter spelling it gives the intelligible sense "urger of the hounds" and may be compared with Κυνόρτας. According to Moeris *tooth-ache* is in Attic ἠμωδία, in Hellenistic αἰμωδία[1]; but the Attic form is perhaps an invention of someone who found the imperfect of the verb αἰμωδιᾶν written ΗΜΩΔΙΑ[2]. The form σημαία (*standard*) for σημεία is erroneous: all the older inscriptions such as the Monumentum Ancyranum, and also the oldest manuscript of Polybius, shew either -εί- or, which comes to the same thing, -ή- or -έ-, which latter form explains the false -αί-[3]. The extraordinary contrast to the confusion in the case of ΕΙ -Ι is unmistakeable.

SECTION 18.

Subsequent history of ΟΙ.

ΟΙ appears to have become confounded with υ at about the same time, that αι was confounded with ε. It had never been very far removed from this sound; if the attempt is made to

Steph. Byz. Ἀβάκαινον: πόλις Σικελίας, οὐδετέρως καὶ προπαροξυτόνως, καὶ ἡ παραλήγουσα διὰ διφθόγγου, ὡς Ἡρ. ἐν ῑγ περὶ οὐδετέρων. Are these the ipsissima verba of Herodian, or has he not rather merely set Ἀβάκ. under the neuters in -αινον? Theogn. XII. 26 (Lenz II. 409) etymology of χαίτη from Ἡρ. ἐν τῇ ὀρθογραφίᾳ. Is it really likely that he intended by the etymology (from κρατῶ κράτη) to guard against the barbarous writing χέτη? P. 410, an etymology of ἄχρι is cited from the same work. Eustath. 1392. 23 (L. ib.) on γαιήοχος and γεοῦχος γηοῦχος, from Didymus and Herodian. This is an isolated case if one at all. The 4th passage (Jo. Alex. 18. 23)

Lenz himself ceases on mature consideration to reckon as belonging to the fragments of Herodian. And now with these compare the abundance of instances, even out of περὶ μονήρους λέξεως, in the case of ει -ι, ᾳ -α etc.! In the same way Marius Victor. (see above p. 62, n. 2) says that the orthography of the Greeks had to do for the most part with ι mute and ει; there is no mention of αι.

[1] Moer. 198.15; αἰμ. is in many cases the traditional reading in Aristotle.

[2] Timokles in Ath. VI. 241 A uses the form ἠμωδία in such a context, that any one might well take it for the substantive.

[3] Dittenberger *Syll.* p. 480.

pronounce οι really with the closed *o*, as must be done in accordance with what has been said above, the small interval separating it from *ü* will be remarked. Consequently Eustathius may be right in seeing intentional alliterations in the Homeric Σκύλλη κοίλης, Χάρυβδις ἀναρροιβδεῖ[1], and there is a close connection between words like λοῖγος λυγρός, κοίρανος κύριος[2]. Accordingly there is no more need to assume any intermediate step, in order to explain the common Greek transition of οι to υ, than to assume such a step between αι and ε. The transition through *ui* assumed by Curtius and others was destitute of actual traces even in Bœotian; that through *ö* must be decidedly rejected both for that dialect and for the Greek dialects taken as a whole[3]. For it is always open to suspicion to enrich a language with a new sound taken from other languages; moreover *ö* that is the sound intermediate between *ǫ* and *ę* is no nearer to *ǫi* than is *ü*, which forms the middle point between *u* and *i*. Latin *oe*, by which οι is regularly represented except in *Troia* and *anquina* (ἄγκοινα)[4] which were taken over at an early date, was in my opinion[5] just as much as *ae* and for as long a time as the latter a real diphthong, but afterwards passed not like *ae* into an open but into a closed *e*[6]. Whether it was at any intermediate period *ö*, I do not venture to decide; still it seems dangerous even here to assign this special sound to such an extremely small number of words in the language. As regards the time of the transition of οι to υ, we find isolated examples of the simple spelling so early as a papyrus of the second century B.C., but only where it is accompanied by very negligent orthography and grammar: ἀνύγετε, ἀνγύω[7]. The later inscriptions in general interchange οι with υ in the same degree as αι with

---

[1] Eustath. on *Il.* A. 406, *Od. μ.* 104 (long ago cited by the followers of Reuchlin).

[2] Curtius *Etymol.*[5] p. 658 f.

[3] This transition is favoured by Beermann, *Curt. Stud.* IX. 41 f.

[4] On *anquina* see Boeckh *Seewesen* 152.

[5] K. L. Schneider *Gramm.* I. 1, 77,

Seelmann *Auspr.* 226 f. hold the same view.

[6] This is shewn by its representation in Romance by *e* (Diez *Gramm.* I.[2] 170), while *ae* corresponds to Romance *ie*; *oe* and *ē* are treated entirely alike, and *ē* was closed, Schuchardt *Vulgärlatein* III. 151. Seelmann 227.

[7] Pap. L. 50 (160 B.C.), 51.

ε η[1]; the orthographic rules on οι υ belong to the period of the Byzantine writers[2]; this statement however according to what has been said before applies equally to the case of αι ε. οι has shared with υ the fate of becoming first *ü* and finally *i*.

Section 19.

Pronunciation of genuine ΟΥ.

Of the three corresponding diphthongs with ό, ΑΥ ΕΥ ΟΥ, we have already had occasion to treat of the rarest and the first to disappear, namely ου. It is self-evident that its second element was *u* not *ü*, and that accordingly simplification took place by *ἐπικράτεια* as in the case of ει. An *ou* occurs as is well known in old Latin (*douco, ious*), in old German, in English, in Portuguese and other Romance dialects; it is nearly related to *au*, which arises from[3] it as in German, or forms its origin as in Portuguese, *cousa ouro*[4]. This *ou* however is related rather with the Greek ωυ (*ọu*) than with ου (*ọu*); moreover in the case of the latter there is hardly any appearance of contact with αυ[5]. The genuine diphthong ου is found in οὐ, οὗτος τοῦτο etc., where it is formed by the addition to ο of the same υ, which in αὕτη ταῦτα produces with *a* the diphthong αυ; also in τοιοῦτος τοσοῦτος τηλικοῦτος; next in σπουδή (cp. σπεύδω), in ἀκόλουθος (cp. κέλευθος), in βοῦς (βούτης) Βουτάδης, in δοῦλος (written so in Bœotian too, not δῶλος), in Σούνιον[6], ξουθός στροῦθος

---

[1] Λυπά νεοπυῶν πεπύημαι C. I. Gr. 2824, 2826 Aphrodisias; ἀνῦξαι ἀνύξι Cephallenia C. I. Gr. 1933; ἀνύξας by γυνεκί and κή Bull. de corr. hell. IV. 514 (Thracian Chersonese). οἰπό Lyd. 126 A. D. ib. VIII. 378. The earliest example from Attica is Ποιανεψιῶνα (about 238—244 A.D.) Meisterh. p. 46[2].

[2] Even according to Lenz, Herod. I. p. ciii., who allows the possibility of an exception only for certain words such as δροίτη δρύτη. In B. A. p. 1204

(L. II. 645, 13) Herodian speaks of the pronunciation (ἐκφωνεῖσθαι) of the ι in οι in contrast to its silence in ωι.

[3] Cp. p. 7 above.

[4] Diez Gramm. I.[3] 171, 379.

[5] In the Athenian tribute lists the forms Αὐλιᾶται and Οὐλιᾶται interchange in a Carian name.

[6] Cauer C. Stud. VIII. 258 f.; ΔΟΥΛΙΟΝ C. I. A. I. 333; on Gortyn. Inscr. it is true we find ΔΟΛΟΣ.

etc.[1]; all these instances rest on the testimony of ancient, especially ancient Attic, inscriptions, which continue to distinguish ου and ō. It must be admitted, as we have said before, that the line of demarcation is not exceedingly sharp, and accordingly we find both ΤΟΤΟΝ *τοῦτον* and ΒΟΝ *βοῦν*[2], and in the case of ΦΡΟΤΡΟΣ ΦΡΟΡΟΣ[3] (from προϜοράω) it is difficult to say which is correct. In *ἄρουρα* the genuine diphthong is shewn by the Cyprian writing *a-ro-u-ra*[4].

SECTION 20.

Pronunciation of ΑΤ ΕΤ.

There remain ΑΤ ΕΤ, diphthongs, whose fate was notably different from that of all the others, inasmuch as here there took place not a simplification, but a hardening of the second element into a consonant. The Greeks of the present day pronounce them as *av ev* before vowels and soft consonants (βγδ, λμνρ, ζ) that is according to their usual writing *αβ εβ*, but before hard consonants (πκτ, φχθ, σ)[5] *af ef*, = αφ εφ, e.g. *ἐβεργεσία*, *ἔβδιν* (*εὔδειν*), *ἀφτός*, *ἔφκολος*, *ἔφκρατος* etc. This sound-development forms a decisive proof, that in ancient Greek the υ in this diphthong, at least in general, had preserved its original *U*-sound free from modification[6], and accordingly must be transliterated by *au*, *ęu* and not by *aü ęü*. For the development of *v* from *ü* would be as difficult as that from *u* is easy. At the same time in the case of ευ traces are not entirely wanting of a modification of the second element: ευ interchanges with ει in Ἰλεί-θυια Ἐλεύθυια Ἐλευθώ[7]; further we find on an inscription of

---

[1] *Ξουθίας* ancient Doric (Sparta?) Röhl no. 68; *Στρουθίης* also with ΟΤ Styra Röhl 372[355].

[2] Inscrip. of Eleusis *C. I. A.* iv. 27[b], 40.

[3] Dietrich in *K. Zeitschr.* xiv. 56; Cauer l. c. Also in the late inscrip. *C. I. A.* iv. 22[a] ΦΡΟΤΡΟΝ and ΦΡΟΡΙΔΕ side by side. Cretic *φρώριον*, *Bull. de corr. hell.* ix. 8, l. 8.

[4] Inscrip. of Idalion. *Dial. Inschr.*

[5] Before σ only in cultivated pronunciation; the popular pronunciation is *ps* (see Appendix).

[6] The same opinion is held by G. Curtius, G. Meyer and others.

[7] Ἐλευθυίας Cret. (Le Bas v. 67, 74, *Bull. de corr. hell.* iii. 293, l. 13), Ἐλευθώ in the Anthology (*A. P.* 7. 604, 9. 268), Ἐλευθία Ἐλευσία Sparta *Mitth. arch. Instit.* i. 162, Dittenb. *Syll.* 191.

Mantinea belonging to the first century B.C. αἰτάν and ἐπισκειάν, side by side with frequent instances of αυ and ευ[1]. The Ionians however were so far from tending to such a pronunciation, that in the fifth fourth and third centuries they wrote with more or less consistency AO, EO: ταῦτα, αὐτός, Καοκασίων, Εὐελθών, λεοκοῖς[2]. This need imply no difference of pronunciation from the Attic, for au could be equally or more correctly represented by ao i.e. aọ as by aυ i.e. aü, and this mode of writing was also made easy by the treatment in Ionic of original εο, which became in pronunciation and for the most part also in writing ευ: καλεῦντες, ἐποίευν. There is an isolated instance of εου, Εὐρυσθένεους from Samos[3]. This very contraction into ευ was in many places usual in Doric[4], and wherever it occurs furnishes a proof, that in the district in question ευ was not eü. ao also in many places became αυ: Arcadian and Cypriot -αυ in the Gen. of the 1st Declension; Σαυκράτεις Σαύμειλος Πραύχα[5] in Bœotian, from Σαο-, Πραόχα. The Ionians on the other hand made ᾱọ first into ηo then into εω: πολίτεω, λεώς, χρεώμενος, certainly implying a sort of diphthong (εọ), since this εω decidedly resists separation into two syllables[6]. The process is this, the second vowel is lengthened and approximates to a, while the first loses some of its a-sound and is shortened. In the Doric Ἑρμοκρηῦν Τιμοκρηῦν from Ἑρμοκρέων we have the converse process[7]. But, to close this digression; the close relationship of ευ αυ to corresponding combinations of an O-sound is sufficiently made clear, and to return to the point from which we started, the value of this υ has been thereby established as distinct from the ordinary

---

[1] Le Bas II. 352[1], 35, 27.

[2] Erman in *Curt. Stud.* v. 294; C. Curtius *Progr.* Wesel 1873; Hausoullier in *Bull. de corr. hell.* IV. 51; G. Meyer[2] p. 135 f. The examples are from Chios, Samos, Erythræ, Halicarnassus and other towns of the Asiatic mainland (also a coin of the Doric Cnidus has Εὔβωλος, Hauss. l. c.); from Phanagoria *C. I. Gr.* 2121, Εὐτάμονος, Amphipolis (ib. 2008). The Ionic papyrus so often mentioned has υ always, but omissions of the preceding

vowel are notably frequent, l. 4 τυτοσαυτο = ταὐτοσαυτοῦ, 6 ενθυτα = ἐνθαῦτα, 9 ικετυουσα, also 14 κελυει.

[3] Bechtel *Inschr. d. ion. Dial.* 217. B. would also explain thus (p. 58) Ἀριστοκλέους (Thasos) no. 72, cp. p. 35, n. 4 above.

[4] Ahrens *D. D.* 213 ff.

[5] G. Meyer[2] p. 136; Πραύχαε Röhl no. 127, who explains rightly.

[6] G. Meyer[2] p. 148 f.

[7] Cauer *Del.*[2] 169.

value. Additional proof is furnished by spellings such as
'Αχιλλεούς ancient Corinthian; ἄνεο ἄνευ Attic, period of
the Empire; Λαυδικεούς Olympia, period of the Empire, and
other similar instances[1]. Moreover in this case alone Latin
has not retained the Greek υ, but has represented it by its own
u[2]. At the same time the other point too, namely that ancient
Greek αυ ευ were not *av ev*, has been pretty nearly proved already
by what has gone before. For how could καλέοντες γένεος have
been contracted to *kalevntes genevs (genefs)*? Or how could *av af*
have come to be written with *ao*? It is indeed just as hard to
say, how if the pronunciation was *av* AT came to be written
and not AF, especially as the digamma continued for a long
time in use in so many dialects. Nevertheless, except in the
case of Crete, as far as we know, it occurred to only one man
among all the engravers and stone-cutters, to write digamma
here, namely the cutter of a Locrian inscription[3], and even he
did so only in one word NαϜπακτίων, and that only once in
twenty possible instances where he had to bring in Naupactus
or its inhabitants. So fixed was the stupid "historic" or
"traditional" orthography among the Locrians! In like manner
ῈϜθετος on a Corinthian clay-tablet is isolated, while on others
'Αχιλεύς, Εὐρυμήδης, Ζεύς, αὐτο- are so written[4]. In Crete
on the other hand such a multitude of examples of αϜ εϜ (οϜ)
have recently come to light[5] owing to the excavations of
Halbherr, that the matter deserves serious consideration. In

---

[1] Cp. p. 29 above; G. Meyer[2] p. 135
(after Dittenberger *Herm.* VI. 306);
Arch. Ztg. 1877 part 2, no. 68. Λαυδι-
κεύς and many others [Empire], Meyer
136. Γονεοῦσι Assos *Archæolog. Inst.
of America* I. p. 33[iv]; also ΕΘΤΤΥΧΟ[Σ
Bull. de c. h. VII. 52 (Thess.) must be
Εὀύτ.

[2] Cp. below p. 81, n. 4.

[3] Röhl no. 321 (Cauer[2] 229) B. 15.

[4] R. no. 20, 101, 43, 48, 66, 68.
I willingly leave undecided the new
reading *o-vo* i.e. *ov* for *ov* on a Cyprian
inscription (Deecke in *Bezzenberger's*

Beiträge VI. 78, *Dial. Inschr.* 68).
Α⋀ΤΑΙΣΙ is found on l. 7 of the great
Pamphylian inscrip. of Syllium (Röhl
505 *Dial. Inschr.* 1267) with a symbol
which on other Pamphylian inscriptions stands for Digamma (Röhl p. 143
Bezzenb. *Dial. Inschr.* 368); here too
we find ⋁ΟΙΚΥ *οἶκον*, Σ(Ε)ΛΤ⋀ΠΟΣ
Seluviyos. The digamma it is true appears as well: Ϝέτ[ι]ια (*vetiya*, *ἔτεα*),
τιμάϜεσα.

[5] Comparetti *Museo Italiano* II.
131, 162 f., 194, 211, 215, 218, 222, 231,
etc.

the first place then on archaic Cretan inscriptions also we find
as a rule αυ ευ, and on the Gortynian law code without exception.
In the next place examples are not wanting of a writing which
was evidently in a state of fluctuation, corresponding to the
instance cited Ἀχιλλεούς, for example ἀμεϜύσαθαι [ἀ]Ϝυτάν¹,
just as an old Naxian inscription also shews AϜVTO αὐτοῦ, an
example of Ϝ in Ionic to which exception has long been taken
though to no purpose². Now this fluctuation points to the
fact, that the sound au was adequately represented neither
by αυ i.e. aü nor by aϜ. In the third place it may be
erroneous to give to the Ϝ the value of the English and
Romance v and not rather that of the English w, which as is
well known belonged to the Latin v. For on a later Cretan
inscription, dating from the time when the digamma was disappearing, νέργων i.e. Ϝέργων, ἔργων is found repeatedly, and the
name of the town Axus, properly Ϝάξος, appears more than once
as Ὄαξος; while on the other hand it is true, that the sound
might be thickened to a spirant, written β, instead of being
resolved into a vocalic syllable: διαβειπάμενος, Βολοεντίοι =
Ὀλούντιοι³. Moreover, the digamma, had it had the fixed sound
of v, would hardly have disappeared so generally from the
language, nor indeed would it have been likely to have existed
in it before, as the only spirant of this sort, without f etc.; but
conversely, if it was a semivocalic u, and the language in general
gave up the u-sound, it is easy to understand, that it did not
follow suit in undergoing the change to ü and consequently had
to disappear. Accordingly there will be to a certain extent
a connection between this sound-change and the disappearance
of Ϝ, and we also see dialects such as the Bœotian retaining

¹ ib. 204, 221 (cp. the doubtful
ΤΙΤΟϜΕΣΘΟ 157, while in 215 we
have ΤΙΤΟϜΤΟΣ, 208 ΤΙΤΤϜΟΣ).
² Röhl no. 408 (the reading quite
certain). Many attempts at explanation have been hazarded (as by Röhl),
see however Bechtel Inschr. d. ion.
Dial. p. 39. A new instance of Ϝ in a
Naxian inscription has lately come to

light: Bull. de corr. hell. 1888, 464:
ᕽᗺᐃᓿᖉᗅᚼᗺᓿᖉ Ϝιφικαρτίδης.
³ Τέργων Comp. II. 678, col. II. l. 5,
8; διαβειπ. 659, no. 21, 11; on Βολοεντίοι Meyer² 233. Cp. also Eretria
Ἐφημ. ἀρχ. 1888, 83 ff. l. 174 ο Ὀαλι-
δίο[υ] nom. proprium = Ϝαλιδίου ('Ηλείου)
while ib. 182 Α it is written Ἀλιδίου.

the digamma with the true *u*, while those like the Attic and Asiatic-Ionic gave both of them up at an early period. If now the digamma was a semivowel, no inference can be made from the writing *a*F *e*F for a modern Greek pronunciation, any more than in the case of the Oscan, which writes the corresponding diphthongs regularly *av ov*, that is to say with the semivowel[1]. The interpolation of a digamma or of a β representing a digamma after ευ when followed by a vowel which occurs regularly in Cyprus and occasionally in various localities:— ΕὐϜάγορας, ΒακεύϜας Bœot., Εὔβανδρος Dodona, Εὐβάλκης Lakon., *e-u-ve-r-(e)-ke-si-a* ἐνεργεσία, *e-u-ve-le-to-to-se* Εὐέλθοντος Cypriot[2], admits of easy explanation. For in this case a semivowel *v* was developed out of a *u* just as easily as a semivowel *y* from an *i*, which likewise appears in Cyprus: *a-no-si-ja* ἀνοσία, and in neighbouring Pamphylia, where two *i*'s are written: ΔΙΙΑ, ΕΣΤϜΕΔΙΙΤΣ Ἀσπένδιος. The same holds good naturally not only of ευ but also of *v = u*; hence we have in Cyprus *tu-va-no-i* δυϜάνοι i.e. διδοίη (formed from ΔΤ instead of ΔΟ), and on a Chalcidian vase ΓαρυϜόνης Γηρυόνης[3]. In case however any should be inclined to infer from what has been cited, that the *v* of these diphthongs tended from an early period in these dialects to harden into a consonant, it must at least not be forgotten, that it was precisely in the Cyprian dialect that the customary pronunciation was really diphthongic; for the manner of writing is *pa-si-le-u-s(e)* βασιλεύς *o-na-sa-ko-ra-u* Ὀνασαγόραυ. The Cyprian dialect also shews by the coexistence of forms such as *e-v(e)-re-ta-sa-tu* and *e-u-v(e)-re-ta-sa-tu* (ἐϜρητάσατυ, εὐϜρητάσατυ i.e. ὡμολόγησεν, from Ϝρήτα = ὡμολογία, ῥήτρα)[4], how Lesbian αὔρηκτος for ἄϜρηκτος ἄρρηκτος, Εὐρυσίλαος for ἘϜρυσ.[5], and similar instances are to be explained. In these the

[1] B. Kruczkiewicz, *d. altlat. u. oskische Diphth. ou, Ztschr. f. öst. Gymn.* 1879, 1 ff.

[2] *Dial. Inschr.* 648, 458 (cp. 1040, 1146); Karapanos *Dodone* Tab. 34, 3; *Mitth. d. archaeolog. Inst.* i. 231; *Dial. Inschr.* 71, 165 ff. (cp. *e-u-va-ko-ro* ΕὐϜαγόρω 153 ff., *e-u-va-te-vo-se* Εὐάνθεος 161 ff.). On the other hand ἀριστεύτοντα, Corcyra R. no. 343, may just as well be an error for ἀριστεύοντα as for -εύϜοντα.

[3] Inscr. of Idalium, *Dial. Inschr.* 60 (Cauer[2] no. 472) l. 6; *C. I. Gr.* 7582.

[4] Idalium l. c. 4, 14.

[5] Ahrens *D. A.* p. 37; Inscr. of Eresus, *Dial. Inschr.* 281 c.

Ϝ was changed into a vowel before the *r*, for which process the Cyprian writing contains the middle step; the υ however must by no means be considered as the representation in writing of a digamma still heard in pronunciation. In many cases a digamma in the middle of a word also has in the dialects become combined with the preceding vowel into a diphthong: e.g. Cyprian *ke-ne-u-vo-n(e)* κενευϜόν κενευόν (κενεόν), Lesbian ναῦος (ναός), αὔως (ἠώς), εὐάλωκε, Homeric εὔαδε, αὔίαχοι; Apollonius Dyskolos bears witness, that in εὔαδε and ναῦος the following υ combined with the ε α into a syllable[1], he accordingly analysed εὔ-αδε, i.e. *eu-ade* not *ev-ade*. It is true that, if the ευ αυ in such words were scanned short occasionally, as in αὐάτα in Pindar and αὐειρομέναι in Alcman[2], the pronunciation could hardly be other than *avata* etc.[3]; why then are they written with υ? But we have not the slightest proof, that in these cases the poets themselves did not really use the digamma; subsequent copyists have in general as far as possible removed the antiquated symbol from the texts. For the rest αυ ευ were neither at the end nor the beginning of a word readily shortened, in marked contrast to the corresponding diphthongs with ι; the examples cited with shortened ευ θηρεύει and εὔωνος are only from the rustic Hipponax[4], and but little can be added from the authors that have come down to us: ἰχνεύων in Pindar, Ζεῦ ἀλεξῆτορ in Sophocles[5]. Yet, if the pronunciation were ἄυ ἔυ, the syllable must have been scanned short where a vowel followed not in isolated instances but always and without exception. How comes it then, that a learned man like Bursian[6] declares, that he finds no evidence, that the ancient Greeks did not pronounce αυ and ευ as *av* and *ev*? The Greeks of to-day pronounce εβο and ευο precisely alike; the ancients are said *si dis placet* to have done the same,

---

[1] ΚενευϜόν *Dial. Inschr.* 20; Apollon. π. ἐπιρρ. p. 559. 29 (p. 149 ed. Schneider-Uhlig); see Giese *Aeol. Dial.* 272.

[2] In the Egypt. frg. col. 2, v. 29. Also in Alcæus frg. 41 Bergk ἐγχεῦε is handed down, Athen. x. 430 A, although in ib. 430 c. xi. 481 A ἐγχεε.

[3] Curt. *Etym.* [5] 569.

[4] Schol. Hephæst. p. 107 Westph.

[5] Pind. *Pyth.* 8. 35; Soph. *O. C.* 143. So also Ζεῦ 'Ολύνπιε in the verse in Röhl no. 75.

[6] *Verhandl. der Philologenvers. im Frankfurt am Main* (1861) S. 187.

but their poets have obstinately scanned the one as a Pyrrhic the other as a trochee. If then Bursian finds no evidence, this must not be ascribed to any real lack of material; whoever will take the trouble to cast about him, will find on this very point *embarras de richesse.* It would moreover be absolutely monstrous, if the pronunciation were as in modern Greek, that the Grammarians should so consistently reckon αυ ευ as diphthongs, although they do not regard αβ εβ as diphthongs; and they are not only counted as diphthongs, but as genuine diphthongs, different from υι, and not only as genuine diphthongs, but actually as diphthongs κατὰ κρᾶσιν[1]. Whoever continues to see no impossibility here, but still hopes to find a way out of the difficulty, may proceed to explain how φεῦγε, Ζεῦ, βασιλεῦ etc. can have the circumflex accent. And why is ΑΤΤΟ to be *aftu,* ΤΟΤΤΟ on the other hand not *toftu* but *tutu?* Or how can the Rhetor Demetrius note the euphonious character of the name Εὔιος, because it consists entirely of vowels up to the last letter[2]? Of what avail against all this are such poor arguments as that drawn from ΑΥΤΟ and the writing ἀτοῦ and ἑατοῦ common after the 1st century B.C. for αὐτοῦ and ἑαυτοῦ[3], which it is alleged can only be comprehended by supposing the pronunciation to have been *avtu* and not *autu?* As a matter of fact this word being troublesome and difficult to pronounce considering its frequency was very naturally made easy in the popular speech and finally lost even the *a* (mod. Gr. τοῦ τῆς etc.): but the most obvious mitigation of its difficulty even if the pronunciation were *autu,* could only be the rejection of the *u.* In the same way in popular pronunciation the German name *Auguste* loses its *u,* in late Latin too we find *Agustus, Cladius,* with which we may compare *Agosto* and *Zaragoza (Caesaraugusta)* and Italian *Metaro* and *Pesaro (Metaurus, Pisaurum)*[4]. Accordingly *au* can very easily produce *a*;

[1] Cp. p. 22 above.

[2] Demetr. π. ἑρμην. § 69 (see p. 66).

[3] So in Greek text of Monum. Ancyr.; further instances from Delos *Bull. de corr. hell.* III. 153; Lemnos ib. IV. 543. Athens *C. I. A.* II. 478 c. 6; 487, 5, Add. 489ᵇ, 15 (G. Meyer[2]

p. 137). ΕΣΤΕΤΩ ἔσται αὐτῷ Phryg. *Bull. de corr. hell.* VIII. 251.

[4] Corssen *Ausspr.* I.[2] p. 664; W. Schmitz *Beitr. zur lat. Sprachkunde* 96 ff.; Diez *Gr.* I.[3] 171. Seelmann *Ausspr. d. Lat.* 223.

indeed if we are to believe the Greek philologist Psichari, we must absolutely recognize in ἀτός, which survives to this day dialectically, a proof of the original diphthongal pronunciation of αυ; for, according to him, ἀτός cannot be explained from *aftos*[1]. Above all how could αυ change to *o*? Nevertheless this vowel has here and there in Doric been developed from αυ: καππώτας from καταπαύω, αὐσωτοῦ from αὐτὸς αὐτοῦ = ἑαυτοῦ[2]. Correspondingly in Cretan ευ becomes ου; ψούδια ψεύδη, ἐπιτά-δουμα[3]. That is to say in the case of αυ we have κρᾶσις, just as αι becomes η by κρᾶσις; in the case of ευ ἐπικράτεια, just as ι arises from ει by the same process. When furthermore we find in the centuries just preceding the Christian era, in various dialects and also in the κοινή, κυριέουσα written for κυριεύουσα, σκεοθήκα κατεσκέασεν, ᾿Εωννμεύς and so on[4], I can well understand, how in pronunciation the υ which was really inconvenient was got rid of, but not how *v* should have been allowed to drop out just in those cases, where it stood between vowels[5]. Accordingly under the assumption, that αυ ευ were *au eu*, our difficulties vanish on all sides; under the other assumption we are absolutely surrounded with difficulties, if not impossibilities.

In Cretan ἀυκά = ἀλκή, ευθῆν = ἐλθεῖν[6]: al el becoming

[1] Psichari *Rev. Crit.* 1887, 266.

[2] Ahrens *D. D.* 185; G. Meyer[2] p. 139. On the other hand Bœotian ἀσαυτῦ *Dial. Inschr.* 385, 391.

[3] Ahrens *D. D.* 187; G. Meyer[2] p. 139; *Bull. de corr. hell.* IV. 354.

[4] Ahrens ib. 188; Curtius *Sächs. Gesellsch. d. W.* XVI. 219; a very complete collection of examples G. Meyer[2] p. 137 ff. Even on the Lam. Styr. Röhl 372[81] ᾿Εαλκίδης (carelessness? cp. no. 36, 73, 104 etc., where all sorts of letters are omitted). *C. I. Gr.* 2909 (Mykale) = Bechtel 144 πρυτανέωντος, trustworthy? Ib. 2107[c] (Pantikapaion) [βασιλ]έοντος. (It must be remembered that Ionic ΕΟ = ΕΥ.) But in 2691de this βασιλ. is certainly not to be read, see Le Bas, and 2919 (Tralles, also with βασ.) is a modern forgery, see Fröhner in Bechtel p. 148.

[5] Before consonants ἐνοίας *C. I. A.* II. 616, 19 (ib. l. 16 ἐπανέσαι for ἐπαιν.), ἀπελεθέρα Osann *Syll. inscr.* p. 440. To these examples and a few others in Meyer I add πολυδέκη Pap. L. 43, χέσομαι for χεύσ. Kaibel 816 (Rome; Wagner *de epigr. Gr.* [Leipzig 1883] p. 45); ᾿Αξάνων Sterret *Arch. Inst. of America*, III. no. 513, 598; Πολύεκτος Rhodes *Bull. de corr. h.* IX. 115; Φάστῳ Phryg. ib. VIII. 246; but ᾿Εθύμαχοs Styra Röhl 372, 114 must be cancelled, see Bechtel 19, 193.

[6] Ahrens *D. D.* III. (from the grammarians, at present no evidence from inscriptions, if ἀδευφιαί on the Gortynian inscrip. [v. 18] is nothing more than a scribe's error). On the supposed Thasian ᾿Αυλωφῶν = ᾿Αγλαο-φῶν see Bechtel *Thas. Inschr.* p. 11.

au eu as in Romance, where in most dialects the next step was for *au* to become *o*, though in some it has remained. In the same way we may explain Bœotian εὔδομος for ἔβδομος and εὐ-δομήκοντα (if really existing) in Corcyra[1]. Similarly we find on some of the most faulty papyri ῥαῦδος and ῥαῦτος for ῥάβδος[2]. The Romance languages furnish excellent analogies on this point also: Spanish *ciudad* from *civ(i)tat-*, *cautivo* from *captivus*; Provençal *paraula* Fr. *parole* from *parab(o)la*, etc.[3] As regards transliteration into and from other languages, Terentianus Maurus speaks of Latin *au eu* and Greek *αυ ευ* as perfectly similar sounds[4]; accordingly *Paulus*, *Aurelius* are represented by Παῦλος, Αὐρήλιος. If then in face of this Bursian has recourse to the argument, that we know nothing of the pronunciation of Latin *au*, that is only evading the matter; he must allow the logical conclusion: *avspices, avt, avrum.* This people are naturally not willing to do[5], in spite of the famous *Cauneas = cave ne eas*[6]; the fact is rather this, that *v* was pronounced as a semi-vowel, like English *w*, and therefore readily combined with *a* before consonants forming *au*: *cau(e)neas, auceps* from *avis, aufero.* It must be regretted for our purpose, that the Romans expressed consonantal and vowel *V* with one symbol; the poets however by scanning *Agāue ēuoe, Ēuander*, have taken sufficient care that

---

[1] Ahrens *D. A.* 174; *C. I. Gr.* 1563, 1845 (*Dial. Inschr.* 491, 17; 3206, 47).

[2] Papyr. L. 40, 41; a stronger instance still ἐμβλεύσαντας Papyr. Lond. (ed. Forshall) II. 11 for ἐμβλέψαντας i.e. ἐμβλέψαντας. The author of the three documents is the hermit of the Serapeum, the Macedonian son of Ptolemy Glaukias.

[3] Diez I. 278, 281, 289 etc.

[4] Terent. Maur. v. 467 ff.: *AV* et *EV, quas sic habemus cum Grais communiter, corripi plerumque possunt*—(481) *AV tamen capere videtur saepe productum sonum, auspices* cum dico et *aurum, sive Graecus* αὔριον. *mira nec putanda nobis talis alternatio est δί-*

χρονον *quod* ἄλφα *notum est, sicut A nostratibus.* (There is no information elsewhere on *āu*, K. L. Schneider *Gr.* p. 58.) Some Roman grammarians wished to transliterate *αυ ευ* by *ay ey*, Curt. Valerianus in Cassiodor. K. VII. 158.

[5] Terent. M. says also very expressly v. 480: *hanc enim* (*EV*) *si protrahamus, A sonabit, E et V*, syllabam nec invenimus ex tribus vocalibus. The alleged testimony of Beda for the pronunciation *avrum* does not exist according to Keil's edition (VII. 228, 20).

[6] On this (Cic. *de Div.* II. 40, 84) vide Henrichsen p. 132.

the difference of pronunciation as contrasted with *ăvus lēvis* should be evident. And supposing that *v* had been doubled in these words we should find the writing *euuoe* (like *Maiia*). Moreover, had Ἀτρεύς been pronounced *Atrefs* or *Atrevs*, the Romans would never have declined these proper names by the second declension, as they do: *Atrei Atreo Atreum*[1]. The Greeks on their side represent consonantal *v* by *ου*, even in cases where it is preceded by *a, e*: Ὀκτάουιος, Σεουῆρος; and side by side with this appears Ὀκτάιος[2]. Yet, if Greek *αυι* had been *avi*, neither mutilation nor monstrous piling up of vowels would have been necessary; Ὀκταύιος, Σευῆρος would have served their purpose. The latter mode of writing occurs after Hadrian's time[3], although so late as the period of Septimius Severus the writing Σεουῆρος far preponderates[4]. There was indeed nothing extraordinary in the representation of *eve* by *ευη* i.e. *eue*, as in the biblical names Λευί, Εὔα, Δαυίδ, and this is quite wrongly used as an argument on their side by the followers of Reuchlin; the Copts also write ⲈⲨⲢⲀ, i.e. *Euha*, where the *h* can only be put in on account of the hiatus[5]. But the fact that Latin *av ev* is written from the second century onwards with *αυ ευ*, though never before, suggests that the modern Greek pronunciation had at that time begun[6], and naturally first before vowels. The only real difficulty in this question is to get any information as to the beginning of the present pronunciation; for the available material is in part of an absurdly questionable character. A bad Attic Epigram of the time of Hadrian, which has tormented our learned men quite unduly, gives ἐν εὐφήβοισι παλαίστραι[ς ?], which is explained by Kaibel in such a manner, that he makes the author scan ἐφήβοισι from metrical necessity and represent this scansion by εὐφ = *eff*, while according to others παλαίστραις is the right

---

[1] The vulgar pronunciation was *Orphaeus* three syllables, as Aristaeus, Mar. Victorin. K. VI. 66 f., Seelmann 229.

[2] Dittenberger *Herm.* VI. 302 ff.

[3] do. p. 306.

[4] p. 306, 3. In Sterret's inscrip-

tions (note 292) we find Σεου. and Φλά-ουιοs no. 279, 345, 426, 534, 536, 613, 620 ; Σευ. 366, l. 56.

[5] Stern *Kopt. Gr.* p. 19. Also Hebrew Vau = English *w*, Stade *Hebr. Gr.* 65.

[6] So Dittenberger l. c.

reading and εὐφήβ. is shortened by the verse-wright from
εὐεφήβ.[1] For my part I have the greatest hesitation in assigning ευ = ef and φ = f to the time of Hadrian; for before consonants, according to what has been said before, the modern
Greek pronunciation cannot have prevailed even in the time
of Terentianus Maurus (end of the third century). The
change must be explained by the endeavour of language to
get rid of all diphthongs, to which end the other means, viz.
krasis and ἐπικράτεια, were not in this case sufficient; it has
however brought with it barbarous dissonances, since the υ
has become sharpened to f before hard consonants. The sound
f, as we shall have occasion to shew further on, was on the
whole entirely foreign to the classical language, and cannot be
shewn to have existed even in the dialects; there is nowhere
anything like *efkratos efstrotos* (εὔκρατος, εὔστρωτος), and also
nothing like *aftos* (αὐτός), since no dialect, even supposing it
had a spirant at that period, allowed this spirant to stand
before a tenuis. According to Dittenberger we have an
instance of the consonantal pronunciation of υ in αυ in Παουλλίνα on a Roman inscription of the late Empire, since, if αυ had
still had the sound of *au*, it would have been written Παυλλίνα,
as always before[2]. However even this argument is a desperate
expedient: Παουλλίνα according to him is to prove this, Θραού-
ΣΙΟΣ (Θραούστος?) on the other hand on another Roman
inscription[3], i.e. *aou* in the case of a *Greek* name, of course proves
the opposite, and the same is true of the above mentioned
γονεοῦσι etc., in all which cases the insertion of the O was just
as much a work of supererogation as in Παουλλίνα. When
however we find in Asia Minor, it is true on a very late inscription, κατεσκεούασαν τῷ Φλαουιανῷ, the author must doubtless

---

[1] *C. I. A.* III. 1104, Kaibel *Epigr.*
956 (the stone is lost): εἰκόνα τήνδε
Ποθεινὸς ἐν εὐφ. παλαίστραι (even the
last s is supported only by one copy)
τεύξας κοσμητοῦ θήκατο Νυμφοδότου. Παλαίστραι[s] Boeckh Dittenb. (cp. the
same *Herm.* XII. 1 f.); on the other hand
Neubauer *Herm.* XI. 139 takes εὐφ.=
ἐφήβοισι with pleonastic υ and a play on

εὐ—. This appears to me at any rate
less monstrous than K.'s explanation,
who moreover takes ἐν ἐφ. = σὺν ἐφ.
(Neub. 'as one of the Ephebi'); both
connect παλαίστρᾳ with τεύξας.

[2] Dittenberger p. 307; *C. I. Gr.*
6665 (on the Via Latina).

[3] *C. I. Gr.* 6669 (epitaph of a freed-
man of Tiberius).

6—2

have pronounced *kateske-vasan* just as *Fla-viano*[1]. But there can be no two opinions about κατεσκέβασε and ἀπελέφτερος on inscriptions of a period later but unfortunately not to be more accurately determined[2]. Moreover a Spanish *Pablo* points with certainty to a Greek *Pavlos*, since *Paulus* would give *Polo*. Ulfilas also represents αυ ευ by *av* and *aiv* (*Pavlus aivaggelyo*), and this Gothic *v* was certainly intended to represent a Greek spirant, although in Germanic words it was rather a semivowel, corresponding to the old German *w*. However Latin *au* also becomes *av* in Gothic : *kavtsyo* for *cautio*.

II. CONSONANTS.

SECTION 21.

Consonantal system in ancient and modern Greek.

As regards the pronunciation of the consonants Bursian again says, that he sees no reason in the case of any of them, except possibly β, to deviate from the modern Greek pronunciation. I on the contrary see many reasons in the case of many of them; indeed I find almost the whole sound-system different. The ancients, as is well known, distinguish between ἄφωνα and ἡμίφωνα, mutae and semivocales, a distinction which corresponds approximately to that which is made by modern phoneticians between explosives and fricatives. According to the ancients λ μ ν ρ σ, according to some also θ φ χ, are ἡμίφωνα; β γ δ π κ τ and according to the ordinary classification φ χ θ are mutes ; three double-consonants are added, each formed by the combination of a mute and a semi-vowel, namely ζ ξ ψ. This distribution according to the modern pronunciation appears in the following shape. Not only θ φ χ, but also β δ γ and ζ, are reckoned among the fricatives; π κ τ are the only explosive sounds, ξ ψ the only double-consonants. There remain to be noted the loss of the spiritus asper, which was

---

[1] Sterret (p. 80, n. 5 above) no. 279.   2015 (Callipolis), *Bull. de corr. hell.*
[2] Κατεσκ. *C. I. Gr.* 3693 (Cyzicus),   1888, 202 (Kios); ἀπελ. 5922[b] (Rome).

not reckoned in the alphabet, but belonged to the fricatives, the new formation of the fricative *y* not only from γ but also from vowel *i*, in many cases diminishing the number of syllables (ἰατρός *yatrós*, ποῖος *pyos*); lastly the universal abandonment of the lengthening of the consonants represented in writing by their doubling: ἀλλά pronounced *alá*, μέλλω *mèlŏ*[1]. I think therefore, that the transformation of the sound-conditions could hardly have been greater, especially as even the explosive sounds which have remained have in certain cases a special pronunciation, conflicting with the writing.—We will begin our more detailed examination with the ἡμίφωνα, under which head we shall reckon the spiritus asper.

SECTION 22.

Pronunciation of the nasals ΜΝΓ.

The Greeks have and had three nasal sounds, corresponding to the three classes of mutes: the labial nasal μ, the dental ν, and the guttural, which has no especial symbol in the alphabet and is represented by γ (ṅ in Lepsius), called by certain grammarians ἄγμα or ἄγγμα. Only ν can be used as a final, but final ν was assimilated in the context to following consonants, i.e. it became μ or γ respectively, and more rarely λ ρ σ: τὸρ Ῥόδιον, ὢλ λέγουσι, ἐς Σιδῶνι, ἐσστήλει or ἐστήληι[2]. Inscriptions preserve abundant testimony to this, and in many, at least before mutes and μ, assimilation is consistently carried out[3]; even manuscript authority is not

[1] In the modern dialects according to Psichari (cp. *Rev. crit.* 1887, 264 n. 4) the vanished nasal has developed a doubling of the consonant: *aθθos ἄνθos, niffi νύμφη, toχχiro τὸν χοῖρον, toyyero τὸν γέρον(τα), torrafti τὸν ῥάφτην.*

[2] *C. I. A.* II. 9. 14[b]. 86, 14, 31. 369 etc. So also ἐστήσαντι i.e. ἐνστ. 834[b II], 28. Cp. Giese *Aeol. Dial.* 83 ff.; Cauer in *Curt. Stud.* VIII. 295 ff.; Meisterhans ed. 2, p. 86; Hecht *Orthogr. dial. Forschungen* 1, Progr. Königsb.

1885. The Ionic Inscript. of Halicarnassus *Bull. de corr. hell.* IV. 303 has sometimes ἐλ Λυρισσῶι sometimes ἐν Λυρισσῶι; the older one R. 500 l. 41 τῶς συμπάντων.

[3] Consistently carried out e.g. on the Megarian inscrip. *C. I. Gr.* 1052 (*Dial. Inschr.* 3003): in the rescript of Cn. Manlius to the inhabitants of Heraclea Latmi, *C. I. Gr.* 3800, Le Bas v. no. 588, Dittenb. 209 (only l. 9 πρόνοιαν ποιεῖσθαι).

wanting on some papyri[1], and doubtless in the Attic and Macedonian periods this mode of writing was largely made use of in the texts of authors. But it appears, that in time the general tendency was, in the cultivated speech, to isolate words more and pronounce each distinctly by itself[2], as is shewn in an especial degree by the dropping of elision and crasis. In any case very few traces of assimilation have remained in our best manuscripts, and in our present manner of writing none; the modern Greek popular pronunciation on the other hand retains certain traces of it, although in general it rejects final ν altogether[3]. Conversely with us assimilation in the interior of words is regular, with the ancients this is not so much the case: it is not only that συνλαμβάνω, ἐνκαλεῖν and in general ἐν- συν- παν- before all sounds is on papyri the more common writing[4], but also on inscriptions Ὀλυνπία, λανβανέτω, ἄνκυρα, ἔπενψεν and such like appear at all periods with greater or less frequency[5]. To infer from this, as some have done, that the Greeks pronounced the nasal before consonants in the French way, is an extraordinary piece of perversity[6]; however

---

[1] Pap. L. 2 (Dialectics) col. 2 τῶμ ποιητῶν, 3 οὐθέμ πῆμα, 5 ἐγ γυναιξί, 7 τόγ γε, 8 προσιδοῖσαμ φάος, 9 ἀγ γίνοιτο, 11 τῶμ ποιητῶν. However it is not frequent on this careful and very old manuscript. Pap. 1 has only μὲγ γὰρ col. 6, and ἐμ βραχεῖ in the acrostic v. 2. On the other hand a Herculanean ms. (Gompertz *Wiener Akad.* Bd. 83, 87 ff.) which also shews ει for ηι : ὅταμ πόρρωθέμ ποθεν. ἐπιτήδιομ πρᾶξιν. τῶμ προλήψεων γιγνόμενον καὶ τῶμ φαινομένων. τὸ λεγόμενόμ ποτε. καταγέλαστογ γὰρ etc.

[2] Hecht l. c. p. 32 cites (after G. Hermann *de emend. rat. gr. gr.* c. IV.) Dionys. π. συνθ. p. 158 R. :—κλυτὰν πέμπετε in Pindar is an instance of harsh juxtaposition, since the dental ν and the labial π do not agree well and do not fuse together at all into the beginning of a syllable.—According to Hecht assimilation ceases at Athens

soon after the beginning of the 3rd century B.C.

[3] Foy p. 24 (τὸν παρακαλῶ pron. tombarakaló, τὸν πόλεμον tombólemo).

[4] On the mss. of Hypereides cp. my table of comparison p. XI. Pap. L. I. 11 ἐνκέκλεικεν ἐνκλίνι. 18, 19 συνκαταδύνει. Philod. π. ὀργ. III. 14 ἐνποιεῖ. XVII. 13 τἀνπολλά.

[5] Ὀλυνπία Ὀλύνπιος is absolutely the usual spelling on the ancient Olympian inscriptions; assimilation in general was much more carelessly carried out in early times than later on. Ἔπενψεν C. I. A. II. 51, πονπῆς 603; ἄνκυρα 811 D, [185]; ἀνπέλων constantly C. I. Gr. 1840 (Corcyra). On the ancient Attic inscr. vide Cauer p. 288 f. On Attic in general Meisterhans ed. 2, p. 85–8.

[6] J. Schmidt *Vokalismus d. indog. Spr.* p. 116 ff., who calls this a nasal vowel and transliterates nȳphe. G.

no doubt before β π φ ψ the μ was not pronounced as a full *m* as at the beginning of a syllable or a word. We have express testimony to this, with reference not only to μ but to Latin *m*[1], and the same applies to the German pronunciation of *mp mb*, the closing of the lips not being completed before the sounds *p b* have been reached. This then and the habit of dividing into syllables, causing the nasal to become in a certain degree final, gives a sufficient explanation of that manner of writing[2]. A yet more undefined pronunciation of the nasal, especially before labials, led to entire assimilation or even omission: Boeot. ἔππασις = ἔμπασις (ἔγκτησις), Ὀλυππίχα[3]; found sporadically in the most various localities Ἀφιτρίτα, νύφη, Ὀλυπικός, Ἄθαββος, etc.[4] The most important phenomenon of this kind is the so-called ν ἐφελκυστικόν, i.e. a nasal after-sound following final -ε (ει) and -ι (especially σι), which was present in Attic and Ionic from an early period and thus made its way into the common language. This nasal, which naturally took a special colouring from the initial letter following, was not strong enough in all cases to exclude hiatus and thereby prevent synaloepha, but it

---

Meyer also opposes this view p. 284, with regard to Latin Seelmann 289 f.

[1] Mar. Victor. VI. 16 Keil: clari in studiis viri, qui aliquid de orthographia scripserunt, omnes fere aiunt inter *m* et *n* litteras mediam vocem, quae non abhorreat ab utraque littera, sed neutram proprie exprimat, tam nobis deesse quam Graecis (i.e. is unrepresented in writing); nam cum illi *Sambyx* scribant, nec *m* exprimere nec *n*. Also in Latin spellings such as *Septenbris Ponpeii*, Schmitz *Beitr. z. lat. Sprachkunde* p. 66-.

[2] κέκρυνμαι can only be explained by division into syllables (Athens), Kaibel *Epigr.* no. 96, καλυνμάτων constantly Inscr. of Epidaurus Ἐφ. ἀρχ. 1886, p. 147 sqq., l. 57 sqq. ἐγραμμάτευεν *C. I. A.* II. 489ᵇ 3.

[3] The latter occurs in *Bullet. de corr. hell.* III. 385 (κοινή διάλ.). Also

in Attic we have ξυββάλλεσθαι, *C. I. A.* II. 52ᶜ; in Crete αφφανω αμφανω, ποππάν, περιαππέτιξ Comparetti *Mus. Ital.* I. 147. G. Meyer[2] p. 267.

[4] Ib. p. 284; J. Schmidt l. c.; cp. Seelmann 273. This rejection of the nasal appears in Modern Greek too, but only before φθχ owing to a special tendency: ἀφαλός ὀμφαλός, ρεβίθι ἐρέβινθος, συχωρῶ, Foy p. 79, 80. In the ancient language constant in Cyprian and Pamphylian, and before dentals and gutturals as well as labials.—On the Corinthian clay tablets (Röhl no. 20; *Dial. Inschr.* 3119 f.) Ἀμφιτρίτα is written twice with μ, twice with ν, and twice without a nasal. Σφίξ, for Σφίγξ, *C. I. Gr.* 8139 (Athenian vase); τυχάνοι and τυχχάνοι *Ion. Papyr.* (cp. p. 44, n. 3 above). Addition of nasal also occurs in ἐμπρίατο *C. I. Gr.* 1840, 2, cp. Seelmann 274.

often did effect this and as time went on its tendency to do so increased; in like manner it did not necessarily make length by position with a following consonant, but it could do so. Homer and after him the whole range of poetry has made free use of the means here presented for convenient versification:— ἔστ᾽ ἔστι ἔστιν; ἔλεγ᾽ ἔλεγε ἔλεγεν; the prosaic language of the Attic inscriptions neglects to denote this weak sound more often at an early period than later on; indeed finally from the Macedonian period onwards the nasal was written regularly in all cases or at all events completely predominates[1]. Accordingly the pronunciation may have undergone a gradual transition from *elegē estī* to a tolerably defined *elegen estin*. Our custom of placing the ν ἐφελκ. in prose to prevent hiatus and in all cases where there is a definite pause, but elsewhere of leaving it out, has no foundation whatsoever.

Initial μ on the other hand in contrast to its weak pronunciation when final or medial is in isolated instances written with aspiration: ΜΗΕΓΑΡΕΙ, ΜΗΕΙΞΙΟΣ, Μέίξιος[2]; in Latin also initial *m* had its fullest sound, and the aspiration of initial liquids appears also in Welsh[3]. Some would assume the guttural nasal, written γ, before μ and ν, on account of the traditional name *agma*; for in this name, a transposition of γάμμα, the sound itself ought according to them to occur[4].

[1] Meisterhans ed. 2, p. 88-9, based on the valuable treatise of Hedde Maassen : de litera ν Graecorum paragogica quaest. epigraphicae, *Leipziger Studien* IV. p. 1 ff.—The use of ν ἐφ. on Ionic inscrip. contrasts sharply with our texts of Herodotus (Ermann Curt. *Stud.* v. 278) ; e.g. the longer Chian inscrip. (Bechtel 174) and that of Halicarnassus (238) have ν in all cases.—Cp. also *Rh. Mus.* XLIII. 279. The name ἐφελκ. is founded on an error, Maassen p. 43: the original mode of expression is τὸ ἐ ἐφελκυστικόν ἐστι τοῦ ν̄.

[2] Röhl no. 514, 344; also on the inscript. of Sillyon in Pamphylia (ib. 505 *Dial. Inschr.* 1266) l. 10, 21, 23

MHO; *C. I. Gr.* 7382 where ΜΗΟΨΟΣ must be read with Stuart for Μαοψοs. G. Meyer[2] § 244 Note. (Cp. Dittenberger *Jahresber. f. AW.* XXXVI. 146.)

[3] Prisc. I. § 36; Lepsius *Stand. Alphab.* p. 172.

[4] Westphal *Griech. Gramm.* 1. 1, 17; Brugman *Curt. Stud.* IV. 103. Evidence as regards *agma* is furnished by Varro in Prisc. I. § 39 (A. Wilmanns *de M. Ter. Varr. libris gramm.* p. 221): ut Ion scribit quinta et vicesima est litera, quam vocant *agma* (ἄγγμα ten Brink and Wilm.), cuius forma nulla est et vox communis est Graecis et Latinis, ut his verbis: *aggulus aggens agguilla iggerunt*. Subsequently he adds to these *agceps agcora*; neither he nor any

For this very reason however others emend ἄγγμα. For our part we are inclined to pronounce throughout, γίγνομαι giṅnomai, signum siṅnum, and Greek γίνομαι γίνωσκω thus receive an immediate explanation; moreover γν γμ, although combinations of mute with liquid, always make syllables long by position. Still the latter is the case also with δμ δν, and on the papyrus πρᾶ -γμα is thus divided where there is a break of the line, not πρᾶγ-μα[1]. This question hardly admits of decision; certainly we cannot regard as decisive the softening of ἐκ to ἐγ before μ and ν, for this softening takes place before other liquids. Modern Greek has in such cases no nasal, omission on the other hand occurs as in γίνομαι: πρᾶμμα (prama) πρᾶγμα[2].

SECTION 23.

Pronunciation of P (*and* Λ).

On the pronunciation of λ there is nothing to note except that it too appears in a few instances initially with an aspirate; ΛΗΑΒΟΝ λαβών[3], ΛΗΕΟΝ. P according to the description given by Dionysius was pronounced with the tip of the tongue[4], and accordingly was as in modern Greek[5] dental, not guttural. Singularly enough its aspiration when initial or doubled is supported by only one example on inscriptions ΡΗΟFΑΙΣΙ of an ancient Corcyrean epitaph[6]; it is however vouched for by Latin transliterations as well as by the Grammarians:

---

other Grammarian says anything about the occurrence of the same sound before *m n*, and in the latter case *g* is written in Latin, while in the former the usual way is to write *n*. On Latin *gn* cp. K. L. Schneider *Gr.* 1. 272 f.; Corssen i. 106; Rumpelt p. 99.

[1] Hypereid. i. 11, 5; 27, 9; 29, 8; 34, 28; ii. 3, 7 etc.; never divided otherwise in this manuscript.—'Ιάματα of Epidaurus ('Εφημ. 1883) l. 49 στί-γματα.—Inscr. of Antiochus (*Ber. Berl. Akad.* 1883, 49 f.) ιvª. 14 διατετα-γμέναις.

[2] Foy p. 77, also ἀναστεναμός (-ασμός), βρεμένος = (βε)βρεγμένος (Psich.).

[3] Röhl no. 360 Ægina, according to Comparetti's reading which is rightly approved by Röhl (*Jahresber. f. AW.* xxxvi. [1883] p. 2). ΛΗΕΟΝ Attic vase (archaic) 'Εφ. ἀρχ. 1886 p. 87.

[4] Dionys. *de compos.* p. 79 R. : τὸ δὲ ρ (ἐκφωνεῖται), τῆς γλώσσης ἄκρας ἀπορραπιζούσης τὸ πνεῦμα, καὶ πρὸς τὸν οὐρανὸν (palate) ἐγγὺς τῶν ὀδόντων ἀνισταμένης.

[5] Foy p. 3 f.

[6] Cauer *Del.* no. 23 (=84)=Röhl 343, = *Dial. Inschr.* 3189.

Rhesus, Pyrrhus, which on their part shew also, that the *h* was heard after the *r*[1]. Aspiration of initial liquids is, not to speak of other languages, not unknown even in German[2], especially where we speak with much emphasis; in Greek we find besides MH PH the Ϝεκαδάμοε of an epitaph from Tanagra[3]. Analogies for the different values of ρ are furnished by Spanish, where also *r* when initial and when doubled in the middle of a word has a quite different and much more emphatic sound than medial *r* alone. Modern Greek, which has lost not only the aspirate but also the doubling of medial consonants, appears certainly to know no such distinction. The ancient language on the other hand not only as a rule wrote double ρ[4] where initial ρ either in composition or by reason of the augment became internal, but also treated initial ρ itself from a prosodial point of view as a double-consonant: ἴσα καὶ τὰ ῥήματα τίκτειν Aristophanes (in anapæstic verse)[5]. On the other hand its aspiration after an aspirate, as taught by some Grammarians (χρόνος, θρόνος, ἀφρός, but κάπρος)[6], is not borne

[1] Varro's doubt whether *hr* ought not to be written (or again *retor* without *h*) was grounded on grammatical theories. Priscian I. § 25; Cassiodorius K. VII. p. 152. The Copts indeed write *hretor* Stern *Kopt. Gr.* p. 19, and Bechtel *Inschr. des ion. Dial.* p. 133 would take ΑΗΡΣΙΩΝ (Amorgos no. 228) as Ἀρσίων, ΦΗΡΑΗΣΟ (Naxos no. 23) as Φράησου.

[2] [This emphatic pronunciation in German is described by Dr Blass as follows:—We are accustomed to pronounce (in emphasis) t-hage (Tage), n-hein (nein), s-hage (sage), and even 'haber (aber), that is to say we pronounce the spiritus asper after the lenis.]

[3] Röhl no. 131. *Dial. Inschr.* 876.

[4] It is true that this rule is often violated; for instance παραρύματα in the *att. Seeurkunden* as *C. I. A.* 74 d, 9, 16, 38, 60, 78 etc.; καταράκτους *C. I. A.* II. 167; ἀποραντήριον etc., s.

Cauer *Curt. Studien* VIII. 282, Meisterh. ed. 2, p. 73, n. 675. Doubling of other liquids in similar position: Ἀρχεννηίδου *Seeurk.* 809 d, 29 f; inscr. from Eleusis Ἐφ. ἀρχ. 1889, p. 49 ff. β, 20 ἀρτήματαρρυμοῖς (i.e. ἀρτήματα ῥυμοῖς); ἀμφιλλεγομένων Crete *Bull. de corr. hell.* III. 290. Cp. G. Meyer[2] § 289.

[5] Cp. ταρριφεντα on a papyrus of the Ptolemaic era, Wessely *Wien. Stud.* 1886 p. 205; in Homer forms like ἀνάρρωγας, κατάρροον, τόρρα, La Roche *Hom. Textkr.* 389, though Aristarchus certainly wrote not only τό ῥα, but διαραίσει (‿ – – –), πολύρηνες. The same fluctuation however appears in Homer in the case of the other liquids.

[6] *B. A.* II. 693: οἱ ἀρχαῖοι γραμματικοὶ τὸ μὲν μετὰ ψιλοῦ εὑρισκόμενον ρ ἐψίλουν, τὸ δὲ μετὰ δασέος ἐδάσυνον· οἷον τὸ Ἀτρεύς καὶ κάπρος ἐψίλουν, τὸ δὲ χρόνος ἀφρός θρόνος ἐδάσυνον.

out by its treatment in prosody, since χρ no more than κρ makes length by position. Among the dialects, aspiration of the ρ as well as the vowels was unknown in Æolic[1]; in other places it was omitted in the few words, where the second syllable began with ρ (aspirated?): 'Ρᾶρος *Rarhos*[2], while θ φ χ in the second syllable produce no alteration: ῥέθος, ῥαφή, ῥαχία.

SECTION 24.

Pronunciation of Σ.

In the case of σ we have no reason not to recognize in the modern Greek pronunciation, which gives to *s* the sharp, or according to present nomenclature surd sound, that current in ancient times. The case, where a medial or liquid follows the σ, is and was an exception: Σμύρνα pr. *Zmyrna*, with the French pronunciation of *z*, i.e. with soft or sonant *s*; in like manner ἐσμέν *ezmen*, σβέννυμι *zbennymi*[3]. A proof of this is given by the writing with ζ not infrequent in antiquity after the Alexandrine period: Ζμύρνα, ζβέννυμι[4]; it was actually a point of controversy among the Grammarians, which spelling was more correct[5]. In this instance Z cannot express a double-consonant but only the soft *s* which had always been contained in it. In the interior of a word before a consonant the Greeks were uncertain, whether the right division of syllables was ἐσ-τί or ἐ-στί[6], and perhaps the pronunciation was *essti* (ἐσ-στί), not unlike the German in similar cases. In fact the doubling of σ

---

[1] Ahrens *D. A.* p. 20. Meister *Gr. Dial.* 100 f.

[2] Herodian 1. 547 L.; G. Meyer[2] p. 176. (According to Herodian himself the ρ was ψιλόν in both syllables, l. c.)

[3] On the modern Greek pronunciation of β γ μ ν Foy p. 50; the same holds good before δ λ ρ, even in the case of words in connection like καλὸς δοῦλος (Psich.).

[4] Franz. *Elem. epigr.* p. 247; G. Meyer[3] p. 224 f.; the oldest example is Πελαϛγικόν (Argos, time of Alexander) Le Bas II. 122. On the corresponding

spelling in Latin (*zmaragdus*) s. K. L. Schneider *Gr.* 1. 381 f., Seelmann 315.

[5] Sext. Empir. p. 638 Bk. (σμιλίον Σμύρνα or ζμιλίον Ζμύρνα). Cp. Lucian, φων. κρίσ. 9.

[6] Sext. Empir. l. c. Ἀρισ-τίων or Ἀρι-στίων (ὄβ-ριμος or ὄ-βριμος, that which follows is certainly perplexing). On papyri and inscrip., which end the lines with a full syllable, the division is sometimes ἐσ-τί sometimes ἐ-στί Prefat. Hyper. p. IX. XVI. The Ἰάματα (Ἐφημ. 1883, 1885) also divide after σ, also the inscr. of Antioch (n. 323).

is found very frequently on old dialectic inscriptions; in isolated cases even on Attic inscriptions: Λέσσβου, γράψασσθαι, εἰσστήν, and instances continue to be found down to a late period[1]. Boeckh[2] was inclined to regard this as an indication of the sound š, English *sh*, and his suggestion has found many to repeat it; it is however as unwarranted as it is unmaintainable and is at present given up[3]. The sound ž is unknown even in cultivated modern Greek; if the ancients had possessed it, they would doubtless have made use of the proper Phœnician symbol to express it.

SECTION 25.

Spiritus asper.

At this point we must treat of the rough breathing, which also belongs to the fricatives or semivocales, although the ancients did not reckon it in among the letters at all. Besides the Æolians of Asia Minor the Asiatic Ionians[4] lacked the breathing, and the alphabet of the latter having the value *e* for H became that used throughout the Greek world. In Magna Graecia however after the adoption of the Ionian alphabet a new symbol was employed for *h*, namely the divided H ⊢[5], and this very symbol was used by the Grammarians perhaps as early as from Aristotle's time onwards[6], not however written in

---

[1] G. Meyer[2] p. 225 f. Attic e.g. ἄρισστα *C. I. A.* I. 9, 20, Ἀσστυπαλαιῆς 233, 28; Λέσσβου II. 52[c]; γράψασσθαι 320; ἐστεφάνωσσαν 567; εἰσστήν εἰσστό 272, 573[b]; even φιλοτιμωσσκαὶ 603. Meisterh.[2] p. 68–9. In a few isolated cases κ is similarly doubled: Ἕκκτωρ Corinth. Vase *Dial. Inschr.* 3122; ἐκκτῶν *C. I. A.* II. 314; ἐκκτ[ο]ῦ 1060; ἐκκπεπτωκότων 224; ἐκκτελέσαντι Thisbe Röhl no. 284; ἐκκταύτας and Ἀσσκλαπιῶι Elateia *Bull. de corr. h.* x. 380; with division of syllables at end of line ἐκ χθέματα (i.e. ἐχθ, ἐκθ.) Cos, *Bull. de corr. h.* vi. 249 l. 59 f.

[2] Boeckh on *C. I. Gr.* I. 25.

[3] For instance by G. Meyer l.c. I

have treated this point exhaustively in the *Satura philologa H. Sauppio oblata* p. 121. See also Seelmann 144 f. on the same point in Latin.

[4] Giese *Aeol. Dial.* 389 ff.

[5] Occurring on inscr. of Tarentum and Heraclea. Also on Vases, so *C. I. Gr.* 7612, 8351, 8391; but ⊢ΙΔΡΙΕΩΣ Tralles *C. I. Gr.* 2919 does not exist; see p. 80, n. 4.

[6] Aristot. *El. Soph.* p. 177 b 3 on ὅρος and ὅρος: ἐν μὲν τοῖς γεγραμμένοις ταὐτὸν ὄνομα, ὅταν ἐκ τῶν αὐτῶν στοιχείων γεγραμμένον ᾖ καὶ ὡσαύτως, κἀκεῖ δ' ἤδη παράσημα ποιοῦνται· τὰ δὲ φθεγγόμενα οὐ ταὐτά.

the same line with the other letters, but written above as a diacritic mark A̰. At a subsequent period the corresponding symbol ⊣ was invented for the spiritus lenis, i.e. the absence of the breathing[1], and the rounding of these symbols gave our present mode of representing the spiritus. Its representation in Latin shews that the *h* was still heard in the Hellenistic dialect; moreover the aspiration of the tenuis in elision was consistently observed, although not always in a way identical with our own; for we find for example, μεθοπωρινός, καθ'ἔτος and δωδεχέτης, ἐφ'ἴσῃ, ἀφέσταλκα[2]. Similar fluctuations are well known in Latin from the first century B.C. and onwards both in the case of consonants and vowels[3]; Catullus' poem on Arrius and his *chommoda, hinsidiae* illustrates this best[4]. In the case of consonants aspiration came in about this time from the Greek, in the case of vowels it must conversely from this time onwards have lost ground in the popular language, so that it was in the cultivated language that uncertainty prevailed, where to pronounce and write *h* and where not. That educated people continued to pronounce the *h* even during the Empire is shewn, to take an example, by a passage of Quintilian, where he laughs at those people as affected, who greet one another with *avē* instead of *havĕ* on account of the derivation from *avēre*[5].

---

[1] The definitions προσῳδία ψιλή or πνεῦμα ψιλόν (the latter properly speaking an unsuitable expression) can mean absolutely nothing else: ψιλός is devoid of breath, and Seelmann p. 262 is mistaken, when he takes the expressions δασεῖα and ψιλή to mean not something absolutely opposite, but only different degrees of aspiration. Latin writers have been (as so often) awkward in their translation of the terms, and the passages spoken of by S. from their grammarians, which would not allow to *h* the value of a letter, have no value for phonetics whatsoever, but only shew like countless others the dependence of Latin grammar on Greek. For my part I see no reason for the as-

sumption, that Greeks or Romans pronounced the unaspirated vowels differently from the Germanic and Romance peoples of to-day.

[2] G. Meyer[2] p. 244. Dittenberger *Syll.* Ind. p. 781 f. 784. Μεθοπ. is the regular spelling Pap. L. 1; δωδεχέτης Kaibel *Epigr.* 112, cp. 190, 205, 222; Rich. Wagner *de epigr. gr.* (Lpz. 1883) p. 90; on ἀφέσταλκα etc. cp. Keil *Schedae epigr.* p. 7 ff.

[3] Corssen *Ausspr.* I.[2] 104.

[4] Catullus *carm.* 84.

[5] Quintil. I. 6, 21: multum enim litteratus, qui sine aspiratione et producta secunda syllaba salutarit (*avere* est enim). In the whole section he is speaking only of correctness of pronun-

But after the second half of the second century A.D. *h* in inscriptions is more and more frequently wrongly put in and wrongly omitted[1]; the letter was therefore evidently disappearing, and the same development took place in Greek. The Copts, it is true, continue to represent the spiritus in Greek loan-words almost without exception with their ϩ (*h*): *hoste, hina, hote* etc.[2]; it cannot therefore have disappeared in the second century. The cultivated pronunciation certainly retained it much longer, just as in Latin, where we find Augustine testifying to the offence taken in his time at pronunciations such as *ominem*[3]. Modern Greek however knows the aspiration no more than the Romance languages; for the French owe their *h* aspiré to the Germans. If however we infer from the growing uncertainty in the use of the symbol in Latin that the sound was beginning to disappear, are we not bound to make the same inference with regard to the Attic of the fifth century B.C.? For here too the cases are very numerous, where H ought to stand and does not[4]. The converse of this is of less frequent occurrence, except on one inscription which was evidently cut by a foreigner, where ἐν, οἰκῶν etc. are written in the most surprising manner[5]. It has indeed actually been maintained, that the breathing was no longer heard among the Athenians of the 4th century[6], and this view receives support from passages of Aristotle, where the

ciation; he comes to orthography in c. 7. The question is also settled by c. 5, 17 ff.; Vel. Long. K. vii. 68 f., etc.

[1] Corssen l. c. p. 110; Seelmann p. 265 f. (the wall inscrip. of Pompeii shew the same uncertainty as early as the 1st cent., op. on the confusion of *ae* and *e* in the same, p. 69, n. 1).

[2] Stern *Kopt. Gr.* p. 19.

[3] August. *Confess.* i. c. 18 § 29 (Seelmann p. 265).—Among Greeks compare (Oros) Prolegomen. Hephaest. p. 93 W.: γίνεται βραδυτής τις τοῦ χρόνου, ὡς καὶ ἐν τῇ δασείᾳ λέγεται, διὰ τῆς ὀξείας (λος in καλός longer than in φίλος).

[4] Collected by Cauer *C. St.* viii.

232 ff. On the inscript. of Eleusis found subsequently (*C. I. A.* iv. 27 b) the symbol is omitted about once in every ten instances. *Bull. de corr. h.* xii. 131 it is always written except in composition; *C. I. A.* iv. 53ᵃ (B.C. 418/7) only in the word ἱερόν, being left out everywhere else, evidently owing to the influence of the Ionic writing, traces of which appear there in other instances.

[5] *C. I. A.* i. 324. (Ἀθηναῖος *Bull.* v. 178 (on vase) is krasis, cp. *C. I. A.* i. 423 ff.)

[6] v. Schütz *Hist. alphabet. Att.* p. 54 ff.; G. Meyer *Gr.*² p. 242.

distinction between οὗ *where* and οὐ is designated as one of pitch without the least mention of breathing[1]. But on the opposite side we have another passage of the same author, according to which ὅρος and ὄρος were identical in writing but not in sound[2]; moreover we find the aspiration of tenues in elision constantly taking place in Attic, in contrast to the Ionic κατάπερ, THPHI (τῇ ῞Ηρῃ), ἀπήγησις[3]. Moreover Plato's *Kratylus* contains two important passages, of which the reading is it is true corrupt, but the sense of which cannot be mistaken. Socrates derives the word ἐπιστήμη on one occasion, starting from the philosophical standpoint of Heraclitus, from ἕπομαι, according to which it must be ἑπιστ., on another occasion however, considering it from the Eleatic standpoint, from ἵστημι, that is ἐπ-ἰστήμη. The former is expressed according to the recorded text thus: διὸ δὴ ἐμβάλλοντας δεῖ τὸ εἶ (ε) ἐπιστήμην αὐτὴν ὀνομάζειν; the latter: ὀρθότερόν ἐστιν ὥσπερ νῦν αὐτοῦ τὴν ἀρχὴν λέγειν μᾶλλον ἢ ἐμβάλλοντας (ἐκβ.) τὸ εῖ (ε) ἐπιστή-μην, ἀλλὰ τὴν ἐμβολὴν ποιήσασθαι ἀντὶ τῆς ἐν τῷ εῖ (ε) ἐν τῷ ἰῶτα[4]. Since ἐμβάλλειν often occurs in the *Kratylus* of the interpolation of a letter, and that which is here interpolated is the breathing, the object to ἐμβάλλοντας in both places must have been the name of the breathing. I suggest therefore that the symbol Ⱶ was already known to Plato, as a παράσημον written over letters, and that the name answering to its form was the first half of ἦτα, accordingly ἤ. If then we substitute τὸ ἤ (or τὸ Ⱶ) in both places for τὸ ει, I think we shall have restored these much abused passages. To return, the chief point is, that such an inference proves too much. For there is scarcely a dialect, where there is not fluctuation[5]; even on the tables

---

[1] Aristot. *El. Soph.* p. 166 b l. 178 a 2 (τὸ μὲν ὀξύτερον τὸ δὲ βαρύτερον ῥηθέν). K. E. A. Schmidt *Beitr. z. Gesch. d. Grammatik* p. 155 f. wishes to explain this on the assumption, that in the combinations μὲν οὐ (*me-nu*) and τὸ οὐ mentioned by Ar. the spiritus was not perceptible; but in that case where was it? Only at the beginning of a sentence?

[2] Here also Aristotle is speaking of τροσῳδία, and must therefore have used this word in the same more general sense as later writers (cp. Schmidt l. c. 187 f.).

[3] Röhl no. 500, l. 19 (Halic.), 384 (Samos), *Bull. de corr. h.* IV. 115 = Dittenb. 349 (Teos).

[4] Plat. *Kratyl.* 412 A, 437 A.

[5] Hiero's helmet, R. 510, Ἰάρων and ὁ —; Locris R. 821, Ὀπουντίων and Ὀποντίων. Thespiæ R. 146, μ' ὁ and ὅς (ο[?] R.).

of Heraclea we find ἴσος and ἴσος side by side. But if the breathing began to disappear at an early period in all the dialects, it could not very well have continued to exist in the Alexandrine and Roman periods in the common Hellenistic language. We must therefore seek for some other explanation ; such an explanation is furnished by the weakness of the breathing, which also serves to make the great inconsistency and capriciousness in the aspiration of isolated words more intelligible. We say ἵππος but Γλαύκιππος Λεύκιππος, and as the cognate languages shew, the spiritus has no etymological warrant whatever. We find too side by side ἄγω (in Locrian it is true ἅγω) and ἡγέομαι, ἦμαρ and ἡμέρα, ἠώς and ἕως ; there is no etymological reason for the fact, that initial υ is always aspirated[1]. This weakness of pronunciation also made it natural, that the Athenians and most of the other stems on adopting the Ionic alphabet should not trouble themselves about any new symbol for the sound of the breathing. In the interior of words in Laconian and other dialects the breathing was a late development from σ: Ἀγηΐστρατος, ἐποί- Ϝηέ = ἐποίησε[2]; according to the Grammarians the Attic dialect knew this internal spiritus only in the foreign word ταῶς[3]. In composition it was not generally written in Attica[4], on the Heraclean tables not always[5]; Latin as a rule represents it even here : *exhedra* (*exedra*), *parhippus, Panhormus, Euhemerus*[6]. It had undoubtedly in this position a still slighter sound than at the beginning of words; the Alexandrine Grammarians themselves, who wrote the ' interaspiration ' in the texts of the poets for the sake of clearness, renounced the rough breathing, if the real significance of the word lying hidden in the compound appeared to be no longer felt: ὠκύαλος νηῦς from ἅλς, Εὐαΐμων from αἵμων.

---

[1] G. Meyer[2] p. 243.

[2] The latter is Argive, R. no. 42, 44 a.

[3] Athen. IX. 397 EF. (Attic vase inscription υἱὸς, *C. I. Gr.* 8202, cp. 8203.)

[4] Cauer *Stud.* VIII. 240 f., Meister-hans ed. 2, p. 67. In Elision ΠΑΡΗ-ΕΑΡΟΙ *C. I. A.* I. 34 and IV. 116ᵃ, 10, ΜΕΔΗΕΝΙ I. 77, 6 (also with pleonasm

ΚΑΘΗΑΠΕΡ IV. 51ᵃ, 43), although Giese *Aeol. Dial.* p. 333 maintains, that the aspirate in this case was quite inaudible.

[5] ταρεξόντι once by ταρεξόντι (the preposition in this dialect took the form τάρ).

[6] K. L. Schneider p. 192 f. Also Coptic *ahoratos*, Stern *Kopt. Gr.* p. 19.

Section 26.

Pronunciation of the Tenues.

Among the nine mutes the Tenues (i.e. ψιλά, the surd
letters) have on the whole retained their pronunciation. At the
present day however the media appears in pronunciation after
a nasal: λαμπρός pr. *lambrós*, ἐντρέπομαι *endrépome*; ἀναγκάζω
ἀνάγκη *anangazo anangi*[1]. The same thing takes place in
close combination of words: τὸν πόλεμον *tom bólemo*, τὸν
τόπον *ton dópo*, τὸν κόσμον *toñ gózmo*[2]. The assumption of
a similar pronunciation in ancient Greek leads at once to pure
impossibilities: how could the ancients have kept ἐντός and
ἔνδον, ἀναφανδόν and -φαντο- so strictly distinct, as they
certainly did? For we are not entitled to appeal to the
Aristotelian ἐντελέχεια by the side of ἐνδελεχής: the word
must have been ἐνδελέχεια, but being of infrequent usage it
was remodelled on the analogy of τέλος. Next we are con-
fronted with ἀμπλακεῖν and ἀμβλακεῖν, Ἀμπρακία and Ἀμ-
βρακία, finally the Aristophanic pun βλέπειν Βαλλήναδε (Παλ-
ληνάδε, Παλλήνη and βάλλειν)[3], those who cite these instances
not perceiving that the very infrequency with which they occur
contains a full refutation of the inference they draw. For tenuis
and media or as we now say surd and sonant explosives approximate so closely in sound, that to say nothing of the license of
word-plays, actual instances of interchange are not wanting in
Greek any more than in other languages, for instance on Attic
inscriptions τότω for δότω, ἀγροπόλει, Μεκακλῆς[4]. Above
all in Egypt τ and δ could not be kept distinct owing to the
peculiarity of the national language, which did not possess a
d, although it had *b*; accordingly mistakes such as τίδυμοι,
τόδε for τότε, Εὔτοξος are among the commonest on papyri[5].

[1] The pronunciation of κλ as γλ
which has often been maintained is
denied by Psichari for the general
language.

[2] Foy p. 47.

[3] Aristophanes *Acharn.* 233; E.

Curtius *Gött. Nachr.* 1857 p. 303.

[4] *C. I. A.* II. 603,272. *Bull. de corr.
h.* II. 552 (ib. III. 64 Scyros κυνή for
γυνή).

[5] Praefat. Hyperid. p. XVII.

P. 7

But the position in which the sound occurs, makes in these cases no difference whatever. Apart from this in the case of *k* a twofold pronunciation is current in modern Greek[1]: guttural before consonants and before *a o u*, and inclining to palatal before *e i* (i.e. *k'* according to Lepsius' alphabet, being to *k* as *ch* in *ich* is to *ch* in *ach*). Consequently in the καί of the present day a sound is heard somewhat like *kye*, in which the *k* is produced so far forward on the palate, that it approximates to *t*. In many cases this palatal *k* like the *c* in Romance was and is further developed to *ch ts*, so that Psichari gives four further pronunciations for κε καί:—*chye che tsye tse*[2], and this pronunciation as Italian *ce*, although at the present day it is not considered worthy of imitation[3], nevertheless made itself distinctly felt side by side with the other at the period of the revival of letters[4]. Something analogous to *k k'* might be found in ancient Greek in the contiguous use of ϙ (*koppa*) and K; this however seems in point of fact to have been more a matter of orthography than pronunciation. The syllables κο κρο κτο were written with ϙ, because the letter was called koppa, κα κρα etc. were on the other hand written with kappa for the same reason[5]; the rest of the work fell to the share of the latter, as standing before the other in the alphabet, except where a *u* still retaining its proper *u*-sound appeared to demand similar treatment to *o*[6]. Subsequently ϙ was given up as superfluous, just as *k* in Latin gave place to *c*.

SECTION 27.

Aspirates and mediae; contrast between ancient and modern Greek.

The pronunciation of the aspirates Θ Φ X is one of the most difficult points. The name *aspirata littera*, δασὺ γράμμα points

---

[1] Foy p. 5.
[2] Psichari *Rev. Crit.* 1887 p. 265.
[3] Foy p. 56.
[4] Cp. the edict of Chancellor Gardiner (p. 3 above), which on this point allows a certain licence; Smith *Sylloge*

p. 530.
[5] BOϙΑΣ (?) Bœot. Röhl 183 stands alone; Meister *Dial.-Inschr.* 881 βω[λ]ᾶς?
[6] Cp. p. 35 above.

to the addition of a breathing, i.e. an *h*; accordingly they are written in Latin *th ph ch*. In pronouncing *ph* as *f*, and *ch* in the German fashion, we make out of the aspirate a spirant, and such also is the English *th*. Modern Greek also makes them spirants, θ being pronounced as English *th* in *think*, φ as *f*, χ before consonants and before *a o u* with a guttural sound like the *ch* in German *ach* (χ in Lepsius' alphabet), before *e i* on the other hand with a palatal sound like *ch* in German *ich* (χ'). It has however also made the mediae into spirants in the same way. Media, μέσον, denotes the intermediate pronunciation between ψιλόν and δασύ, that is to say neither quite without breathing nor yet with a particularly strong breathing[1]. But in modern Greek δ is the soft English *th* as in *this*; β is *v*, that is to say the soft sound corresponding to the hard *f*; γ either a soft guttural *ch* or a soft palatal, being wholly analogous to the χ; Lepsius writes these sounds too with Greek letters: γ γ'. The Germans give the *g* this pronunciation in many cases, especially in the interior of words, and make γ γ' when medial correspond to χ χ' at the end, just as in German other consonants which are soft when medial are pronounced hard when final: *Tage, Tag* (Ταγε-Ταχ), *Berge Berg* (Βergʹε-Βerχ') corresponding to *Leid* pronounced *Leit* while *leiden* has the proper *d*-sound. Palatal γ' is identical with English *y* German *j*, and accordingly the Greeks now pronounce γένοιτο *y(é)nito*, γῆ *yi*. The explosive pronunciation, as a media in the Latin sense, only remains to the modern Greek mediae where a nasal precedes, consequently at the present day ντ νδ, μπ μβ, and partly also γκ γγ are identical in sound[2]. Such a sound-

---

[1] So Dion. Thr. *B. A.* 631; Dionys. *de compos.* p. 83: ψιλὰ μὲν τό τε κ καὶ τὸ π καὶ τὸ τ, δασέα δὲ τό τε χ καὶ τὸ φ καὶ τὸ θ, κοινὰ δὲ ἀμφοῖν (repeated subsequently as μέσον ἀμφοῖν, τοῦ μὲν γὰρ ψιλότερον τοῦ δὲ δασύτερον) τό τε γ καὶ τὸ β καὶ τὸ δ. Cp. also Aristid. Quintil. p. 89 f. Meib. (54 Jahn), 44 (29 J.), p. 101, n. 1 below.

[2] Psichari *Rev. Crit.* 1887, 266, according to whom the pronunciation

komvos (κόμβος), *anðros* is simply artificial and owes its existence to the written form. Another instance of artificial pronunciation according to Ps. is the sounding of the ν of the article in τὸν γάμον, τὴν γυναῖκα: dialectally this is assimilated (*toŋŋamo, tiŋyineka*), in the ordinary language it disappears without any compensation (*to ŋamo, ti yineka*).

system as this transferred to the ancient language must of necessity alter its character most violently. It is however perfectly impossible to transfer it. For all spirants are fricatives, that is according to the ancient nomenclature ἡμίφωνα, having even without the addition of a vowel a certain perceptible sound; but in ancient Greek β γ δ are always and φ χ θ generally reckoned among the ἄφωνα. That the latter were by some, apparently by the Stoics, considered as ἡμίφωνα[1], is fully explained by the fact, that the added breathing is of itself a ἡμίφωνον; in like manner ξ ψ ζ are reckoned as ἡμίφωνα owing to the σ which forms one of their component parts. In the modern Greek pronunciation on the contrary no one could ever maintain these letters to be mutes. Moreover Dionysius of Halicarnassus gives a closer description of the pronunciation[2]; he says that in the case of π β φ the mouth is shut and then suddenly opened, in like manner in τ θ δ the tongue is pressed against the teeth; in κ χ γ it is raised to the palate, and there is no further distinction between these letters according to him beyond that of the breathing[3]. Aristides Quintilianus also writing in the third century expresses himself to the same effect:—in the case of the media β and the related sounds π and φ the stream of air, he says, breaks through the closure of the lips in the centre, and so on, he too making the only difference between the related sounds to consist in the fact, that the tenues were articulated in the front part of the

---

[1] Sext. Empir. p. 621 f. represents the aspirates as ἡμίφωνα, adding, that 'some' reckon them as ἄφωνα; Priscian I. 14 says conversely: hic quoque error a quibusdam antiquis Graecorum grammaticis invasit Latinos, qui φ et θ et χ semivocales putabant, nulla alia causa, nisi quod spiritus in eis abundet, inducti. The Stoics according to Dion. L. VII. 57 reckoned only six ἄφωνα, β γ δ κ π τ. Dionys. Halic., Dion. Thrax etc. reckon the aspirates as mute without expressing any doubt on the subject.

[2] Dion. Hal. *Comp.* p. 78 R.

[3] Dion. Hal. *Comp.* p. 83 f.: π φ

β are pronounced, ὅταν τοῦ στόματος πιεσθέντος τὸ προβαλλόμενον ἐκ τῆς ἀρτηρίας πνεῦμα λύσῃ τὸν δεσμὸν αὐτοῦ. —ΤΘΔ: τῆς γλώττης ἄκρῳ τῷ στόματι προσερειδομένης κατὰ τοὺς μετεώρους ὀδόντας, ἔπειθ' ὑπὸ τοῦ πνεύματος ἀπορριπιζομένης καὶ τὴν διέξοδον αὐτῷ κάτω περὶ τοὺς ὀδόντας ἀποδιδούσης.—ΚΧΓ: τῆς γλώττης ἀνισταμένης πρὸς τὸν οὐρανὸν ἐγγὺς τῆς φάρυγγος καὶ τῆς ἀρτηρίας ὑπηχούσης τῷ πνεύματι, οὐδὲν οὐδὲ ταῦτα διαφέροντα τῷ σχήματι ἀλλήλων, πλὴν ὅτι τὸ μὲν κ ψιλῶς λέγεται, τὸ δὲ χ δασέως, τὸ δὲ γ μετρίως καὶ μεταξὺ ἀμφοῖν.

mouth and softly, the aspirates energetically from the larynx, the mediae with moderate force in the central part[1]. Accordingly all these sounds were instantaneous and explosive; *f ch* etc. on the other hand are fricatives, being produced by a contraction not amounting to complete closure of the vocal passage; for neither are the lips closed in producing *f*, nor in making the *th*-sound is the tongue pressed against the teeth, but only brought near. It is then already placed beyond doubt and will receive further confirmation, that the aspirates and the mediae during the classical period had a different pronunciation from that now in vogue.

SECTION 28.

Pronunciation of the Aspirates.

To understand what the aspirates really are, we must turn our attention to the living oriental languages, especially those of India. There exist in Sanskrit as in the derived languages combinations both of the tenuis with the breathing: *kh th ph*, and of the media: *gh dh bh*; both classes are considered in the alphabet as simple sounds, but are really formed by a combination of mute with breathing. Germans in general pronounce their so-called tenues when initial with a similar breathing, generally without being themselves aware of it; other nations however, as for instance the Hindoos, perceive the distinction between their own true tenues, and the approximation to their own aspirates. We must then, as G. Curtius especially has shewn[2], consider this to have been the character of the Greek aspirates, their prior member being a tenuis: *k p t*.

---

[1] Aristid. Quintil. p. 89 Meib. (54 Jahn): τῶν ἀφώνων τὰ μὲν διὰ τῶν χειλέων χεῖται μόνων, τοῦ πνεύματος τὴν ἔμφραξιν αὐτῶν κατὰ μέσον ἐκβιαζομένου, ὡς τὸ β καὶ τὰ τούτου περιεκτικά, τὰ δὲ κτέ. (The description is less lucid in the case of the gutturals and dentals.) Then: τούτων δὲ τὰ μὲν ἠρεμαίως προάγοντα τὸν ἀέρα κἀκ τῶν περὶ τοὺς ὀδόντας τόπων κέκληταί τε ψιλὰ καὶ ἔστιν εὐφω-

νότερα· τὰ δ' ἔνδοθεν ἐκ φάρυγγος ὠνόμασται δασέα καὶ ἔστι λίαν τραχέα· τὰ δ' ἐκ μέσου τοῦ φωνητικοῦ τόπου μέσα τε εἴρηται καὶ τῆς ἀμφοτέρων εἴληχε φύσεως. Similarly only more briefly expressed before p. 44 (29).

[2] Curtius *Grundz.*[5] 414 ff.; W. Schmitz, *Beitr. zur lat. Sprach- und Litteraturkunde* p. 118 ff.

Out of this a spirant has been developed by assimilation and fusion of the elements, the breathing according to the view usually held being changed to a spirant of a nature homogeneous to the tenuis (*pf* or *pv*, *tθ*, *kχ*), the latter finally crowding out the tenuis. It is still a matter of dispute, whether this assumed intermediate pronunciation : *pf kch tth*, had already begun in the classical period, a view maintained first by R. von Raumer and finding after him its principal champion in W. Roscher[1]. This question too ought however to be decided by the classification of letters discussed above; for *pf* etc. are certainly not mutes, and one may go further and say that they are clearly double-consonants, just as much as ξ ψ ζ. In the next place if this view had been correct, it must have been possible to have cited in its support transliterations, especially in Latin, since *pf* or *ts* or something similar would have been written, if only in sporadic instances, for Greek φθ; but as a matter of fact nothing of the kind is found. And I fail to understand how v. Raumer and Rumpelt can argue, that, because according to Quintilian Cicero in the speech for Fundanius laughed at a Greek witness, who could not pronounce the first letter of *Fundanius*[2], Greek φ was at that time *pf* or according to Rumpelt a simple spirant[3]. According to Quintilian we must suppose that the man said *Hundanius;* but even supposing that he had, as they think, made the *f* into a φ, his representation of the foreign sound by *p + h* would not have been any further from the mark, than the Slavonic and Lithuanian representation of late Greek φ or German *f* as *p*[4]. The only inference that can be made from the passage is that there was a fundamental

---

[1] R. v. Raumer *Aspiraten und Lautverschiebung* p. 96 ff.; W. Roscher *Curtius Stud.* 1, 2, 117 ff.

[2] Quintil. I. IV. 14: quin *fordeum foedosque* (scil. was the pronunciation in the mouths of ancient Romans for *hordeum hoedos*), pro aspiratione velut (other mss. vel *f* ut ; Christ. Halm) simili littera utentes; nam contra Graeci adspirare *ei* (others read φ for

ei ; ita adspirare without *ei* also has authority ; *f* ut φ Christ. Halm ; Spalding rejects *ei*) solent, ut pro Fundanio Cicero testem, qui primam ejus litteram dicere non possit, irridet.

[3] Rumpelt p. 56.

[4] Kurschat *Litt. Gramm.* p. 22, 50. (*Franzose Prancuzas, Christoph Kristups*); Miklosich *Altsloven. Lautlehre* p. 236.

distinction between Latin *f* and Greek φ, more fundamental
than between labial *f* (pronounced entirely with the lips) and
dentilabial *f* (pronounced by laying the under-lip against the
teeth, as we do), and also certainly more fundamental than
between *pf* and *f*; for any one who can pronounce *pf* can also
pronounce *f*. The fact that the Greeks always represented *f*
by φ, is easily intelligible, since the simple breathing did not
even exist as a Greek letter, and among the aspirated tenues the
labial enjoyed a distinct preference. The whole theory of the
pf is also overthrown by metrical considerations. For when we
find in isolated passages of Homer, Hipponax, and Aristophanes
words like ὄφις φιλόσοφος used with the penultimate long[1],
we are not to infer, that φ was a double consonant. Rather
the fact that, if we except this dozen or so of instances, the
aspirate in the countless other cases does not form length by
position, ought to shew clearly, that it was only the breathing,
which cannot produce length by position, which was added
to the tenuis. In like manner no Latin writer thinks of
treating the aspirates *ph th ch*, which made their way into
the language after the 1st century B.C., as double-consonants.
We can explain the fact, that the Greeks here and again
actually do this, by a doubling of the tenuis which in this
case was not at all unnatural: we may compare the spellings
ὄκχος, ὀκχεῖν, σκύπφος, observing that this doubling also is
found only in a very few words among a very large number
not so affected, and is accordingly a special peculiarity or
licence[2]. The fact, that φρ χρ θρ form length by position in
no higher degree than πρ κρ τρ[3], alone forms an irresistible

[1] This is the principal argument
of Roscher (p. 121 ff.). Ὄφις as trochee
Hom. *Il.* 12. 208, Hipponax fr. 49 (Anti-
machus fr. 78?); φιλόσοφος Arist. *Eccl.*
571 (in a hexameter, consequently as a
matter of necessity). Christ *Metrik*,
p. 24.

[2] Spellings such as δεδόκχθαι (Samos, Cauer *Syll.* 134, 26), which are
appealed to by Roscher, are in the
first place extremely infrequent, in the
second place the accumulation of let-

ters is in no way different from that
in ἔξς, Βυσξάντιοι, exstra. The later
forms συνδιαπεφύλακχεν (Mylasa *Bull.
de corr. h.* v. 102), μετηλλακχότες (Ala-
banda ib. x. 302 l. 39), εἰσαγειωκχότα
(-κχεν) thrice ib. xii. 84 f. (Stratonikeia)
belong to the grammarians.

[3] The remark of Aristides Quintilianus (p. 46 Meib. 30 Jahn), that a
final short vowel can be used as long
with especial ease when an aspirate
follows, can scarcely have any founda-

refutation of the theory. I am not myself convinced, that this transitional stage obtained general acceptance at any period whatsoever. At all events I can not find it absolutely established for any period, and it may accordingly for our purpose be disregarded. The following facts may serve as a confirmation of the pronunciation as $p + h$ etc. Those Greek races, which did not possess the non-Phœnician symbols $\phi \ \chi$, in those cases where they were not satisfied with the simple tenuis, adopted the writing ΠΗ ΚΗ, exactly as the Romans did, when the representation of the aspirates by the tenues $p \ c \ t$ usual at an early period seemed to them not sufficiently accurate and aspiration of consonants had ceased to be regarded as strange. Secondly the contact of tenuis with aspirated vowel produces aspirates : ἐφ' ᾧ, ἀνθ' οὗ (ephōi, anthu). On the other hand aspirates readily pass into tenues according to a definite rule in inflexional formation and composition: τεθέαμαι, ἐτέθην, μνήσθητι, ἐκεχειρία, ἀρκεθέωρος, Ἀμπιθάλης, Ἀρκεφῶν[1], and if on the other hand violations of this principle are not infrequent[2] on inscriptions, these errors and the other very numerous alternations of aspirated and unaspirated mutes[3] only serve to shew, how slight was the distinction between the two. Moreover the doubling of aspirates gives tenuis + aspirate, which is quite regular, supposing that the latter consists of tenuis + breathing[4]; in like manner the Germans write quite correctly *tz* for double *z*. It is true that a difficulty arises from the fact that before an aspirate a tenuis pronounced with a different position of the vocal organs becomes likewise aspirated; for to many it appears impossible

tion, although this treatment would not be unnatural in the case of the pronunciation $p + h$ etc.

[1] The two last examples from Delos *Bull. de corr. h.* VI. 25, 27.

[2] Roscher l.c. p. 98. So ἐνθαυθοῖ and ἀνεθέθη on the Eleusinian inscription *C. I. A.* IV. 276. Cp. also Meisterhans p. 78[2] f.

[3] Roscher p. 79 ff.; Schmitz p. 114 ff.—The βάρβαροι in Aristophanes, the Scythian in the *Thesmoph.* and the Triballian in the *Birds* always put tenuis for aspirate; see also the Athenian vase *C. I. Gr.* 8076[3]. On a Phrygian inscrip. *Bull. de corr. hell.* II. 255 f. 'Ρουπῖνος, Τρόπιμος, ὄκλος; Sterret *Arch. Inst. of America* III. no. 366 l. 35, 100, 39 Διοπάνης Τειμότεος, l. 109 Κτιμενηνός, for which subsequently Χθιμ.

[4] There are naturally here and there violations of this rule, Roscher p. 89.

to pronounce *ekhthos* (ἔχθος), *phtheiro* with doubled breath-ing[1]. Σ also has a similar aspirating power, at all events at an early period; hence arises the writing ΦΣ, ΧΣ for ψ and ξ; Plato says, that φ ψ σ ζ are letters with a strong breathing[2]. Is it possible then to pronounce *p h s* in succession? We must however be on our guard against speaking too readily of impossibility; for to others, as for example to Lepsius, *khth*, *phs* appears perfectly possible, and only *khkh* impossible, since here the organ is the same; where the organ is different on the other hand, the breath, according to them, comes out simul-taneously behind the first letter, before the mouth assumes the new position. Accordingly we have no need of the way out of the difficulty, which was adopted by G. Curtius[3] following the lead of others. This was that the breathing heard after the *t* or with the *s* in combinations such as *pth ps* was liable to be transformed in the sensorium of the hearer and consequently also in script to the *p* which was equally susceptible of aspira-tion, and these combinations being of frequent occurrence habit did the rest to establish an orthography ΦΘ etc.[4] This form of writing is as a matter of fact much too well established for such an explanation to hold water; the four or five exceptions on archaic and later monuments: ΑΠΘΙΤΟΝ, ΚΑΤΑΠΘΙΜΕΝΗΣ etc. can hardly count[4]. On the other hand the entirely different treatment of such combinations in modern Greek must be made prominent. The modern Greek spirants shewing an exactly opposite tendency combine with the tenues: φτάνω ‹φθάνω, κλέφτης ‹κλέπτης, ὀχτώ ‹ὀκτώ: neither a combination of hard (surd) spirant with spirant nor of tenuis with tenuis is in accordance with the genius of the language. In like manner σ admits of a surd spirant neither

---

[1] Ebel in Kuhn's *Zeitschr.* xiii. 266 ff.

[2] Plato *Kratyl.* 427 A: διὰ τοῦ φεῖ καὶ τοῦ ψεῖ καὶ τοῦ σῖγμα καὶ τοῦ ζῆτα, ὅτι πνευματώδη τὰ γράμματα, πάντα τὰ τοιαῦτα μεμίμηται αὐτοῖς ὀνομάζων (the giver of the names), οἷον τὸ ψυχρὸν καὶ τὸ ζέον καὶ τὸ σείεσθαι κτλ. The passage is quoted by v. Raumer p. 101,

who uses it (for want of better proof) to establish a spirantic element in φ in Plato's time.

[3] Curtius *Grdz.*[5] p. 414 ff., after W. von der Mühl *Aspiration der Tenues* (Lpz. 1875) p. 21 f. See on the other side J. Schmidt *K. Z.* xxviii. 179 ff.

[4] Röhl no. 314 (Phokis), 382 (Chios).

immediately preceding nor following it: -ευσα i.e. -εφσα becomes εψα—epsa, σχίζω becomes σκίζω, μισθός μιστός, αἰσθάνομαι στάνομαι[1]. In the same way a surd spirant does not allow a preceding nasal: either this is assimilated and in some cases expelled as ἄνθος αθθος αθος, νύμφη niffi nifi[2], or a tenuis took the place of the aspirate and then a media the place of the tenuis, as in the word Κόρινθος which I have myself heard pronounced Korindos (written Κόριντος). Finally we must remark the effect produced in many cases by a preceding ρ: ἦρτα for ἦρθα ἦλθα, Κόρτο popular name for Corinth, ἔρχομαι pronounced erkome or eryome[3]. The same applies to the voiced spirant in combination with a nasal, neither is this spirant allowed without exception to stand combined with ρ. Where the phonetic laws are so different the sounds themselves of ancient and modern Greek must be fundamentally distinct. In the next place there remains to be produced in support of the long continuance of the real aspirates not only Quintilian's testimony, who regarded φ as a dulcissime spirans littera, Roman f and also the v in servus on the contrary as odious and offensive sounds[4], but also that of the Coptic mode of writing which arose at the end of the second or the beginning of the third century. The Egyptian Christians, when they devised a new alphabet, mainly borrowed from the Greek, for their national language, employed the symbols Θ Φ X for the real aspirates which are found in Egyptian; on the other hand for the sounds f and ch, which they likewise possessed, they adopted peculiar symbols which were annexed to the Greek alphabet. In the numerous words borrowed from the

---

[1] Foy p. 134. Σφ holds its ground according to Psichari (Mém. de la Soc. linguist. vi. 305) in the ordinary language, but in Trapezus has become στ.

[2] See p. 85, n. 1.

[3] Psichari Rev. crit. 1887, 265.

[4] Quint. xii. 10, 27: jucundissimas ex Graecis litteris non habemus (υ and φ)—, quibus nullae apud eos dulcius spirant. He goes on to speak of the grecizing spellings Zephyrus, Ephyra,

and adds: quae si nostris litteris scribantur, surdum quiddam et barbarum efficient, et velut in locum earum succedent tristes et horridae, quibus Graecia caret (f and u). Nam et illa, quae est sexta nostrarum, paene non humana voce vel omnino non voce potius inter discrimina dentium efflanda est.— Aeolicae quoque litterae, qua servum cervumque dicimus, etsi forma (f) a nobis repudiata est, vis tamen nos ipsa persequitur.

Greek Φ X occur, but instances also are found of the resolved spelling, ΕΠΣΟΣΟΝ as well as ΕΦΟΣΟΝ, just as in the case of native words the combination of tenuis with *h* alternates with the aspirates[1]. At what time then did the spirants appear in the ordinary speech? Priscian about 500 A.D. evidently found it difficult to adjust to his satisfaction the difference between φ and Latin *f*, which he found emphasized by the earlier grammarians; it appears to him quite absurd, that φ should be a mute and *f* a semivowel, and accordingly he ends in making *f* likewise a mute[2]. A spirantic pronunciation of φ χ θ is unmistakeably described by the Byzantine scholiast of Dionysius Thrax, who brings into prominence the decisive absence of closure in contrast to π κ τ[3]. The description is entirely at variance with that of Dionysius of Halicarnassus. But even Ulfilas makes no difficulty about representing φ by Gothic *f*, θ by þ. Latin monuments with very few exceptions shew *ph* and *f* unconfused up to the time of Severus; after that however the alternations become numerous, and after the middle of the fourth century there is no longer any distinction even in the best documents[4]. Before this and

[1] Lepsius *Stand. Alph.* p. 202; Schwartze *Kopt. Gramm.* p. 79 ff.; Stern *Copt. Gr.* 16 f. On hieroglyphics the name of Philip Aridæus was written according to Lepsius with ☐⌷ *ph*, at a later period Φιλωτέρα, Τρύφαινα only with *p*.

[2] Prisc. i. 13: quare cum *f* loco mutae ponatur (in *fama* φήμη etc.), miror hanc inter semivocales posuisse artium scriptores—(14) sciendum tamen, quod hic quoque error a quibusdam antiquis Graecorum grammaticis invasit Latinos, qui φ et θ et χ semivocales putabant.—Hoc tamen scire oportet, quod non fixis labris est pronuntianda *f*, quomodo *ph*, atque hoc solum interest. This sounds quite differently from what Quintilian says, although Priscian also, true to his predecessors, makes φ pronounced with closed lips.

[3] *B. A.* II. p. 810, on φ χ θ in succession. Π is pronounced with closure of the lips; ἀνοιγομένων δὲ τῶν χειλέων πάνυ, καὶ πνεύματος πολλοῦ ἐξιόντος, ἐκφωνεῖται τὸ φ. In the case of κ the tongue is pressed against the palate, in *t* against the teeth; χ on the other hand is pronounced τῆς γλώττης μὴ προσπιλουμένης μηδ' ὅλως συναπτομένης τῷ οὐρανίσκῳ, and θ ἀποχωρούσης τῆς γλώσσης τῶν ὀδόντων καὶ παρεχούσης ἔξοδον τῷ πολλῷ πνεύματι. v. Raumer puts a right value on this testimony, p. 103 f.

[4] W. Schmitz p. 122 f.; Th. Mommsen *Herm.* XIV. 70 ff. The graffiti of Pompeii furnish only four exx. Orthographic precepts on *f ph* are given by Caper VII. p. 95 K. (time of Trajan but not preserved in its genuine form) and Diomedes p. 423 f. K. (4th. cent.), Schmitz p. 126; cp. also Mar. Plot.

as long as *ph* and *f* were distinguished *ph* and *p*, *th* and *t*, *ch* and *c* had been liable to be interchanged: the contrast between the earlier and later pronunciation is therefore evident. This later pronunciation however will not have arisen all at once, it must have needed time to have made its way from the lower to the upper stratum of the people and to have become general. But its beginning or, if you prefer it, its prelude, is perhaps already to be found in the ancient Greek dialects; on this point we go on to speak in connection with the transformation of the mediae.

SECTION 29.

Pronunciation of the Mediae ; dialectal pronunciation of the Mediae and Aspirates.

We have seen above, that the name *media* denotes a half aspirated sound, and not by any means a weak or voiced sound, with which names *b d g* are now denoted in contradistinction to *p t k*. The Greeks then heard a certain breathing in their $\beta \gamma \delta$; and who shall maintain, that their ears deceived them? Moreover there is this confirmatory fact, that the mediae as well as the aspirates became spirants. It certainly may be maintained that the name mediae suits the present pronunciation also, in so far as the breathing in βv is really weaker than in ϕf[1]. On the other hand, since Latin *b g d* and Greek $\beta \gamma \delta$ correspond to one another with perfect regularity, and the value of the Latin mediae is certainly identical with that of the present Romance and German, the pronunciation of Greek $\beta \gamma \delta$ must have been approximately the same as that of our mediae. In the case of δ this is made especially clear by the fact, that it is so frequently confused with *t* by Egyptian scribes; consequently there can have been no such wide difference as that between

---

Sacerdos (3rd. cent.) K. vi. 451.—
Schmitz p. 134 furnishes examples for
the confusion of *th* and *s* from the

notae Tironianae, also *Sehuderico* for
Theoderico on an inscrip.
[1] Cp. also *B. A.* 810, n. 2.

modern Greek τ and δ[1]. Strangely enough it is only the pronunciation of the β which has really been made a matter of controversy. However that this was during the Attic period not *v* appears sufficiently proven, in case there is still any doubt, by Plato[2], who calls it a mute, and by the βῆ βῆ of the comic dramatists, and it is by no means the case, as has been stated, that in the Roman period it was employed without scruple for *v*. On the contrary the inscriptions of the time of the republic shew almost without exception Οὐαλέριος, Φόλουιος, and this mode of writing, tedious though it was, even in the period of the empire was never quite ousted by the far more convenient β[3]. There existed then a pretty considerable difference between β and *v*, greater than that between semivocalic *v* (English *w*) and consonantal *v* (English *v*), for this would not have prevented the universal adoption of the writing with β. In the time of the Empire, especially from the second century onwards, this difference must have become smaller; otherwise the earlier usage would have been preserved. The Latin *b* too in many places had a similar development, being pronounced in the same way that survives at the present day among the Spaniards and many of the French of the south, whose *vivere* is according to the well known witticism *bibere*[4]. This indistinguishable confusion of the two sounds gave rise next to such spellings as Σεουαστός, which is often met with on Greek inscriptions in Italy[5]. But in the fact, that even at the present day β is an explosive sound when following

---

[1] See Plat. *Crat.* 427 A: τῆς τοῦ δέλτα συμπιέσεως καὶ τοῦ ταῦ καὶ ἀπερείσεως τῆς γλώττης.

[2] Theaet. 203 B: τοῦ δ' αὖ βῆτα οὔτε φωνὴ οὔτε ψόφος (cp. Dion. *συνθ.* 72).

[3] S. Dittenberger *Herm.* VI. 302 ff., who has only two exx. from the time of the republic of β for *v* (yet in Delos about 180 B.C. *Bull. de corr. h.* VI. 38, 43, Dittenb. *Syll.* no. 367, 86, 130 Λίβιου Βιβλου); the Monumentum Ancyranum also still shews ου consistent-

ly. The same writing was used in verse also; *C. I. Gr.* 67 sq. Σιλουίου εὐξάμενος with consonantal pronunciation. The name of L. Verus is commonly written Οὐῆρος, much more rarely Βῆρος, Dittenberger p. 304. In many exx. also *v* internal is omitted, Φαώνιος, Βόλλαι, in short it is quite evident that the Greeks possessed no quite appropriate expression for *v*.

[4] Corssen 1[2], 131; Diez *Gr.* 1, 280. 376; Seelmann p. 239 f.

[5] Dittenberger p. 304.

a nasal, Psichari[1] rightly finds a proof, that it was originally this in all cases ; for *komvos* could not have produced *kombos*, but an original *v* would have done away with the nasal. As regards γ, this letter seems at all events when between vowels to have become a spirant at a very early period in the popular pronunciation. For a frequent misuse of it on papyrus is to bridge over a hiatus: ὑγιγαίνις = ὑγιαίνεις, κλαίγω = κλαίω, Ταύγης Τάγης for Ταύης Τάης, Σαραπιγῆον[2], and conversely it is frequently wrongly omitted: ὑιαίνης, ὀλίος[3], which latter form is also attested as Tarentine and is cited by the Attic comic poets as a barbarism of the demagogue Hyperbolus[4]. Compare further Φιάλεια = Φιγάλεια, ἀγήοχα for ἀγήγοχα, Bœotian ἰών for ἐγώ, ἄγεθλα in Pamphylian[5]. All this points to a softening of the guttural explosive to a *y*, or in the case of a back-vowel to the *g*, which the Germans usually pronounce in *Tage;* but the sound was so undefined and weak, that it was thrust in and left out at will[6]. The phenomenon was however in any case strange to the standard Attic, as is shewn by the sneer at Hyperbolus and probably neither Hyperbolus nor any one else at Athens who pronounced ὀλίος, on the same principle pronounced λέγω as λέω, any more than a Bœotian said λίω because he had ἰὼν for ἐγὼν. Such cases as these have their source in isolated words of frequent occurrence— compare Italian *io* from *ego*, but not *lio* from *lego*—and may subsequently develope into a principle of universal application. In some of the dialects however other mediae also and not less other aspirates to all appearance became at an early period

---

[1] Psich. *Rev. crit.* 1887, 267.

[2] Pap. L. 63 col. 1 ὑγιγαίνις and conj. ὑγιγαίνης; κλαίγω 51; Ταύγης Τάγης 23. 55 Bis; Σαραπ. 40. 41.

[3] ὑιαίνομεν and ὑιαίνις 42, ὀλίος 63, 4; 26 twice.

[4] Herodian 1, 141, 19; Plat. com. frg. 168 K. (in Herod. II. 926); v. Herwerden 60 (*C. I. A.* II. 594, 8). Also on the inscr. of Chersonesos on the Crimean Peninsula (*Bull. de corr. hell.* v. 70 Dittenb. 252), ὀλίωι is found at l. 10; see further Ἐφ. ἀρχ. 1884 p.

39 l. 22 (Peiraieus, decree of Macedonian Period); *Bull.* VII. 166 (Imbros) Meisterhans, p. 59².

[5] G. Meyer *Gr.*² p. 218; ἄγεθλα Röhl no. 505 l. 24.

[6] Cp. Wessely *Wiener Stud.* 1882 p. 197, who draws the general conclusion, that γ was pronounced like *y* before an *E*- or *I*-sound. The indications or suggestions of such a pronunciation are however found with much greater frequency in the earlier than the later period.

spirantic. In the first place so early as the pre-Roman period Laconian employs β in the place of the digamma: Βοινε[ίδας], Βαστίας (from ἄστυ Ϝάστυ)[1]; it also appears with this function in numerous Laconian glosses[2]. In the latter instances it might have been used as a matter of necessity, the scribes who wrote at the dictation of the populace not possessing the usual symbol for the digamma: but the Laconians themselves must have preserved the symbol with the sound, as the Heracleots of Italy did, had not the appropriate symbol ceased to be indispensable owing to the similar sound of β. We must accordingly believe this to have been the case. These same Laconians had a θ, which they themselves wrote certainly for a long period with the old symbol, but which the other Greeks at an early time represented with σ, as in the well known ναὶ τὼ σιώ[3]. It can hardly be doubted that this was at least for a time the modern Greek spirant; if it had been a real σ it would have been so written by the Laconians themselves, while it is quite natural, that the Athenians should have represented the strange spirant in Laconian words by the allied sound of σ. This mode of writing has also made its way into Alcman's poems, and we are able here, in the Egyptian fragment, to make out the limits of the phonetic change: θ remains after σ (ποτήσθω), after ν (ἐπανθεῖ and four other examples), before λ and ρ (ἀεθλοφόρον, ὀρθρίαι), after φ (φθέγγεται), where the next syllable begins with σ (θωστήρια)[4]. T appears

---

[1] Inscr. of Taenarum R. no. 84 (fifth cent. ??); Βαστίας εμπολέΜΟΝ ib. 78 (epitaph of one fallen in war; period ??). Further Εὐβάλκης ib. p. 33, n. 1 (Εὐάλκης 77ᵇ, epitaph of a warrior killed at Mantinea); Βιόλας Εὐρυβάνασσα Εὐβάλκεος Le Bas II. 163ᵃᶜ, Φάβεννος a Lacedaemonian Delphi Dittenb. *Syll.* 189 (beginning of 2nd cent. B.C.); Müllensiefen *de titul. Lacon. dial.* p. 46 f.

[2] Ahrens *D. D.* 424 ff.

[3] The first instance of this σ is in Ἐλευσία = Ἐλευθία = Ἐλειθυία (Ross, Keil), Le Bas 162ᵉ = Dittenb. 191, in

case the Machanidas, who appears here as the dedicator, is the well-known tyrant 210—207 B.C. But here we find also ἀνέθηκε. The other inscrip. with σ in proper names (not without exception) Le Bas 163ᵃᵇ etc., are placed by Foucart in the second or first century B.C.

[4] The last case is attested as an exception in Cramer *An. Ox.* I. 197, 7 (Ahrens *D. D.* 66). The Lakon. gloss ἀκκαλανσίρ (ἀκανθυλλίς) in Hesychius shews change after ν; we have on the other hand a proper name in -νθίς Röhl no. 72.

to be found for θ after σ on an old Laconian inscription[1]. In the next place Apollonius testifies, that in Doric poets, among whom judging by the character of the quotations we must understand Alcman to be included, the tenuis in elision and crasis is ' times without number' not altered before the spiritus asper: κὼ τοξότας, κάλλιστ᾽ ὑπαυλέν[2]. Now this cannot be explained in the same way in the Laconian dialect as the same phenomenon in Ionic; for in that dialect the spiritus had disappeared, in Laconian it was still living when medial. If on the other hand the aspirates had become spirants, it would be quite natural, that in this case the tenuis should not become a spirant, but should remain. Did the Laconian dialect then really have the modern Greek sound-system? We cannot reconcile this view with the phenomena we have described in Alcman, corresponding, as we must assume, with the cultivated Laconian of about the fourth or third century B.C.; for we do not find there anything like ἐπαντεῖ, φτέγγεται, so that the sound must be considered as the aspirate which has stood its ground in these cases. But if θ was still often an aspirate, why should not the same be true of φ χ? Moreover οὐχορης (οὐχ ὁρῆς)[3] on the Alcman-Papyrus goes against the argument taken from Apollonius. I would therefore prefer the following explanation. In Laconian in cases of elision and crasis the breathing might disappear together with the elided vowel, instead of as in other dialects changing its place; in οὐχ ὁρῆς, where there is no elision, aspiration naturally took place. According to this there remains for this dialect a spirantic β and a partly spirantic θ. Similar phenomena are to be found also in other Doric dialects. Cretan, especially as we know it from the Gortynian inscription,

---

[1] Röhl no. 72, infinitive in -εσται.

[2] Apoll. *Synt.* p. 335 (Bergk *Lyr.* III.⁴ p. 697): ἀπειράκις γὰρ τὰ Δωρικὰ διὰ ψιλῶν ἀντιστοίχων τὰς συναλοιφὰς ποιεῖται· κὼ τοξότας Ἡρακλέης. κάλλιστ᾽ ὑπαυλέν κτέ. Bergk refers at least the first three fragments to Alcman.

[3] Col. II. 16; ὦιτ᾽ ἄλιον II. 7 (with Lenis, cp. *Rh. Mus.* XL. 2) obviously stands apart. In the other fragments there are not very many examples for the one or the other; in frg. 60 Bergk φύλλα θ᾽ ἑρπετά θ᾽ ὅσσα, but the mss. φῦλά τε ἑρπετά θ᾽ ὅσα. But 76 χὠπάραν =καὶ ὀπώραν (cp. Ὀπωρίς on a Laconian inscr.) seems to be rightly preserved.

entirely ignores the usual and well-founded rules, according to which the aspirate is neither doubled, nor does it begin two syllables in succession: -σθ is assimilated to θθ, for which we have sometimes θ, but never τθ, and the forms from τιθέναι always shew repeated aspirates: θιθῆι, θιθεμένωι, καταθίθεθθαι, μήπιθιθέτω[1]. If then θ was a spirant, all is perfectly clear; for modern Greek also knows forms like χάφτω (κάπτω), χαχανίζω (cp. καχάζω), χαχλανίζω (cp. καχλάζω), χοχλάκι (cp. κόχλαξ) etc.[2] The Gortynian inscription has T for Θ before and after ν: ἄντρωπος, τετνακός[3], which again agrees admirably. Here then we seem to be really on safe ground; it is however absolutely wrong, to go further and explain φ χ as spirants; for the Cretans wrote for these right on to a rather late period π κ, which they certainly would not have done, if they had been *f* and *ch*. It is evidently rather the case that the one dental aspirate had become a spirant, and that this was the only one which had a special symbol in the national alphabet. With regard to the mediae we have not sufficient material for drawing any conclusion; for even the replacing of F by β only occurs in isolated instances[4]. On the other hand a spirantic δ appears certainly to have existed in Elean: for many of the old Olympian inscriptions use ζ for δ, which can only signify the spirant: ζέ, ζίκαια, Ὀλυνπιάζων. β also occurs for F in the same dialect: Βαδύ place-name = ἡδύ[5], βοικία on the great Damocrates inscription belonging to the Hellenistic period[6]. The latter has also ποιήασσαι for ποιή-σασθαι; on the older inscriptions on the other hand στ appears regularly for σθ: λυσάστω; πάσκοι also for πάσχοι appears

---

[1] Καταθίθ. Gortyn. inscr. c. 6, 4; θιθῆι θιθεμ. Gort. Comparetti *Mus. Ital.* II. 635; μήπιθ. Cnossus ib. 678.

[2] Psichari *Mém. de la soc. de linguistique* VI. 303 f.; who sums up as follows:—en grec moderne, les spirants sourdes s'attirent au commencement de deux syllabes consécutives; quand les deux spirantes sont contiguës, la seconde se change en l'explosive correspondante. Nous avons le traitement inverse dans les aspirées anciennes.

[3] Ἄντρ. ἀντρώπινα Gortyn. inscr. XI. 24; X. 43; τνατῶν ib. v. 39; τετνακός τετνάκηι Gort. *Rh. Mus.* XLI. 119 f. But ἄνθρωπος Cnossus *Mus. Ital.* II. 677/8.

[4] See p. 76 n. 3. G. Meyer assumes spirantic δ 2nd ed. p. 262 (on Cret. φ as spirant cp. ib. 261).

[5] Ahrens *D. A.* 226.

[6] *Dial.-Inschr.* 1172[33].

to be a corresponding instance[1]. Whether this στ σκ is an indication of spirantic pronunciation, I do not know[2]; στ is found just as regularly in Lokrian, which is allied to Elean, and sporadically also on Phokian and Bœotian inscriptions. In the case of Lokrian we again find the same apparent indication which we found in Alcman; that is to say although the symbol for the aspirate is in use, the tenuis is never aspirated in cases of elision and crasis, as for instance ΗΟΡΚΟΣ πεντορκία, ΗΑΓΕΝ (ἄγειν) ΟΠΑΓΟΝ ὠπάγων, ἐπάγειν; κατιϟόμενον καθικόμενον[3]. Finally here also θέθμιον occurs with doubled aspirate; in Olympia we have for the same word ΘΕΘΤΜΟΝ with one of those perplexing errors which characterise these bronzes[4]. On the other hand νθ etc. are found in both places quite as usual, and on an inscription which is apparently Elean τυτθόν[5]. It might be safer, with regard to Lokrian to maintain nothing and with regard to Elean only a spirantic δ and β.

Section 30.

Pronunciation of Ξ Ψ.

Of the three double-consonants Ξ Ψ Z the two first demand but very little discussion. The older Greek races, as the Athenians and Bœotians, employed as has been mentioned above χσ φσ for the symbols which they did not yet possess; the grammarians on the other hand unanimously consider this first member to have been a tenuis κ π[6], and according to Theophrastus this was done even by Archinus, the reformer of Attic orthography in the archonship of Euclides[7]. Ξ being a γράμμα

[1] ΣΤ Röhl no. 109, 111, 117, 119, 121 (*D.-I.* 1147, 1157, 1159, 1161, 1168), τάσκοι R. 112 (*D.-I.* 1152).

[2] G. Meyer[2] p. 262 is much too precipitate: "which proves a pronunciation as in modern Greek."

[3] R. 321, 322 (*D.-I.* 1478, 1479). Also 321[14], αἴ κ' ὁ; but the aspirate is never found written in the case of the article.

[4] R. 321[46]; 113[b] (*D.-I.* 1154). Also on the Xuthias inscrip. (R. 68)

θεθμόν twice; but always σθ. Θεθμὸν Epidaurus Ἐφημ. 1885, 65/66. G. Meyer[2] p. 291.

[5] R. 552 (*D.-I.* 1161).

[6] Dion. Thrax *B. A.* p. 632: (σύγκειται) τὸ ξ ἐκ τοῦ κ καὶ σ, τὸ δὲ ψ ἐκ τοῦ π καὶ σ. Dion. Hal. *Comp.* p. 82 R τὸ ξ διὰ τοῦ κ καὶ τὸ ψ διὰ τοῦ π τὸν συριγμὸν ἀποδίδωσι, ψιλῶν ὄντων ἀμφοτέρων (cp. p. 78, 79).

[7] Syrian Schol. Ar. *Met.* p. 940: ταύτῃ δὲ τῇ ἀποδόσει (that these are

πνευματῶδες[1], χ φ were liable to be heard instead of κ π; but that actual assimilation also took place dialectically and absolutely destroyed the explosive, is shewn by the ancient boustrophedon inscription of Naxos where ἔ⊦σοχος, Να⊦σίο (Ναξίου) are written with the symbol for the spiritus asper[2]. Unfortunately ψ or a substitute for it does not occur on the inscription; on the island of Amorgos, which was colonised by Naxians, on inscriptions in the same alphabet the tenuis occurs in the case of ξ as well as ψ: κσ, πσ[3].

SECTION 31.

Pronunciation of Z.

The third double-consonant Z presents a most difficult problem. In modern Greek this is always a simple sound, namely a soft or sonant *s* (French *zéro*, German *sagen*, English *zeal*); the ancients from the time of Archinus and Aristotle[4] always regard it as a double-consonant, just as much as ξ ψ; and indeed the grammarians make it consist of σ and δ[5] (in

three double consonants, owing to the three positions of articulation, as laid down by Aristotle himself *Metaph.* 1093 A, 23) καὶ 'Αρχῖνος ἐχρῆτο, ὡς ἱστορεῖ Θεόφραστος· ἔλεγε γὰρ ὁ 'Α. ἢ ἔξω τι παρὰ τὴν μύσιν τῶν χειλῶν ἐκφωνεῖσθαι, ὥσπερ τὸ π, καὶ διὰ τοῦτο τὸ ψ πρὸς τῷ ἄκρῳ γεννᾶσθαι τῆς γλώττης ὡς ἐκ τοῦ π σ συγκειμένον· ἢ τῷ πλατεῖ τῆς γλώττης παρὰ τοὺς ὀδόντας, ὥσπερ τὸ δ, καὶ διὰ τοῦτο τὸ ζ κατὰ ταύτην γεννᾶσθαι τὴν χώραν· ἢ τῷ κυρτῷ καὶ πιεζομένῳ ἐκ τοῦ ἐσχάτου, ὥσπερ τὸ κ, ὅθεν τὸ ξ προιέναι (cp. for inscriptional forms note 4 below, and Styra Bechtel 19⁹⁶ Χάροπς, though on 263 Μοφσίδης; ἀναγράπψαι Mykale B. no. 144 does not tell us much).

[1] Plato, cp. p. 105 n. 2 above.
[2] Röhl no. 407 = Bechtel no. 23.
[3] Bechtel *Inschr. d. ion. Dial.* no. 29 Λαμπσαγόρεω; ib. note (Dümmler *Mitth.* XI. 99) 'Αλεκσοῖ.
[4] Aristot. *Metaph.* 1093 A, 20: ἐπεὶ

καὶ τὸ ΞΨΖ συμφωνίας φασὶν εἶναι (the three double consonants are compared with the three musical chords, octave, fifth and fourth), καὶ ὅτι ἐκεῖναι τρεῖς, καὶ ταῦτα τρία, ὅτι δὲ μυρία ἂν εἴη τοιαῦτα (that the possible number of double consonants would be countless) οὐδὲν μέλει· τὸ γὰρ Γ καὶ Ρ εἴη ἂν ἓν σημεῖον (a simple symbol might be devised for γρ). εἰ δ' ὅτι διπλάσιον τῶν ἄλλων (as the others) ἕκαστον (scil. of those three), ἄλλο δ' οὔ, αἴτιον δ' ὅτι τριῶν ὄντων ἓν ἐφ' ἕκαστον ἐπιφέρεται τῷ σ (v.l. τὸ σ, cp. Schol. p. 381), διὰ τοῦτο τρία μόνον ἐστίν, ἀλλ' οὐχ ὅτι αἱ συμφωνίαι τρεῖς (the construction and argument are confused here, the schol. certainly had a different reading).

[5] Dion. Thr. l.c.: τὸ ζ ἐκ τοῦ σ καὶ δ; cp. Schol. p. 780, 814, 815. Dionys. Halic. p. 78: διπλᾶ δὲ λέγουσιν αὐτὰ ἤτοι διὰ τὸ σύνθετα εἶναι, τὸ μὲν ζ διὰ τὸ σ καὶ δ, τὸ δὲ ζ διὰ τοῦ κ καὶ σ, τὸ δὲ ψ διὰ τοῦ π καὶ σ συνεφθαρμένων ἰδίαν φωνὴν

this order). Archinus also says that it contains a δ, and on this point certainly there ought to be no dispute. The German pronunciation giving it the sound (*ts*) of their own *z* is of course a mere misuse and is not defended, but many modern philologists imagine its sound to have been somewhat like *zz* (double sonant *s*) and endeavour not without a little violence to bring the authorities into harmony with their theory[1]. Such speculations as these I cannot follow but rather believe, that the sound, which men like Aristotle and Dionysius of Halicarnassus heard, must have really existed. But with reference to the sequence of the two elements G. Curtius also has entered the lists against the ancients supporting the pronunciation *ds* (more correctly *dz*, with the French value of *z*)[2]. This pronunciation too can be designated as traditional; for in Italian the *z* of Greek words has still this sound (*zelo, zeta*), and it is easy to shew that the tradition goes back to an early period[3]. On the other hand, according to that excellent authority Psichari, the pronunciation of ζ as *dz* which is at present current among the Greek islands is not to be regarded as in any way traditional, any more than the pronunciation of σσ σ as *ts* (τέτσαρα, ἀτσήμι = ἀσ. "silver"). Psichari states that in Chios, the various stages of this modern development may be observed side by side: *nomi"zo, nominzo, nomindzo*[4]. Moreover, as *dy* is etymo-

---

λαμβάνοντα, ἢ διὰ τὸ χώραν ἐπέχειν δυεῖν γραμμάτων ἐν ταῖς συλλαβαῖς παραλαμβανόμενον ἕκαστον.—p. 82: τριῶν δὲ τῶν ἄλλων γραμμάτων ἃ δὴ διπλᾶ καλεῖται τὸ ζ μᾶλλον ἡδύνει τὴν ἀκοὴν τῶν ἑτέρων· τὸ μὲν γὰρ ζ διὰ τοῦ κ καὶ τὸ ψ διὰ τοῦ π τὸν συριγμὸν ἀποδίδωσι, ψιλῶν ὄντων ἀμφοτέρων, τοῦτο δ' ἡσυχῇ τῷ πνεύματι δασύνεται (on account of the media δ contained in it), καὶ ἔστι τῶν ὁμογενῶν γενναιότατον (the noblest, most euphonious sound). This passage is wrongly interpreted by Ascoli *Krit. Stud.* p. 365 f. of the German trans., who finds in it an indication of the sound *z'z').—Sext. Empir. p. 662, Bk.; Bekk. *Anec.* p. 1175 (ζ cannot like ξψ stand as a final, διότι ἐκ τοῦ σ καὶ δ δοκεῖ

συγκεῖσθαι, οὐδέποτε δὲ λέξις Ἑλληνικὴ εἰς ἄφωνον καταλήγει). The evidence from Greek sources is therefore unanimous except the scholia on Aristotle, in which certainly (p. 331 B, 33, 42) the σ is denoted as the second sound for all three double letters. For the Scholiast thus understands the ἐπιφέρεται of Arist., which however in this author (s. Bonitz Index) by no means has the later meaning 'follow'.

[1] Ascoli (see preceding note).

[2] Curtius *Grdr*[5]. p. 615.

[3] We have also the testimony of the Latin grammarians, see below.

[4] Mondry Beaudouin *Bull. de corr. hell.* IV. p. 366 (Carpathus).

logically at the root of ζ, *dz* may easily have been developed
from this just as in Italian *mezzo* i.e. *meddzo* comes from *medius*
(*medyus*), *orzo* from *hordeum* (*ordyum*); *diurnus giorno* (*dzorno*)
also is essentially analogous. Accordingly this pronunciation
too has its claims, and moreover the origin of the modern
Greek pronunciation as simple *z* requires illustration; the
third and not the least warranted pronunciation is that maintained by the grammarians, namely *sd* or more accurately, since
s must be soft before the media, *zd*. Let us endeavour then to
do justice to each one, assigning to it its province and period.
It is a well known rule that in Attic and Hellenistic Greek
the preposition σύν loses its ν in combination with initial ζ:
συζητεῖν, συζευγνύναι, συζῆν. If now *d* was the prior element
in the compound letter ζ (*syn-dsēn*), there was no reason for
the rejection of the ν; we find συγξέω, σύμψηφος. But if the
pronunciation in Attic was *sd*, *sy(n)sden* is perfectly analogous
to συ(ν)σπᾶν, συ(ν)σκευάζειν. Here then we have our first
confirmation of the tradition of the grammarians[1]. In the
next place the preposition ἐξ must of necessity lose its *s* before
δ; before σ it need not. Now we find on the Attic maritime
documents in big letters as a title ἐξ Ζέας, i.e. *eks sdeas*[2].
Moreover the distortion of ὦ Ζεῦ δέσποτα into ὦ Βδεῦ δέσποτα
by an Attic comic poet would be very harsh if the pronunciation
were Δσεῦ, but quite easy if it were Σδεῦ. We often find in
Attica, Bœotia, Delphi, that is in central Greece generally, the
spelling σζ for ζ: Βυσζάντιοι, συναγωνισζόμενοι, ἐπεψήφισζεν[3].
If ζ = σδ, this is analogous to the spellings mentioned above
Λέσσβον, γράψασσθαι etc.; for σζ is then equal to σσδ. We

[1] *C. I. A.* ii. 793 f. 54. I can not
appeal to ἐξ ζωῆς Kaibel *Epigr.* no.
155, since judging by the very late
date of the epigram we must rather
suppose the simplified pronunciation
as *z* to have belonged to the ζ. It cannot be denied however, that the assimilation of ἐξ sometimes does not
take place or takes place wrongly: ἐξ
'Ρόδου ἐξ 'Ρηνείας *C. I. A.* i. 259; ii.
814, 27; ἐγ Πειραιῶς often 834ᵇ ii. (ib.
ἐγκαίδεκα).

[2] Meineke *Frg. Com.* iv. 688.

[3] Thebes *Dial.-Inschr.* 705, 20;
C. I. A. ii. 352, 315; καταδουλίσζοιτο
Delphi W. F. 218, 11. Cp. my *Miscell.
epigraph.* in the *Satura philologa Herm.
Sauppio oblata* p. 124 f. (καρπίσζεσθαι
consular letter to the Oropians, Ἐφ.
ἀρχ. 1884 p. 101 ff. l. 28; also Monum.
Ancyr. μείσζονα, col. 15, 15; other
later exx. G. Meyer² 225.) (Old Attic
ζζ in Βυζζάντιοι, Κλαζζομενίοι, Ἀζζεῖοι,
C. I. A. i. 230, 238.)

find similar pleonasms in ἔξς on an inscription of Chios[1] and the *xs* which is so common in Latin for simple *x*; *sx* and σξ on the other hand still require authentication, as also ζσ. The *s*-sound then preceded in ζ, while in ξ it followed.—ἔζων for ἔστων on a Delphian inscription is a very instructive error in writing, which would be impossible if the pronunciation of ζ had been *ds*, but is easily intelligible supposing it to have been σδ². In the next place in cases of contact σ + δ frequently become ζ. It is true that as a rule διόσδοτος θεόσδοτος are written just as ἐκσώζω not ἐξώζω; but we find on Boeotian inscriptions side by side with Θειόσδοτος, Θιοζότα Θέζοτος Θεόσζοτος Διόζοτος[3], and in Attic inscriptions as well as in authors Θεόζοτος Θεοζοτίδης[4]. βύζην also appears to me to be undoubtedly equal to βύσδην, cp. βέβυσμαι and πλέγδην; and 'Αθήναζε χαμᾶζε ἔραζε θύραζε to 'Αθήνασδε θύρασδε etc., although now there is a tendency to analyze them rather into βύ-ζην, 'Αθήνα-ζε etc. For if this supposed ζε had been added, the word would have been 'Αθήνηζε just as 'Αθήνηθεν and in Homer θύρηζε like θύρηφι θύρηθε[5]. According to our view ἔραζε χαμᾶζε are formed on false analogy, just as 'Ολυμπίασι from the singular 'Ολυμπία, Μεγαροῖ from the plural Μέγαρα.—Lastly we find the *zd sd* of foreign names represented by ζ: 'Ωρομάζης *Auramazda*, Ἄζωτος *Ashdod*, 'Αρταουάζης *Artavasdes*, in Plato, Herodotus and later writers[6]. Accord-

[1] Röhl no. 381 A, 5 (Bechtel *Inschr. d. ion. Dial.* 174); *Dial.-Inschr.* 3130, 3136. Cp. Ναξσιον (=ιων) on an old coin of the Sicilian Naxians, Eckhel *D. N.* I. 226; ἀναγράπψαι Mykale *C. I. Gr.* 2909 (Bechtel 144).

[2] Wescher-Foucart 189, 13; also in 253, 11 not ΕΤΩ which the transcription gives, but ΕΤΩ no doubt is to be found on the stone.

[3] Θειόσδ. Röhl no. 151 = *Dial.-Inschr.* 567; with ζ Tanagra *D.-I.* 982 two sepulchral pillars; 914 col. 3 (= R. 157); 1043 (-σζ-); Thebes 708, 714; Thesp. 807ᵃ; Διόζ. Kopai 556; Thebes 700 (R. 300); Thessaly 345⁷¹, *Mittheil.*

d. arch. Inst. 1889, 59 sq.

[4] Dem. 21, 59; Plat. *Apol.* 33 E; *C. I. A.* II. 944 A, 39; *C. I. Gr.* IV. 821, 1 ff.

[5] χαμᾶθεν (Att. Ion., not in Homer) might be cited in opposition. But the other form χαμαῖθεν (from χαμαί) appears to me correct (accordingly at most χαμᾶθεν). Cp. Osthoff, *z. Gesch. d. Perf.* 596 ff. Forms like 'Αχαρνῆζε (Lentz Herodian 499) have been found neither in authors nor inscriptions as yet.

[6] 'Ωρομ. Plat. *Alc.* I. 122 A, Plut. *Mor.* 369 D; מזד coins of the Satraps, Mazdak head of a sect 500 A.D., see

ingly from all this I infer that in Attica and central Greece
generally ζ, so far as it occurred in the dialects, had the sound
of *zd*, and that this pronunciation was circulated and maintained at least in the case of the grammarians in the Hellenistic
period up to the second century A.D.

But we must now go back to the oldest form of Greek and
especially of Ionic, as we find it in Homer. Here ἔρδω is found
beside ῥέζω from the stem Ϝεργ; why not ἔρζω, if ζ = *ds*?
It is on the other assumption quite intelligible[1], that ἔρσδω
should not remain, but that the σ should fall out. Moreover
initial ζ does not make length by position in Ζέλεια Ζάκυνθος,
from metrical necessity; the same is true of σκ in Σκαμάνδριον,
σκέπαρνον, σκιή. Now here the reading Καμάνδριον has
authority[2], and ὑπεὶρ ἅλα κίδναται ἠώς is read universally;
moreover σ often falls out before π and φ, and accordingly it
could easily be dropped in Σδάκυνθος also[3]. I do not think
its omission in Δσάκυνθος would be so easy.—Δα stands in
the place of the prefix ζα in δαφοινός and δάσκιος. This is
quite natural and easy, if ζα = σδα, σδαφοινός, just as Ζάκυνθος
and σδάσκιος, is difficult to pronounce.—Also it is admitted
by all that ὄζος comes from ὄσδος (Germ. *Ast*); according
to my view there is here no change of sound whatsoever.
Μαζός is the Homeric and Ionic form for μαστός, μασθός of
other dialects: the former is μασδός. We must add ἴζω i.e. ἴσδω,
ἑζόμην i.e. ἑσδόμην which are analogous to ἴσχω, ἔσχον, where
likewise, in Homer as in Attic, the original sound has simply
remained. And, I think, in Ionic also; ἔρδω at all events is
used by Herodotus, and the latter writes Ἄζωτος, where, if the
sound was *shd* and Greek ζ was *ds* or *z*, there was nothing
certainly to prevent him writing Ἄσδωτος.

If the undoubted origin of *z* in *dy* be brought forward in
opposition to this view, it would at once be easy to shew that
zd too may originate in this, since it is a fact that in old

Nöldeke *Ber. Wien. Akad.* 1888, 414 f.
Ἀρταοὐάζης Plut. *Crass.* c. 19, 22, according to cod. N Matrit. (see Charles
Graux, *de Plut. codice Matrit.*, Paris
1880, p. 55). Ἄζωτος universal from
time of Herodotus downwards.
[1] Osthoff *Perf.* 596, 1.
[2] La Roche *Hom. Unters.* p. 42 f.
[3] Cp. Thiersch *Gr. Gr.* § 146, n. 8.

Slovenian *dya* regularly becomes *žda*[1]. It is true that there *tya* also becomes *sta*, whilst in Greek τya becomes -ττα or -σσα according to the dialect. But those who adopt Curtius' assumption are equally unable to shew any analogy between the treatment of *ty* in Greek and that of *dy*, and they have to explain what is absolutely surprising, namely that the same language admitted *dz* but not *ts*[2]. According to my view, it has (at least universally) admitted even *dz*, since not only has this in many dialects become δ δδ, as *ts* has become ττ in Thessalian, Bœotian, Attic[3] and also Cretan, but also other dialects have transposed the two elements. Attic might very well reject δδ, although it preferred ττ to σσ, and the Doric of Delphi, which had σσ for *ty ts*, might nevertheless avoid the corresponding assimilation in the case of *dz*, especially as the sound of the soft *s* only existed in the language in combination with a consonant, while here it would have been independent. On this side then there is really no obstacle; on the other hand it is certainly perplexing to meet with σδ, i.e. the Attic sound of ζ, as a dialectic peculiarity of the Lesbian and some other poets as Alcman and Theocritus[4]. Be it remarked however, this is only in books, not on in-

---

[1] Miklosich *Altsloven. Lautl.* p. 275.

[2] I would however suggest, that the sound *ts* is hidden beneath the writing T, which occurs in Halicarnassus R. 500 (5th cent.): ΑΛΙΚΑΡΝΑΤ[ΕΩ]Ν and ΑΛΙΚΑ[ΡΝΗ]ΣΣΕΩΝ ΑΛΙΚΑΡΝ-ΗΣΣΟΝ, ΟΑΤΑΤΙΟΣ, ΠΑΝΤΑΤΙΟΣ; also on coins of the Thracian Mesembria: ΜΕΤΑΜΒΡΙΑΝΩΝ (Kirch-hoff[4] p. 12), and according to Röhl's suggestion (p. 139) in ΘΑΛΑΤΗΣ Teos 497 B. 23. For in these Carian proper names on other later inscriptions -ασσις -αξις is written for -ΑΤΙΣ, *Bull. de corr. hell.* IV. 316, V. 580, VI. 191 (Bechtel 104, 239, 240).

[3] I still have no doubt in spite of Ascoli (*Krit. Stud.* 324 ff.) and in spite of G. Curtius' recantation (*Etym.*[5] 666)

that ττ and σσ both go back to *ts*. Ascoli's proofs of the origin of ττ in σσ are all of a very problematical character. It seems to me also sufficiently certain, that ττ was a peculiarity of Euboea and Oropus, although Bechtel *Inschr. d. ion. Dial.* p. 13, 37, still doubts it. Κίσυς Styra no 19,[383] B. and Κισα- do.[382] are too obscure in their derivation, to be of any use as instances.—On Crete see p. 122, n. 4 below.

[4] Ahrens *D. A.* 45 ff.; Meister *Gr. Dial.* I. 129. This usage is not constant either in the Aeolic poets or in Theocritus; the rule which Ahrens tries to institute is doubtful. Cp. Morsbach *dial. Theocr. Curtius Stud.* x. 31 ff.

scriptions; the Lesbian inscriptions as early as the fourth century have always ζ[1]. But an antiquated spelling might easily be transmitted in the manuscripts of poets[2], and be adopted by artificial poets like Theocritus. It appears to me, that considering the few fragments which we possess of the Lesbian poets and the almost entire want of early Æolian inscriptions, we cannot yet expect a satisfactory solution of this riddle. I would suggest however, that the Æolians pronounced *sd* as the Athenians, but wrote this with two symbols, employing ζ for that sound, which in their dialect arose from δι- before a vowel: ζὰ = διὰ, κάρζα; this sound must have been *z* (*dz*)[3], and for such a ζ no one cites any instance of the writing σδ. A difficulty of a different sort is the Delphian καταδουλιζμῶι[4], evidently pronounced -*zmoi*, in a dialect which we have claimed for the pronunciation *zd*. This orthography Ζμύρνα ζβεννύναι is, as was mentioned under σ, very widely circulated in the Hellenistic and Roman period[5]; in itself however it by no means proves the simplification of the ζ. For Σμύρνα did not represent the actual pronunciation *zmyrna* (with soft *s*) with greater propriety than Ζμύρνα, in which latter spelling the *d* became mute spontaneously. Thus in the Attic period also we find beside Ὠρομάζης, where ζ = *zd*, Φαρνάβαζος Τιρίβαζος, with ζ = Persian *z*[6]. It is however noteworthy, that ζμ appears so often subsequently, and moreover the alternations between σ and ζ are not entirely limited to this case. We find on an inscription of Cnidus ζήζαζα (ζήσασα)[7], on

---

[1] προσονυμάσδεσθαι on an inscription of Cyme of the Roman period (Cauer no. 127 = *Dial.-Inschr.* 311) is of course only an affected archaism.

[2] The grammarians themselves regard it merely as a matter of spelling, putting it in the same category with Æolic κσένος Πέλοψ ἱέρακς (Ahrens p. 48 f.; Meister 127, 1; R. Schneider *Bodleiana* p. 43).

[3] With διά—ζά cp. τια (τίνα) σά in Doric (Ahrens *D. D.* 277).

[4] Wescher-Foucart 433, 13.

[5] σζ also occurs occasionally before μ: ἐνδέσζμους Ath. (Macedonian period) Ἐφ. 1883, 125 f. γ, 12; Ἐρασζμία *C. I. A.* III., 1553; χρησζμόν Cos *Bull. de. corr. h.* v. 228 (to be divided as χρησ-ζμόν).

[6] Coins of the Satraps פרנבזו, תריבזו, Nöldeke *Ber. Wien. Akad.* 1888, 415, 419.

[7] Kaibel *Epigr.* 204[b]; a few other exx. Keil *Bullet. de l'acad. de St Pet.* 1857, p. 179 (*Mél. Gréco-rom.* II. 38 f.).

ordinary papyri ὕβριζαν, ἐσύγη (ἐζύγην)[1]; as a general rule it is true the writers of the papyri know how to distinguish the two letters. In the next place, against the value *zd* we have the Hellenistic spellings Ἀσδρούβας, Ἐσδρας, Ἀσδώδ, Ἀρταουάσδης, Ὠρομάσδου[2]; for in the case of *ks ps ξ ψ* are always used in these transliterations and adaptations, and I would also confidently suggest, that the presumably Carthaginian name ΑΞΙΟΤΒΩ (gen.) on a Theban inscription is really ΑΙΡΟΥΒΩ[3]. So far then we should conclude that the modern Greek pronunciation prevailed in the Hellenistic *popular* language, while for the preceding era we have as yet only found the sound *zd*. And certainly *zd* could be simplified to *z* by a gradually weakened pronunciation of the *d*; but this is true to a still greater degree of *dz*, the claims of which must now be put to the test. Now ζ occurs to all appearance with such a value, *ts* or *dz*, on old Cretan inscriptions: ὄζος i.e. ὄσος (from ὄτγος = ὄτσος), ἀνδάζαθαι = ἀνδάτσαθαι ἀν(α)δάσσασθαι (ζωῶ = ζωοῦ)[4]. But this disappeared in Crete at an early date, and ττ or δδ according to the circumstances, and initially δ was written for it. Thus the Gortynian inscription; later on we

---

[1] Pap. L. 40, 41 (ὕβρ.); pap. Weil col. 4, 14; ib. 5, 1 φορντίζειν φροντίσιν. All these pieces are more than averagely faulty; e.g. the Papyrus of Hyperides on the contrary shews nothing of the kind. (The attic ψηφίσεσθαι for -ζεσθαι Boeckh *See-Urkunden* p. 467 does not exist; see *C. I. A.* II. 809ᵇ, 35.)

[2] We find on the Monum. Ancyr. col. 5, 26 *Artavasdis* Greek Ἀρταουάσδου, 29 *Artaba(zi)* Ἀρταβάζου, 30 *Artavasdi* Ἀρταουάσδη, 6, 11 *Artavazdis* Ἀρταβάζου. Cp. Mommsen p. 110, 1; p. 118, n. 6 above.—Ὠρομάσδου Inscr. of Antiochus of Commagene (69—34 B.C.), Puchstein *Berl. Monatsber.* 1883, 49 ff., col. 1ᵇ 19; II* 10.—Ἀριοβαρζάνης is written by Greeks and Latins with *z*; the pronunciation was probably here, where in any case there was position-length, generally simplified. In Herodotus however (7, 2 f.) we find (Ἀρτο)βαζάνης, and I think the Athenians wrote it thus, though now we find in the texts Ἀριοβαρζ. (the latter also *C. I. A.* II 481 c¹, 1st. cent. B.C.)

[3] Νώβαν (Accus.) 'A. *Dial.-Inschr.* 719; Meister writes here Ἀ(σδρ)ούβω. The inflection according to the 2nd decl. is certainly strange, especially beside Νώβαν.

[4] Comparetti *Mus. Ital.* II. 131, 142, 162, 172, 194, 202 f., 210, 212, 224, 674; hitherto ζ had not occurred on old Cretan inscr. Further discoveries are certainly pressingly wanted, in order to throw light on ἡλιζίαι (= ἡλικία) Fοιζηα (= Fοικηα) and such monstrous forms.

find also θάλαθθα and also Τῆνα Ττῆνα Δῆνα (Ζῆνα)[1]. Of these θάλαθθα with spirantic θ appears to be a sort of compromise between real Cretic θάλαττα and the ordinary θάλασσα; but Ττῆνα might be something like *ddena*, with a stronger articulation of the initial letter, to express which the tenuis was brought into requisition. In any case the original *ts dz* in Crete disappeared in later times without leaving any trace, and where in the Greek-speaking world can it be said to have continued its existence? As a matter of fact we find no trace of it on Greek soil, but only on Italian. For the Italian peoples, the Latins, Faliscans, Oscans and Umbrians, employ Z always either for the soft *S*-sound or, and this must be the more original, for *ds ts*; consequently those Greeks too, who brought the alphabet to them, that is especially the Chalcidians, must have possessed the ζ with the value of *dz*[2]. Whether they retained it with this value, or later on like the Cretans rejected the sound-combination *dz*, is of course another question; in Italy however *z* may have been maintained as *ds ts*, whatever the Chalcidians did, and this would explain the fact, that this value appeared again in the time of the Empire and has continued to the present day. The Latin Grammarians, although sometimes under Greek influence they resolve *z* into *sd*[3], nevertheless maintain elsewhere, that it is equivalent to

---

[1] Meyer[2] p. 217, 256, 273. It is best however not to venture on such far-fetched solutions of the riddle as Meyer, who finds a palatal *ǵ* in the initial sound of Ττῆνα.

[2] On this cp. Corssen *Auspr.* 1[2] 395 (Osk. *horz hortus, -azum -arum;* Umbr. *pihaz piatus, menzaru mensarum*). The whole subject of ζ in the Italian languages has been worked out by L. Havet, *Mémoires de la société de linguist.* III. 192—196; I owe my knowledge of this to a kind communication of the author himself. Besides the three values of ζ which we have discussed he gives as the fourth and most universal *zz*, as an instance of which he gives the Latin *badisso*; but

this I cannot at once follow. The curious Oscan Νιυμσδιηις (Messana, Mommsen *Unterital. Dial.* p. 192), where σδ represents the simple soft *s*-sound (the name is written elsewhere *Niumsi-, Niumpsius,* Νύ(μ)ψιοι), is explained by Havet by the assumption, that with certain Greeks σδ too had become the simple sound *z*. It is quite as possible however to say that the Greeks not possessing the simple *z* without δ interpolated a *d* after it, *zd* being familiar to them. (For σδ instead of ζ cp. on the same inscr. τσ in ουτσενς for ψ.)

[3] Victorin. K. VI. 196, on the Virgilian *Mezentius* with the vowel of the first syllable long by position : quae

ds (*ts*), if they do not actually deny altogether the compound nature of the letter[1]. Moreover in the vulgar writing of the later empire *z* appears representing *di* followed by a vowel: *Aziabenicus* or *Azabenicus, zeta* (*diaeta*), and also for *j* (*y*):— *cozugi, Zanuari*[2], no doubt in the same way and having the same value as in the common Italian *mezzo* and the Venetian *mazore*.

To sum up then, the following seems to be the result of the whole investigation. In ancient times the Greeks possessed the sound-combination *zd*, in ὄζος ἐζόμην etc., and beside it a *dz* which was developed from *dy*, to which corresponded a *ts* from *ty*. The latter sound-combinations however did not hold their ground, the result being that *hizdo* and *nomizdo*, the former original, the latter from *nomidzo*, coincided in sound. To denote *zd* the Phoenician Sain was taken, which in Semitic signifies simple *z* (soft *s*), partly also as it seems *dz*; similarly Samech (*s*) had to serve for *ks*. In those places where *dz*

(*z*) si adsumpta non esset, per *s* et *d* *Mesdentium* scriberemus. Cp. Terent. Maur. v. 921.

[1] Mar. Victorin. K. vi. p. 6: sic et *z*, si modo latino sermoni necessaria esset, per *d* et *s* litteras faceremus (obscurely p. 34). Vel. Long. K. vii. 51: atque has [tres] litteras (*x* also as well as *z*) semivocales plerique tradiderunt. Verrio Flacco (time of Augustus) placet mutas esse, quoniam a mutis incipiant, una a *c*, altera a *d* (mss. a *p*). quodsi quos movet, quod in semivocalem desinant, "sciant," inquit "*z* litteram per *sd* scribi ab iis qui putant illam ex *s* et *d* constare, ut sine dubio muta finiatur." mihi videtur esse aliud *z*, aliud σίγμα καὶ δέλτα, nec eandem potestatem nec eundem sonum esse, sed secundum diversas dialectos enuntiari. Dores enim scimus dicere μελίσδειν, alios μελίζειν, nec ideo tamen eadem littera est, non magis quam cum alii κεβαλήν, alii κεφαλήν, alii ὅππατα alii ὅμματα, alii θάλατταν, alii θάλασσαν dicunt, cum

idem dicant. He goes on to deny that *z* is according to its actual sound a double consonant; for it is, he says, susceptible of being doubled and in pronunciation it has not, like *x*, a distinct sound at the beginning and end of its utterance. This grammarian then (time of Trajan) evidently pronounced a simple modern Greek ζ. For the very reason that *z* in itself was not a double consonant, some wished to write *Mezzentius* in Virgil, K. L. Schneider p. 380.—Martian. Cap. iii. § 257 considers the sound of Greek ζ to be ΤΣ.—Against Seelmann *Auspr.* 308 I remark, that the passage Quintil. xii. 10, 27 f. does not refer to ζ and υ, but to φ and υ: *quos mutuari solemus* refers to speaking, while he comes afterwards to writing, and in doing so speaks of *f* (and *u*) as compensatory letters belonging to Latin, *wanting in Greek*. So Spalding and before him Gesner.

[2] Corssen 1², 215 f.; Seelmann p. 239, 320 ff.

was in use, as long as it held its ground, it too and also *ts* were represented by Sain = Zeta; with this value it reached the Italians. In other localities it was otherwise, according to the wants of the dialect; in Elis Z was used for spirantic δ[1]. In the pronunciation *zd* however the sibilant gradually over-powered and extinguished the *d*; if in spite of this the sound continued to form length by position, the sibilant must have been doubled, and this certainly presents difficulties in the cases where it was initial. There is however no reason to assume that the simplification of the compound took place before the Hellenistic period; possibly the Macedonians were the originators and propagators of the change, the sound *zd* being strange to them. During this period there is no cause for surprise, if we find ζ for Sain in transliterations, as in Γάζα and the numerous Hebrew names such as Ζαχαρίας, or for English *j = dž*, in Indian names such as 'Οζηνή *Ujjayini*. Correspondingly on a bilingual Attic inscription we find Sain as the Phoenician equivalent of ζ in Βυζαντία[2].

SECTION 32.

Assimilation in Word-nexus; Hiatus.

We have yet to make some general remarks on the combination of words and on their accentuation. With regard to the first point the Greek language appears to stand midway between the Sanskritic method, where the single word is modified by the surrounding words in the main in the same way, as the elements of a single word are modified by one another, and the method of our own language, which allows single words, and indeed any separable parts of a word, entire independence. We have spoken above of the assimilation of the final nasal, probably this was carried out still more in pronunciation than in writing. On the other hand in the case of final ρ and σ, as well as ξ and ψ, assimilation does not take

---

[1] See p. 113 above.

[2] *Corp. Inscr. Semitic.* no. 120 (3rd. cent. B. c. ?): הרנא כעלת בזנתי =E(*l*)- ῥήνη Βυζαντία.

place or only in a very slight degree. For instance the combination κσθ is not suffered in the interior of words, but σ is rejected (πεπλέχθαι for πεπλέκσθαι); in the case of final ξ however this takes place only in very close combination, namely in the case of ἐξ and at most also in ἔξ πύξ λάξ. As regards the prepositions we must remark beforehand that the language, and this is true of Latin as well as Greek, made no distinction between their combination with a verb, where we write one word, and that with a noun; there was the same close connection and consequently the same assimilation[1]. The only way in which we practise this in the case of ἐξ, is to write ἐκ before a consonant, i.e. to reject the σ; but the Greeks even in writing assimilated the mute to the following sound with great regularity, the tenuis only standing before κ τ π χ σ, before θ φ, and at an earlier period before σ also, ἐχ was written, before media or liquid ἐγ[2]. And this was so established as a usage in writing, that it is found regularly even on the papyri, though there in the case of ἐν and σύν contrary to our custom the assimilation is omitted. Ἔγγονος also comes under this head, i.e. ἔκγονος, certainly not to be pronounced engonos and derived from ἐν[3]. The Bœotians and Arcadians however assimilated the ξ in quite a different way, namely by rejection of the κ: ἐσδέλλειν (ἐκβάλλειν), ἐς τοῖ ἔργοι Arcadian, ἔσγονος and also before a vowel ἐσσάρχι (ἐξάρχει) Bœotian. The absence of the preposition εἰς ἐς, for which ἐν Arcad. ἰν was employed, made this possible without ambiguity. The numeral ἔξ can in Attic in like manner become ἔκ ἔγ: ἔκ ποδῶν, ἐγδάκτυλος[4]; still even in composition it is just as often or

---

[1] On those early inscriptions, where the words are still separated by punctuation, the preposition is never separated from the noun; in Latin also such separation is often omitted, or on the other hand it is extended to the prepositions compounded with the verb, v. Corssen *Auspr.* II.[2] 863 ff.

[2] Meisterhans 2nd ed., p. 82–4; Dittenb. *Syll.* Index p. 781. Before ρ ἐγ 'Ρυμοῦ Athens 'Εφ. ἀρχ. 1883, 123 l. 58, on the other hand two instances

of ἐξ (above); other irregularities also appear (ib. and Meist. 2nd. ed., p. 84), and the intermediate form ἐκγ: e.g. ἐκγ Μαγνησίας Ditt. 171[106, 108]; omission of consonant before σκ in ἐ Σκύρου, Athens 'Εφ. ἀρχ. 1883, p. 123, l. 62.

[3] 'Εγγόνοις, Dittenb. 132,[25] is a blunder due to ἐγγ.—Cp. ἐγγράψασθαι ib. 126,[61]=ἐκγρ. l. 63.

[4] Cauer *Curt. Stud.* VIII. 294 f.; Meisterh. 85, 125, 2nd ed.; Lebadea (Vulgar dialect) 'Αθήν. IV. 369 ἐκπέδους.

oftener written ἕξ. According to a similar rule we have λακ-
πατεῖν from λάξ, πυγμάχος from πύξ.—Since assimilation went
no further than this, very harsh consonantal contacts always
remain possible in Greek, for instance not infrequently that of
final σ with πτ, φθ, κτ, χθ, a contact which even in composition
the language has no means of obviating: προσπταίω. The
author however was to a great extent at liberty either to avoid
or to permit such contacts, and thus give to his composition
either a harsher and stronger or a softer and more polished
character[1]. The Greeks were in general far more sensitive
about the contact of vowels. But they avoided a very close
combination of words by contraction of the vowels which came
in contact, as was the practice in the interior of words, and
preferred to slur quickly over the first vowel, so that in the
case of prepositions and such small words it entirely disappeared: πάρεστι, ἐπ' αὐτῷ. Short initial vowels disappeared
after long ones in the case of such words and in familiar daily
combinations; an inscription of Chios has ἦ'ς, an Attic inscription ὀκτὼ 'βολῶν[2]. Proper contraction generally takes place in
the case of preceding monosyllabic words, which in any case are
closely dependent but whose presence must somehow be made
evident: τοὔργον, κἄστι. It is quite another question, how far
these processes appear in writing; in the earlier period men
preferred to spare their material and trouble, later on they
thought more of clearness[3]. Thus even in poems we frequently
find such combinations written in extenso on old manuscripts
and inscriptions, where in pronunciation elision must have taken
place[4], and the Romans always write in extenso, but according
to the testimony of Cicero pronounced in ordinary conversation
just as in verse, that is they slurred so quickly over the first
vowel, that it formed one syllable with that following and a

[1] Dionysius of Halicarnassus in-
vestigates this point in his treatise περὶ
συνθέσεως.

[2] Röhl no. 381ᵃ 2; C. I. A. II.
834ᵇ II. 70.

[3] For this reason the preposition is
commonly not elided before proper

names, also before titles of office,
Meisterhans p. 32, after Geyer Obs.
epigr. de praep. Gr. forma et usu, Lpz.
(Altenburg) 1880, p. 5 ff.

[4] Kaibel Epigr. 39: ἀρετῆι τε οὐκ,
49 τε ἑταίροισιν, 52 δὲ ἔργων, 53 γυναικὶ
ἐσθλὴν, 55 δὲ ἀρετῆς etc.

hiatus did not take place[1]. The Greek poets were at all
periods except the latest one, that of Nonnus, contented to allow
only those vowels to come into contact, in the case of which
elision or crasis was possible; but when the prose writers began
to pay attention to this point, they went farther and put limits
even to this kind of combination of distinct words, leaving all
words that had any importance and independence separated.
Accordingly we find ἀλλ᾽, δ᾽, ταῦτ᾽, or δηλώσαιμ᾽ ἄν, but
according to strict observance nothing like ἐκτήσατ᾽ Ἀριστοτέλης was readily allowed, but Ἀριστοτέλης ἐκτήσατο was
substituted, so that the hiatus did not present itself at all.
The same punctiliousness as is well known characterised the
Roman poets from the time of Augustus onwards. Moreover
it appears that in the time of the empire the Romans avoided
this combination of vowels, which had been customary before,
no less in ordinary conversation, while the pronunciation on the other
hand was no longer avoided; the pronunciation at that time
must have been, so to speak, purer giving every word and every
syllable of a word its proper expression and value. Quintilian
gives rules as to how far the use of hiatus is permitted to a
speaker, discriminating between the several cases; nevertheless
in the nexus of early Latin neither the quantity of the vowels
nor their quality made any appreciable difference, except that
in an example such as that cited in the *ad Herennium* as to
be avoided, *baccae aeriae amoenissumae impendebant*, people
in ordinary conversation must have omitted the harsh combination and allowed hiatus[2]. But Quintilian cites as an example
of dexterous hiatus in opposition to synalepha, the occasional
advantage of which he allows, *pulchra oratione acta*[3]. The

[1] Cic. *Orat.* 150: quod quidem
Latina lingua sic observat, nemo ut
tam rusticus sit, qui vocalis nolit con-
jungere (in pronunciation), 152 : sed
Graeci viderint : nobis ne si cupiamus
quidem distrahere voces (i. e. vocales)
conceditur. Indicant orationes illae
ipsae horridulae Catonis (in which
therefore a hiatus must frequently
have been suppressed even in script),
indicant omnes poetae, etc. This is

scarcely contradictory to § 77 (on the
occasional use of hiatus by the humilis
orator).

[2] Quintil. ix. 4, 33 f.—*Ad Herenn.*
iv. § 18: fugiemus crebras vocalium
concursiones, quae vastam et hiantem
orationem reddunt, ut haec est: *Baccae*
etc.

[3] § 36: et coeuntes litterae, quae
συναλοιφαί dicuntur, etiam leviorem
faciunt orationem, quam si omnia

case must have been the same with the Greek of that period. Dionysius of Halicarnassus found the hiatus μᾶλλον δὲ ὅλον in his Demosthenes, and imagined that this was really intended by the orator[1], evidently only because there were speakers at that period, who allowed this in speaking and did not get rid of it by synalepha. Demetrius who is somewhat later considers it actually more euphonious, to pronounce the vowels separate in the sentence πάντα μὲν τὰ νέα καὶ καλά ἐστιν, than with synalepha καλά 'στιν[2]; the people however no doubt even at that period pronounced in the latter way. For even the Greeks of the present day are accustomed to annul the hiatus, at all events in speaking.

SECTION 33.

Transference of final consonants.

In ancient Greek, just as in French, though hardly to such an extent, final consonants were liable to be carried on. The teaching of the grammarians is[3], that where elision of a final vowel has taken place the consonant preceding this must be given to the following syllable: κα-τε-μοῦ, ἀ-πε-κεί-νου, just as in French *en-tr'eux*. Wherever in composition a consonant comes before a vowel it belongs to this vowel without any exception, even in the case of ἐξ εἰς πρὸς δυσ-; on the other hand, if a consonant follow, the final consonant remains with the preceding vowel; thus ἐ-ξι-έναι, δύ-σελ-πις, but δύσ-μορ-φος. In the case of σ indeed, as has been already remarked, the right analysis even in the case of simple words was a matter of doubt; hence these rules, which were of course capricious.

verba suo fine cludantur, et nonnunquam hiulca etiam decent faciuntque ampliora quaedam : ut *Pulchra* etc.

[1] Dionys. *Dem.* 42.

[2] Demetr. π. ἑρμ. § 70: πολλὰ δὲ καὶ ἄλλα ἐν συναλοιφῇ μὲν λεγόμενα δύσφωνα ἦν, διαιρεθέντα δὲ καὶ συγκρουσθέντα εὐφωνότερα, ὡς τὸ πάντα κτέ. εἰ δὲ

συναλείψας εἴποις καλά 'στιν, δυσφωνότερον ἔσται τὸ λεγόμενον καὶ εὐτελέστερον.

[3] Theodosius *Bekk. Anec.* 1127 f.; ed. Göttl. p. 62; Lentz *Herodian.* II. 390 ff., 407 f. Vid. K. E. A. Schmidt *Beiträge* p. 134 ff.

We are at liberty to doubt, whether the pronunciation really was so entirely established and certainly whether it continued the same through the different periods. The writer of the great Hyperides manuscript indeed always separates ἀ | πε- στέλλετε and so on where the line breaks off, but he writes more frequently εἰσ-αγγελία than εἰ-σαγγελία, and moreover sometimes ταῦ | τοὐχ, sometimes οὐδ' | ὅστις[1]. On the long Epidaurian inscriptions, which sing the praises of the miracles of healing worked by Apollo and Asclepius with classic mendacity, the following examples of line-division occur: ὠ | σδὲ (beside τάχισ | τα γασ | τρί[2] ὅ | στρακα), ἐξ | ἐλθηι, ἀ | πά- γοντα, ἐ | νύπνιον, ἐ | κτούτου. The pronunciation and separation οὐ | κέστι οὐ | χήκιστα[3] was certainly established. A transference between article and noun (τῶ | νέργων) and also between other looser connections may have taken place frequently[4], but they did not divide so (in writing) except in rare instances, which are paralleled by instances of the opposite such as ὅσ-ος of equally little significance. A peculiarity worthy of mention, which appears on the Gortynian inscription and elsewhere sporadically, is the doubling of final ν in short words in close connection, so that it belongs to both syllables: ταννήμίναν, συννῆι (i.e. συνῆ), ὤννἄν, ἠννἔχων[5]. Although Bücheler is of a different opinion, I think that this pronunciation gives the explanation for corresponding instances of licence in prosody in the Æolian dialect:—ἀσὐνέτημι, ἐνόχλης, σὺν ὀλίγῳ[6].

[1] Hyper. Praefat. p. ix.

[2] Ἐφ. ἀρχ. 1883 p. 199 ; 1885 p. 15. Cp. later Attic inscr., which also finish the line with a complete syllable: II. 469, 35 ἐ | ν ἀστει, 403, 17 ἐ | κ τῶν.— Inscr. of Antiochus (p. 122, n. 2 above) II.ᵃ 23 προ | σόδους ; IV.ᵃ 15 προσ | καρ- τερείτωσαν is necessary, because on this inscription σ is always separated from τ θ etc.

[3] ib.; C. I. A. II. 467, 81 οὐ | κέἀσας, 379, 3 οὐ | κόλίγα.

[4] Several occur in the second Hyperides mss. Praef. p. xvi.

[5] Gortyn. Insc. 2, 49 ; 10, 41 ; *Museo Ital.* II. 599 col. vi., 9 ; also νσσ in τὀνσσἐπιβαλλόντανς 7, 9 ; but not συνεσσάξαι 3, 16, which comes from ἐκσάττω.—Samos Dittenb. *Syll.* 132, 12, 15.

[6] Meister *Gr. Dial.* I. 148 (Büch- eler *Rh. Mus.* XL. additional fasciculus p. 9).

SECTION 34.

Accent.

With regard to the accent of words it is well known, that in Greek this consisted in voice-pitch, not voice-stress and still less voice-duration, although in both the classical languages the latter was united with voice-pitch in the period of their degeneration[1]. For the Greek of the present day pronounces accented vowels long, unaccented short: *xénŭs* (ξένους), *yénĭtŏ* (γένοιτο), *ăthrŏpŏs, athrŏpŭs.* The period, at which this extraordinarily important transformation took place, may be to a certain extent ascertained from prosody. For the versification of the classical period makes no account whatever of word-accent[2], and indeed, since the accent was purely musical, there was not the slightest reason why it should; but even tunes, according to the testimony of Dionysius of Halicarnassus, were set without regard to the accent, that is the tune (cp. προσῳδία, accentus) of ordinary speech[3]. But in the post-Christian period we find it the rule in Babrius' fables, that the penultimate syllable of the choliambic always bears the accent, and Nonnus (end of the 4th century) never ends a hexameter with a proparoxyton[4]. In the case of the pentameter an ever-increasing effort can be traced right on from the Alexandrine period, to limit accented final syllables, and finally almost to banish them, and this was done for the most part in favour of the paroxyton termination which prevailed also in the Byzantine trimeter[5]. In just the same way in the Latin of the

[1] This is not the place, to enter on the controversy with regard to Latin, for which Seelmann also maintains an original predominance of the factor of stress over the musical. The evidences of the grammarians, to which he appeals (28 f.), are certainly all late, while the musical factor (and that exclusively) is testified to so early as by Nigidius.

[2] Attempts have indeed been made to shew that there was some such regard (v. J. H. Heinr. Schmidt *Metr.* 211 ff.); I cannot however regard his attempts as successful, and see little trace of anything of the kind in Latin versification. Cp. H. Weil *Göttinger Philologenvers.* (1852) p. 85 ff.; Weil-Benloew *Accentuat. lat.* p. 66 ff. 240 ff.

[3] Dionys. *Compos.* p. 63 R., with examples from Eurip. *Orest.*

[4] This law was discovered by A. Ludwich (Fleckeis. *Jahrb.* 1874, 441 ff.).

[5] F. Hannsen *Rh. Mus.* XXXVIII. 226.

same period the transformation in the pronunciation may be ascertained from the metrical phenomena[1]. Further accurate observation of the Greek poets has of late led to the assumption, that there existed in the language from the earliest period side by side with the variety of pitch a variety of stress following laws coinciding with those of Latin accentuation: namely the stress is said never to have rested on the last syllable and on the last but two only when the penultimate was short[2]. It appears to me however still doubtful whether this is the true significance of the observations. With regard to pitch and tone we are told by Dionysius, that the interval between high pitch and low pitch syllables amounts pretty nearly to a fifth[3]. Now our accentual system, based on the statements of Dionysius Thrax, Dionysius of Halicarnassus and others, distinguishes only three kinds of syllables, high pitch (ὀξεῖα προσῳδία), low pitch (βαρεῖα προσῳδία) and those in which high and low pitch are united (in that order) (προσ. περισπωμένη, so called from the 'drawing round' the accent from high to low)[4]. This kind of accentuation or that corresponding to it, in which the sequence is from low to high, occurs in modern languages also; for instance the ancient circumflex is heard in Italian in the case of double consonants (donna, stella). Since the time of Aristophanes of Byzantium the low pitch syllables have been denoted by ⸍, the high pitch by ⸌, the circumflexed by the combination of the two symbols Λ, which gradually became rounded. Originally every syllable had its accent: ΛΕΓΌΜΈΝΟΪ; but in course of time the notation

---

[1] Weil-Benloew p. 255 ff.

[2] Isid. Hilberg, das Prinzip der Silbenwägung, Wien, 1879. Cp. Hannsen Rh. Mus. xxxvii. 252, who, though agreeing in principle, makes the law of accentuation run quite differently; the last syllable, if long, has the strong stress; if not, the penultimate.

[3] Dionys. Comp. p. 58: διαλέκτου μὲν οὖν μέλος ἐνὶ μετρεῖται διαστήματι τῷ λεγομένῳ διὰ πέντε, ὡς ἔγγιστα· καὶ οὔτε ἐπιτείνεται πέρα τῶν τριῶν τόνων καὶ ἡμιτονίου ἐπὶ τὸ ὀξὺ, οὔτε ἀνίεται τοῦ

χωρίου τούτου πλεῖον ἐπὶ τὸ βαρύ. On the contrary, afterwards page 62 : ἡ δὲ ὀργανική τε καὶ ᾠδικὴ μοῦσα διαστήμασί τε χρῆται πλείοσιν, οὐ τῷ διὰ πέντε μόνον, κτέ.

[4] Dion. Hal. p. 60 ff.; Dion. Thrax p. 629 Bk. : τόνος ἐστὶ φωνῆς ἀπήχησις ἐναρμονίου, ἢ κατὰ ἀνάτασιν ἐν τῇ ὀξείᾳ, ἢ κατὰ ὁμαλισμὸν ἐν τῇ βαρείᾳ, ἢ κατὰ περίκλασιν ἐν τῇ περισπωμένῃ. Varro ([Sergii] explan. in Don. K. iv. 531) hands down to us several other names for περισπ. : δίτονος, σύμπλεκτος etc.

was simplified; the gravis being placed only on the penultimate syllables of oxytones and perispomena instead of those accents being used, or on final syllables, where the high pitch was partially suppressed in the speaker's context, to serve to denote such suppression[1]. Here the imperfection of this accentual system becomes evident; for it is obvious that in ὁ δ᾽ ἀγαθὸς ἀνὴρ ἀεὶ... all the syllables do not really have the same pitch. Accordingly even in ancient times more accurate systems were put forward, which, we may say, fortunately never attained general circulation, but unfortunately have not even been properly handed down to us[2]. For example many distinguish a μέση, which was recognized also by the Roman Varro; this middle pitch probably comprised besides the final syllables which properly speaking were oxytone all syllables following next after a high pitch and likewise the second half of a syllable having the circumflex[3]. Glaucus of Samos made the number as many as six: ἀνειμένη (= βαρεῖα), μέση, ἐπιτεταμένη (= ὀξεῖα), κεκλασμένη (= περισπωμένη), ἀντανακλωμένη and a sixth accent, of which not even the name or indeed anything else concerning it is established, except that it belonged to the subdivisions of the circumflex[4]. The ἀντανακλωμένη however has its origin in the union of gravis and acute on the same syllable: δαὶ̈ς δᾷς, ἐάν ἦν, and since the high pitch never occupied more than one mora, appears to have been the

[1] See *Bekk. Anec.* 674; confirmation of the ancient writing in the Egyptian fragment of Alcman. The papyri of the *Iliad* in London (Pap. Bankes and Pap. Harris) have likewise examples of several accents on the same word: ΕΙΙΕΟΟΕΤΟΝΤΟ; still both in them and in the fragment of the *Iliad* in the Louvre (Pap. 3) the βαρεῖα is principally employed to represent the oxytone or circumflex which properly belongs to the following syllable: ΑΦΝΕΙΟΥ, ΔΟΙΟΙ, ΘΝΗΤΩΙ, ΕΙΙΕΙ (Pap. B.); ΕΠΕΙΔΗ, ΥΠΟΔΡΥΙ, ΕΦΕΤΜΑΟ (Pap. H.); ΠΑΡΑ, ΑΥΤΑΡ, but ΥΨΟΥ (Pap. L.). In these instances it is remarkable, that this gravis is often pushed so far to the right; but this must not lead us to suppose that it belongs to the last syllable; for we also find ΠΟΛΙΟΝΤΕ (the symbol being over ιο), and in words with more than one gravis ΑΜΟΙΒΗΑΙΟ, ΔΑΦΟΙΝΕΟΝ.

[2] See Varro l. c. p. 528 f.

[3] Weil-Benloew p. 13 ff.; Misteli *Ueber gr. Betonung* (Paderb. 1875), J. Hadley *Curt. Stud.* v. 417 ff.

[4] The mss. give HC (joined to the preceding word); early editions give νήτη after a conjecture of Wase, Weil suggests ἴση, Keil περικεκλασμένη.

accentuation of all long vowels to which we give the acute[1]. The grammarians, who only employed the accent for the texts of poets who wrote in some particular dialect, rightly considered the system of Glaucus too complicated; but the real language may nevertheless have been still more complicated in this respect, and this illustrates well, what terrible difficulties Greek pronunciation must have presented to foreigners. Our position is easier, since no one can control us, and though perhaps it is not right to be entirely indifferent as regards a better or worse pronunciation, there is no need on the other hand to be pedantic, as though the ancient Greeks might some day rise from their graves and call us to account for murdering their beautiful language.

---

[1] Boeckh *de metr. Pind.* p. 47, 52; Weil-Benloew p. 12 ff.; Corssen II[r] p. 803.

APPENDIX.

M. J. Psichari of Paris has placed at my disposal, besides other abundant information as to the pronunciation of the Greeks of the present day, a translation of the Lord's Prayer (Matth. vi. 9 ff.), prepared by himself, together with an accurate phonetic transliteration, which is fundamentally the pronunciation of a Greek, who, born in Chios like M. Psichari himself, has spent ten years in Athens and speaks the common language of Greece. It will be of interest, if I give this translation here, with the necessary explanations which also I owe to M. Psichari. In order to remove any ambiguity I have myself changed the transliteration into Roman letters.

Πατέρα μας, ποῦ εἶσαι στὸν οὐρανό, νάγιαστῇ τὄνομά σου, νάρθῃ ἡ βασιλεία σου, νὰ γίνῃ ἡ θέλησή σου, ὅπως στὸν οὐρανό, ἔτσι καὶ στὴ γίς. Τὸ ψωμί μας τὸ καθημερνὸ δόσμας το σήμερα, καὶ συχώρεσε μας τὶς ἁμαρτίες μας, σὰν ποῦ καὶ μεῖς συχωρνοῦμε τῶν ἀλλωνῶν τὶς ἁμαρτίες. Μὴ μᾶς φέρῃς σὲ πειρασμό, μὰ σῶσε μας ἀπὸ τὸν πονηρό· Ἀμήν.

Transliteration.

Pătĕră măs, pwísĕ stǫn ūrănǫ́, năyăstí tǫnǫmắ sǔ, nắrθī văsllíă sǔ, năyínī θĕ̇llsí sǔ, ŏrǫs tǫn ūrănǫ́, ĕtsl k'ĕ stĮ yĮs. Tǫ psǫmí măs tǫ kăθímĕrnǫ́ dǫ́zmăs tǫ símĕră, k'ĕ slχǫ́rĕsĕ̇ măs tĮs ămărtíĕs măs, sābǔ k'ĕ mĮ slχǫrnǘmĕ̇ tǫn ălǫnǫ́n (ălǫnǫ́) dĮs ămărtíĕs. Mí măs fĕ̇rĮ sĕ̇ plrăzmǫ́, mă sǫ́sĕ̇ măs ăp tǫn bǫnĮrǫ́. Ămí.

It will be seen that Psichari distinguishes the open (a) and the closed sound (ạ) in the other vowels also, and not only in the case of *e o*; the former is predominant throughout, except in the case of *i*. Those vowels remain without any special designation in this respect, which are spoken too quickly to allow of their exact quality being observed ("voyelles réduites"). With regard to *mas* (plural of oblique cases of *ἐγώ*), when it is itself unaccented and follows an accented syllable, Psichari remarks, that it would be more correctly represented by *más*, the *a* here inclining towards the *e*.—*ā ĩ* denote nasal vowels similar to the French sound.—The quantity is however according to our authority just as fluctuating as the quality; it depends on quickness of pronunciation, on context, on the intention of the speaker; a word may have a different quantity and quality of its vowel when isolated to that which it has in connected speech.—In the case of the consonants I have made use of the Greek letters δ θ χ to denote the spirants (English *this, think*; German *ach*); *k'* expresses the palatal *k* (*ky*, articulated in the middle of the palate); *s* and *z* the hard (voiceless) and soft (voiced) sounds.

As regards matters of detail I add (after Psichari) the following definitions and rules of pronunciation :

(*a*) *O* is in general open ; thus in all cases above with the exception of the final syllable of *ἀλλωνῶν*, where owing to the nasalized sound (*-nõ dis*) produced by the closely connected *τίς* (*dis*), the sound became closed in the pronunciation of the individual taken as a standard. Psichari himself however does not pronounce so, though he uses an analogous pronunciation in the case of *e*: δὲν ἔχω, but δὲν τρέχω. In his own pronunciation he gives the closed sound to final *o*, whether accented or not; ὀκτώ *ŏχtǒ*, πτερόν *ftĕrǒ*, πίπτω *pĕftŏ*. This as will be seen does not agree with the notation given above, but Psichari states that this pronunciation of final *o* as *ọ* is very widely spread. On the other hand he gives *ftẹ̆ŏ* as his pronunciation of *πταίω* ; in the case of *ftĕrǒ* (*πτερόν*) he leaves the *e* without designation.

(*b*) Accented *i* is almost always given as closed; when unaccented it appears to fluctuate; in both cases the origin of *i* (from ι η υ etc.) is perfectly indifferent. With reference to the dialectal pronunciation of υ (οι) as *ü* noticed above Psichari remarks that the statements of G. Meyer (*Gramm.*[2] p. 108) are very accurate ; M. speaks there of the pronunciation as *iu* and gives as examples from the dialect of Attica κιουλιά κοιλιά, ἄχιουρα ἄχυρα, κιούρτος κύρτος. Psichari however is inclined to regard this *ü* in all cases as a modern development after palatals, not as a survival from an older period; *τυρί* will be found to be in the dialect, where such phenomena occur, not *türi* but *tsüri* with palatalisation of the *t*.

(*c*) The transcription πονηρόν *boniró* militates against the rule we have mentioned above, according to which unaccented *ir* (*ιρ, ηρ, υρ*) must become *er*. I assume that the Chiot thought it necessary to pronounce this word with its ecclesiastical associations ("the Evil One") in accordance with the writing. The apparent retention of the *e*-sound of *η* in the dialect of Trapezus is much doubted by Psichari: τέν = τήν, Ἕλλενες etc. might rest on modern phonetic laws; a scientific investigation of the matter has yet to be undertaken.

(*d*) Both βασιλεία and ἁμαρτία remain free from the detrition of *ι* before a vowel following, which has been referred to above (*vasilyá, amartyá*). The reason again appears to be, that they are ecclesiastical words, which are not subject to popular treatment.

(*e*) Νάγιαστῇ *nayastí* is written by Psichari with *τ*, though as a rule in such cases the written form contrary to the pronunciation retains the *θ*. The rule that two voiceless spirants, just as two tenues, are not tolerated in immediate proximity, is in general extended to *σ* also, except that the ordinary pronunciation does not follow this out consistently in the case of *σφ*. On the other hand *φσ* is not allowable (except in the artificial pronunciation of the educated): δουλεύσω pr. δουλέψω, and so always in the interior of words, while in the case of final syllables *ευς*, i.e. *εφς*, becomes *ες*: βασιλές, Ὀρφές. There are indeed no words, which terminate with two consonants in the nominative.—No exception is taken to the collision of voiced spirants (such as βδ, ευδ *evd*).

In order to place in a true light the contrast of the old and the new, I add myself a transliteration of the Lord's Prayer, according to the original text, in the Hellenistic pronunciation of that period, without however venturing to denote the quality of the vowels; for the popular pronunciation of the first century A.D. is not known with sufficient accuracy to render that possible. Only in the case of *οι* I have given the closed pronunciation of the *o*. I denote the aspirates by k', p', t' ($=k+h$, $p+h$, $t+h$); s and z are the hard and soft s-sounds. I give the accents in the ordinary manner, except that I dispense with the grave in the case of monosyllabic words.

Pătĕr hēmôn hŏ ĕn toi̇s ūrănoi̇s, hă(g)ĭăst'étō tŏ ŏnŏmấ (tōnŏmá?) sū, ĕlt'étō hē băsĭléä (băsĭlíä) sū, gĕnēt'étō tŏ t'élēmấ sū hōs ĕn ūrănô kai ĕpĭ̇ gês. Tŏn ắrtŏn hēmôn tŏn ĕpĭúsĭŏn dŏs hēmin sémĕrŏn, kai ắp'ĕs hēmin tă op'ĭlémătă hēmôn (tōp'ĭlémăt'ēmôn ?), hōs kai hēmi̇s (k'ēmis?) ăp'ékămĕn toi̇s ŏp'ĭlétais hēmôn, kai mē īsĕnĕṅkēs hēmâs ī̇s pīrăzmŏ́n, ăllă rhûsai (rhûsĕ?) hēmâs ăpŏ̀ tû pŏnērú.

GREEK INDEX.

A

Αβαεόδορος (Tanagra) 56

ἄγ(γ)μα, name of nasal γ 85, 88

ἄγεθλα (ἀεθλα) 110

ἄγω Locrian for ἄγω 96

AE Bœot.= αι 56

AE diphth., its phonetic value and history 67 ff

AϜ EϜ for αυ ευ 75 ff

AϜϜTO αὐτοῦ Naxian inscr. 76

Ἄζωτος Ἀσδώδ 118, 122

Ἀθήναζε 118

AI diphth., phonetic value and history 52 ff, 64 ff; αι in verb-endings 65; ἄι for ᾱι Bœot. etc. 45; change of αι to ᾱ before a vowel 52; αι seldom confused with ε in script 65

ĀI diphth. phonetic value and history 43 ff; ᾱι before vowel becomes ᾱ 52

Αλαίη 66

Αἰγείς for Αἰγής 47; Αἰγηίς poet. 47 n. 5; became later Αἰγίς ib.

Αἴγιρα not Αἴγειρα 59 n. 2

αιετός Att., not ἀετός 53 n. 1

AIH (AIE) for AH (AE) Ionic 53

αἰμωδία not ἠμ. 70

αλ ελ in Cretan became αυ ευ 80

ἀλάθεα (Lesb.) 52

ΑΛΗΟΝ (ἀλλέων) 26

ΑΛΙΚΑΡΝΑΤΕΩΝ 120 n. 2

Ἀμπιθάλης 104

ἀμπλακεῖν and ἀμβλ. 97

ἀναιραιρημαι? Thasos 64 f.

ἀνδάζαθαι (Cret.) 122

ἄνεο (ευ) 75

ἄντρωπος (Cret.) 113

ἄνω not ἄνῳ 50 n. 1

AO EO Ionic for AΤ EΤ 74; αο contracted to αυ 74

AOT for AT 83

ἀπελέφτερος 84

Ἀριστηΐδης -είδης 48

Ἀρίστηχμος (Bœot.) 27, 57

Ἀρκεφῶν 104

ἄρουρα with real ου 73

Ἀρρενήΐδης -είδης 48

ἀσάλεα (Dor.) 52

-ασι (ᾱσι) dat. plur. Att. 45

ἀτοῦ ἑατοῦ for αὐτοῦ ἑαυτοῦ 79 ff

ἀτσήμι 116

AT diphth., phonetic value and history 73 ff; αυ contracted to ω 80

αὐάτα, αὐειρομέναι, αὔως 78

αὐκά (ἀλκή) 80

αὔρηκτος (Lesb.) 77

αὐσωτοῦ (Dor.) 80

Ἀφιτρίτα 87

ἀφτός (αὐτός) 73

ἄχυρα 21, 42 n. 3

B

B its phonetic value and history 108 ff, in the dialects 111 ff; β for Ϝ dialect 76, 111, 113; the same after ευ 77; β for Latin v 109

βαδύ 113

βασιλεία (acc. of βασιλεύς) 34

βαστίας 111

βδεῦ, distortion of Ζεῦ 117

ENGLISH AND LATIN INDEX.

themselves, who, now that the German pronunciation has been adopted even in Russia, are in fact the only people who still cherish itacism.   Among them however there are not wanting enlightened investigators of language, who do not refuse to take a scientific view even of this subject.

SECTION 3.

Genuine and counterfeit Erasmian principle.

It is however worthy of remark, that the Erasmian pronunciation, in the actual form which it has taken in various countries, is by no means identical with that theoretically developed by Erasmus and his adherents.   In reality the axiom which has been more or less followed is this, that the symbols and combinations of symbols are to be pronounced as the corresponding symbols in the various languages ; but this is an axiom of convenience not of science.   The genuine teaching of the Erasmians is on the contrary really scientific ; they endeavoured, independently of the modern Greek tradition, to recover the ancient pronunciation from direct evidences, from transcripts into and out of foreign languages, and from linguistic precedents. They also, as was right and fair, called in to their help the analogy of modern languages ; Erasmus heard the sound of $\alpha\iota$, i.e. $a + \iota$, in the German *Kaiser*, that of $o\iota$, i.e. $o + \iota$, in the *moi toi soi* of certain Frenchmen, while Beza expresses the pronunciation of these words by *moae toae soae* (triphthongal), and recognizes the genuine $o\iota$ $(o + \iota)$ in *soin* and *besoin.*   The train of thought then is this, various modes of writing such as $\iota, \eta, \upsilon, \epsilon\iota, o\iota, \upsilon\iota$ cannot possibly from the beginning have stood for the same sound, but rather, when the writing was diphthongal, the pronunciation also was diphthongal, i.e. the members of the diphthong were pronounced distinctly but united into one syllable, as they are heard in numerous instances in living languages.   But finally in practice only so much as was convenient, was retained from those scholars' scientific discovery, namely the freedom from modern Greek tradition and the employment of West European analogies, the most obvious being

P.

10

CAMBRIDGE: PRINTED BY C. J. CLAY, M.A. & SONS, AT THE UNIVERSITY PRESS.

Printed in the United States
84950LV00005B/75/A